BEARS
IN THE
STREETS

BEARS
IN THE
STREETS

~∞~

THREE JOURNEYS
ACROSS A CHANGING RUSSIA

LISA DICKEY

ST. MARTIN'S PRESS 📖 NEW YORK

BEARS IN THE STREETS. Copyright © 2017 by Lisa Dickey. All rights reserved. Printed in the United States of America. For information, address St. Martin's Press, 175 Fifth Avenue, New York, N.Y. 10010.

www.stmartins.com

Map of Russia by Amy Turner

Text design: Meryl Sussman Levavi

Cataloging-in-Publication Data is available at the Library of Congress.

ISBN 9781250092298 (hardcover)
ISBN 9781250092304 (e-book)

Our books may be purchased in bulk for promotional, educational, or business use. Please contact your local bookseller or the Macmillan Corporate and Premium Sales Department at 1-800-221-7945, extension 5442, or by e-mail at MacmillanSpecial Markets@macmillan.com.

First Edition: January 2017

10 9 8 7 6 5 4 3 2 1

In the papers every day there were thousands of words about Russia. . . . And it occurred to us that there were some things that nobody wrote about Russia, and they were the things that interested us most of all.

—John Steinbeck, *A Russian Journal*, 1948

Contents

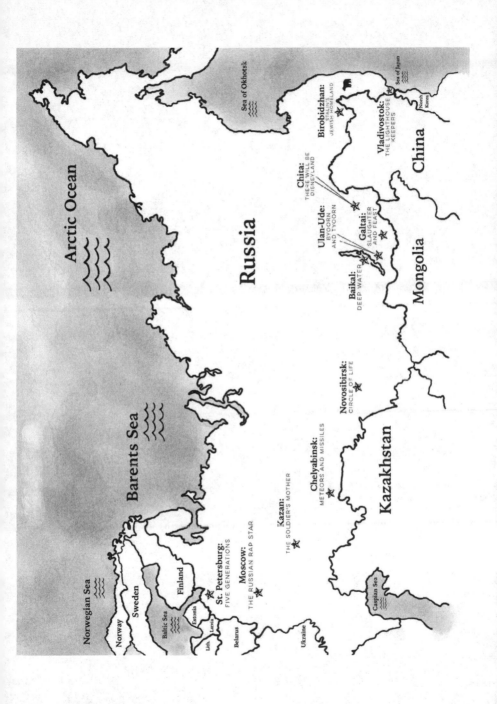

Prologue

I'M WALKING DOWN VLADIVOSTOK'S ADMIRAL FOKIN Street, a tidy, tree-lined pedestrian mall with a view of sparkling Sportivnaya Harbor in the distance. It's a brilliant late-summer day, the sun beaming down on shops and souvenir stands, the street packed with people. At this time of year, Vladivostok is a warm, inviting seaside city, the smell of salt air mingling with the aroma of freshly flipped blini and coffee wafting from cafés.

Strolling beside me are Valya and Katya, a couple of older Russian women wearing pedal-pusher pants and sensible shoes.

"How's your trip so far?" Katya asks me.

"It's my third day," I say, "so there's not much to tell." I've only just arrived in Vladivostok, the first stop of a planned three-month journey across Russia. I'll be traveling by train, dropping into 11 cities to visit people I interviewed first in 1995, then again in 2005, and now in 2015. Valya is one of the people I met 20 years ago, but her friend Katya, who's tagging along for our walk, is the one asking the questions today.

"I'm just happy to have gotten my Russian visa without any problems," I tell her, adding that I hope to be allowed to travel freely throughout the country over the coming months.

"Of course you will," Katya says brusquely. "Why wouldn't you?" I tell her that with U.S.-Russian relations at their lowest point in years, I'd recently read a few articles suggesting that Russian officials have been clamping down on unstructured travel.

"*Pffft!*" she retorts, waving her hand. "That's just the American press. You can't believe what they write, especially about Russia. Listen, Americans think that in Russia, we have bears roaming in the streets!"

I laugh, amused at the image of wild bears running amok down this nice pedestrian avenue. "Well, I'm not sure Americans think that," I say. "But I take your point." She's right that, for the most part, Americans have no idea what her country is really like—which is the reason I've come here. U.S. media coverage of Russia tends to focus on the economy, political situation, and leadership. In contrast, I'm hoping to paint a portrait of not only how ordinary Russians live today, but also how their lives have changed over the past two decades.

In all my years of coming here, I can't remember ever hearing this "bears in the streets" comment. I probably wouldn't have remembered it this time, except that another Russian said the exact same thing to me a couple of weeks later. Then another one said it a week after that. Then another, and another. By the end of my trip, no fewer than six people in six different cities (and four different time zones) had informed me that this is what Americans think. "Bears in the streets," I realized, was the apparently ubiquitous shorthand for the Russians' feeling that the West doesn't take them seriously enough—that we think they're primitive or backward.

Of course, the bear has been a symbol of Russia for centuries, in everything from fables to political cartoons to the 1980 Moscow Olympics mascot, Misha. And Russians occasionally refer to themselves as "bears"—as Vladimir Putin famously did in December 2014 at his annual televised press conference. When asked if there was a connection between Russia's struggling economy and the upheaval in Crimea, he responded with this convoluted metaphor:

> Imagine a bear who's guarding his taiga. If we
> continue the analogy, maybe it would be best if our
> bear just sat still. Maybe he should stop chasing pigs
> and boars around the taiga, but start picking berries
> and eating honey. Maybe then he will be left alone.
>
> But no! He won't be. Because someone will always
> try to chain him up. As soon as he's chained, they
> will tear out his teeth and claws . . . And then, when
> all the teeth and claws are torn out, the bear will be
> of no use at all. Perhaps they'll stuff him.

It's hard not to feel sorry for the bear in this story. But the fascinating thing about bears is that they can appear either fierce or cuddly; even a seven-foot-tall grizzly seems huggable if he's in the right mood. This seems fitting given the current state of affairs between Russia and the United States: we're allies, but also mad at each other, so even though we try to play nice, the claws keep coming out.

This felt like a tricky time to be an American in Russia, and as I began my third trip across the country I wasn't sure what I'd discover. But starting with Katya's comment, it seemed likely that bears—metaphorical or otherwise—would figure into the answer.

ONE

—⚭—

Three Journeys

IN THE SPRING OF 1995 I WAS LIVING IN RUSSIA, TRYING
to launch a new career. I'd spent the early nineties in the
liberal arts major's first circle of Hell, suffering through dreary
administrative jobs in Washington, D.C., while wondering how
I got through college without learning a single marketable skill.
I answered phones and filed paperwork until I was a paper cut
away from insanity. Then, at age 27, I booked a one-way ticket
to St. Petersburg, rented an apartment in the city center, and set
about trying to turn myself into a writer.

Moving to Russia wasn't as random as it sounds. I'd studied
Russian in college, and had even lived at the U.S. embassy compound in Moscow for seven months from 1988 to 1989, working
as a nanny for a U.S. diplomat's family. Those were the "bad old

days": the Soviet Union was our mortal enemy, the KGB was listening to our conversations, and the embassy's security people spent hours trying to scare us out of getting too cozy with Russians. It was overwhelming—as was Moscow itself, which was massive, gray, noisy, and dirty. So, five years later, when I decided to find my fortune in post-Soviet Russia, quaint old St. Petersburg seemed the logical choice.

I had everything planned out. Best-case scenario, I'd sell feature stories to newspapers and compile enough clips to continue a writing career back home. Worst-case scenario, nobody would buy my stories, but I'd have fun living the bohemian life in Russia for a while. With my rent just a hundred bucks a month for a two-bedroom apartment, and subsisting on a diet of potatoes, carrots, cabbage, and beer, I figured I had enough money to last a year.

Six months into my grand experiment, nobody would buy anything I wrote. I eagerly penned fluffy little pieces about music festivals and adventures on trolleybuses, but I was stuck in a chicken-and-egg conundrum: no one would publish my stories until my stories had been published elsewhere. Even the small, poorly written English-language newspaper, the *St. Petersburg Press*, wasn't interested, though in response to my shameless hounding they finally offered me part-time work as a copy editor. I started going in to the newsroom a few hours a week, and that's where, posted on a bulletin board in April 1995, I saw this printed-out e-mail:

> My name is Gary Matoso. I am an American photojournalist currently based in Paris . . .
>
> I have a project that I am in the early stages of planning . . . The basic idea is a trip across Russia by car, St. Petersburg to Vladivostok (maybe the other way around). I plan to take two to three months to complete

the journey, stopping in big cities, small towns and villages. I want to shoot a very personal b&w photo essay, a sort of photo journal that documents the people, places and experiences that will make up the trip . . .

How can you help? First of all, ADVICE. Have any of you been out to the far reaches of Siberia? What can I expect as far as roads? (Are there any?) PLACES TO GO. Do you have any ideas on places that I should definitely see or someone I should meet along the way? . . . CONTACTS. This will be a real road trip. I am trying to put together a list of friendly faces, a place to crash for the night, or just someone who knows the area . . .

By this point, I was hyperventilating. What an adventure this guy was going to have! I was afraid to read further for fear he hadn't written the words I was desperate to see. Fortunately, he had.

Lastly, and this is a biggie, I am looking for candidates to be my traveling partner . . .

Here is the scoop. I need someone who's fluent in Russian. I speak some but not enough to attempt this trip on my own. I will cover all of the expenses for the trip and get you back to Petersburg. This offer is directed at but not limited to journalists . . .

It will be a long and hard trip, with no luxurious hotels or fine restaurants (well, maybe one or two restaurants) . . . Anyhow, spread the word, I am sure there are enough crazy people out there . . .

Sincerely,

Gary Matoso

He must pick me. In all my months in Russia, I'd spent very little time outside Moscow or St. Petersburg. I was desperate to see more of the country, and this trip would be a great opportunity to write—and, let's be honest, *sell*—stories from the road. Sure, it would be weird to travel with a total stranger; for all I knew, this Gary Matoso person was a kook, or worse, an over-caffeinated alpha male. I didn't care. I was ready to pack my bags and hop the next train for Siberia. All I had to do was convince Gary that I was the perfect travel companion, using a passel of carefully picked white lies: I e-mailed him that I was fluent in Russian (not quite, though I was getting there); an accomplished writer (false); and, most important, unflappable (way false).

There were several candidates, but lo and behold, the photographer picked me. Forget boho St. Petersburg—I was going to the hinterlands and beyond.

Gary wanted to start with a remote lighthouse he'd heard about at the farthest southeastern tip of Russia, so we booked flights to Vladivostok for September 1, 1995. From there, we planned to meander back to St. Petersburg, stopping in 10 to 12 cities along the way. Our goal was to find an interesting cross-section of people to profile, then post photos and stories to a website as we traveled.

This last part sounded bold, futuristic, and quite possibly insane—at least until Gary arrived in St. Petersburg with an unusual piece of equipment. Standing in my kitchen, he pulled out a 35 mm Nikon camera with a hardware attachment roughly the size of a Buick, then snapped a photo of me. He ejected a little diskette, popped it into a slot in his Apple PowerBook laptop, and when my face magically appeared on the screen, I actually shrieked.

Not only had I never seen this technology, I'd never even heard of it. Digital cameras weren't widely available in 1995, but Gary had scored an expensive prototype from Kodak—and this, he told me, was the real motivation behind the trip. He wanted to demonstrate how these newfangled digital cameras could be used to create documentary projects on the brand-new World Wide Web. If all went well, our website, which we dubbed "The Russian Chronicles" (having decided "A Trans-Cyberian Journey" was a little too cute) would be one of the first real-time Web travelogues.*

We set off the next day for Vladivostok with only the barest notion about how the next few months would unfold. I'd managed to scrape up contacts in a few cities, mostly Russian friends of friends intrigued at the idea of hosting actual Americans in their rarely visited towns. The rest of the time we'd be winging it, asking everyone we met whether they happened to know anyone in the next town over, as we made our way across the country on the Trans-Siberian Railway. (We'd quickly given up on Gary's idea of driving once we learned there were few decent—meaning paved—highways in the Russian Far East.)

Over 12 weeks, more than 5,000 miles, several screaming fights, and approximately 6,000 vodka shots, Gary and I created a portrait, in words and photographs, of the lives of contemporary Russians. In the course of the trip, we had adventures beyond what we'd ever imagined.

We spent four days on a research ship on Lake Baikal, watching freshwater scientists collect species that exist only in that magnificent lake. We stood by in awe as a Buryat farmer slaughtered a sheep for us, slicing open the animal's chest and plunging in his bare hand to pinch shut its aorta, then prepared a feast of mutton and vodka that went on until the sun rose. We attended services in the last remaining synagogue in Birobidzhan, the capital of Russia's Jewish Autonomous Region, listening in

---

* The original website, including its quaint advisory that "this site is best viewed using Netscape 1.1N or later," is still online: http://www.f8.com/FP/Russia/.

Gary and me in Moscow in 1995, weary travelers near the end of our "once-in-a-lifetime" trip (COURTESY GARY MATOSO)

confusion while a self-styled rabbi named Boris exhorted elderly women in headscarves to pray to Jesus Christ. And we watched with delight as two closeted gay men in Novosibirsk put on a spectacular drag show for us in their living room.

It was truly a once-in-a-lifetime trip. Which was why, in 2005, I decided I wanted to do it again.

Gary couldn't join me this time because of work commitments, so I brought in another photographer, David Hillegas, to make the trip. Washingtonpost.com agreed to publish our updates as a daily blog, and a communications company called I-Linx sponsored us with a few thousand bucks and a satellite phone. I didn't tell the Russians I'd met in 1995 that I was coming back, opting instead to surprise them. Miraculously, through a combination of decade-old hand-scribbled notes, Google, manic perseverance, and stupid luck, I found almost everybody we'd done stories about on that first trip. The only exceptions were an elderly pensioner in Chelyabinsk (who was likely no longer alive) and a truck driver. Everyone else, we were able to interview and photograph.

In 2005, people seemed better off, materially and financially, than they'd been ten years earlier. Most were enjoying fruits of middle-class life that were previously out of reach: trips to Turkey, cell phones, Visa cards, Italian leather shoes. Many seemed more at ease speaking to me than they had before. In 1995, just four years removed from the collapse of the Soviet Union, people in Russia had seemed to be in a state of existential shell shock. By 2005, they were settling comfortably into their new capitalist reality, members of a growing middle class in a country that had arguably never had one before.

Even before that trip ended, I knew I'd want to go again in 2015. But when the time drew near, I decided to do things a little differently: I wanted to go alone, rather than with a photographer, and write a book instead of blogging. Apart from that, I'd do the same trip, and see all the same people, as before. I was eager to find out how everybody's lives had changed, now 20 years after that first visit.

Yet I was nervous too. Relations between the Russian and U.S. governments were more poisonous than they'd been in decades. We were furious at Russia for annexing Crimea, Russia was furious with us for the sanctions we subsequently levied, and everybody was pointing fingers after a Malaysian airliner was shot down over a disputed part of Ukraine. On March 8, 2015, the *Washington Post*'s Michael Birnbaum reported that "after a year in which furious rhetoric has been pumped across Russian airwaves, anger toward the United States is at its worst since opinion polls began tracking it. From ordinary street vendors all the way up to the Kremlin, a wave of anti-U.S. bile has swept the country, surpassing any time since the Stalin era, observers say."

This was a crazy time for a lone American to set off on an extended ramble across the country. On the other hand, maybe it was the perfect time. In the midst of the PR flame war, I'd be able to see what was really happening on the ground in Russia. And I'd be doing it through face-to-face conversations with people I'd been dropping in on for 20 years.

—⁕—

Something about this particular contradiction—this presumed enmity between Russians and Americans, even as people connected easily on a human level—had always fascinated me. It was the reason I became obsessed with Russia in the first place, back when I was a patriotic young military brat.

In the summer of 1976, my mother announced that she was going to visit the Soviet Union. This was an unusual choice for an American during those Cold War years, and especially for the spouse of an active-duty U.S. military officer. But she was curious, so she booked a tour and went to explore Moscow, Leningrad, and Kiev for a couple of weeks while my dad, a U.S. Navy pilot who'd just got done fighting the Communists in Vietnam, took care of my brother and me at home.

I was nine years old and deeply confused. Weren't the Russians our enemies? Why would my mom want to go visit the people my dad was fighting against? The whole time she was away, I was terrified; I truly feared I'd never see her again. But when she got back, she told us that she'd had a wonderful time and Russian people were lovely, and she showed us pictures of candy-drop-colored churches and gave us gifts, including a beautiful hand-carved wooden box that I treasured.

So, Russians were our enemies, but they were also really nice

My mother in Red Square, 1976 (FAMILY PHOTO)

people? Now I was more confused than ever. From that moment on, I needed to see the place for myself, to understand how both these facts could possibly be true.

I wanted to learn Russian, with its weird letters and incomprehensible sounds, but to my disappointment neither my middle school nor my high school offered classes. So for many years, the closest I could come was to painstakingly copy the Russian translation of John 3:16 from the front pages of the Gideon Bible whenever we happened to be staying in a motel. I'd carefully trace out the Cyrillic letters, wondering what it would sound like to speak them aloud, then marveling that one day I would actually know.

At last, in college, I got my chance. I earned my bachelor's degree in Russian Language and Literature, though even after four years of study, I still spoke it atrociously. My language skills improved during the seven months I spent at the U.S. embassy in Moscow, but it wasn't until that first year in St. Petersburg, 1994–95, that I became fluent.

So, when I went on the 1995 trip with Gary, my Russian skills were very good. On the 2005 trip, they were pretty good. Now, as I prepared for my third trip, they were decidedly not good. I hadn't set foot in the country for ten years, and apart from the occasional tipsy vodka toast, I hadn't spoken a word of Russian. What I needed was a chance to practice everyday conversation with native speakers. Fortunately, the neighborhood where I was living—West Hollywood, California—happened to be chockablock with Russian immigrants.

I found my way to the small Russian Language Library on Santa Monica Boulevard, where I met Sofia, a white-haired, bespectacled émigré who agreed to chat while she minded the desk. We started simply, telling each other where we were from, where we lived, what kind of work we did. *Good*, I thought. *This is easy.* Then, she asked if I had a family. And I froze.

I remembered that in Russian, you can't simply say "I'm married." It's a gendered construction, meaning you either say "I am wifed," or "I am husbanded" (technically, "I am behind husband," which deserves a dissertation of its own). So I looked Sofia in the eye and said, in Russian, "I am wifed."

She smiled indulgently. "No, you are husbanded." She figured I'd misspoken.

"Actually," I said, "I am *wifed*."

"Ohhh," she said, then paused thoughtfully. "Well, these things happen. There are many such people in West Hollywood.

It does not bother me. But I don't think you should tell anyone in Russia."

Her advice didn't come as a surprise. Ever since Russia passed a law in 2013 outlawing the "propaganda of nontraditional sexual relations to minors," a new wave of anti-gay sentiment, including episodes of violence, had reportedly swept the country. Even though the law didn't criminalize homosexuality outright, it was written in a way that seemed to justify anti-gay backlash. After all, even simply telling someone you're gay could be legally construed as "propagandizing," if some random child happens to be within earshot.

Living in St. Petersburg in the mid-1990s, I'd never worried too much about anti-gay attitudes—but I didn't exactly broadcast anything, either. I was single, so I didn't have to lie when asked if I was married or had a family. On the 1995 trip, whenever people asked about boyfriends, I'd just smile coyly and change the subject. This works well when you're 28. But returning in 2005, at age 38, I found it harder to shake off people's queries, which started to take on a tone of grave concern. Really? I was almost 40 and still didn't have a man? That was sad enough; I could only imagine the looks of horror and pity I'd get this time, at age 48, still having failed to get "behind husband."

The problem could be avoided with a simple white lie, but it was one I couldn't bring myself to utter. I once lost a job because I was gay, and throughout my adult life I'd endured countless conversations with homophobic colleagues, acquaintances, and relatives about whether I could or should "change." When I finally did get married, in 2010, my own brother refused for religious reasons to come to the wedding. This was a battle I'd been fighting for a long time, and I was proud to have a stable, loving relationship with my wife, Randi. I hated the idea of denying her existence, or worse, making up a fake husband. But it now seemed, for safety's sake, I might have to.

As I continued to plan, other worries popped up. For one, how safe would I be traveling alone? I'd never felt unsafe on those earlier trips, but of course I had been with Gary and David. In general, street crime didn't seem like a big problem in Russia, though I'd actually had my suitcase stolen in St. Petersburg just two days before the 2005 trip launched. I'd been staying in a friend's apartment, and while neither of us was home, a thief broke in through a window and lugged the entire bag back out with him, making off with my clothes, winter coat, boots, backup software, antibiotics, cash, and, most irritatingly, all of my underwear. I was devastated by the theft, oddly hurt that some Russian asshole would steal my stuff when I was here trying publicize the human side of his country. The saving grace was that I'd had my laptop and passport with me. Everything else, I'd had to replace on a manic, deeply resented shopping spree.

I'd have to be careful traveling alone, especially since the Russian economy was now in the toilet. On January 1, 2014, one U.S. dollar bought 33 rubles. On June 1, 2015, three months before my trip, a dollar bought 53 rubles. And on September 2, 2015, the day I arrived in Vladivostok, a dollar bought a breathtaking 67 rubles—meaning that U.S. dollars were now worth twice as much as they'd been less than two years earlier. How safe would a lone American woman, traveling across Russia during a wave of anti-American sentiment, carrying dollars (and a backpack full of expensive Apple products) in the midst of an economic meltdown, truly be?

And even if street crime didn't turn out to be a problem, going alone raised other concerns. How would it feel to be alone on those long train trips? Who would look after my stuff when I needed to go use the loo? In cities, would I be safe taking taxis alone back to wherever I was staying after the inevitable vodka-fueled reunion dinners? My brain began whirling with questions I'd never had to consider before: Should I bring pepper spray? Are you allowed to pack it on international flights? If not, should I buy some there? Do they even sell pepper spray in Russia?

I started to make myself crazy, thinking of the horrifying possibilities. And then, in addition to questions of safety, I had another worry: the battle with Russian officialdom.

The Russian government had recently tightened its visa restrictions, making it unclear whether I could even get permission to travel to all these cities without official invitations to each. One friend told me about an eminent American journalist who'd been desperately trying to get a visa so she could research a book, only to be stonewalled without explanation for more than a year by the Russian embassy.[†] A Google search instantly revealed that I was an openly gay American who'd written extensively about Russia—probably not the kind of person Putin's government wanted wandering around the country right about now. Should I take down my website? Scrub my Facebook page? Delete my Twitter feed? Or was I being unnecessarily paranoid?

For the first two trips I'd traveled on three-month business visas, arranged for a small fee, with no questions asked, through a company in St. Petersburg. But this time I'd be making the arrangements at home in Los Angeles, and I didn't even know where to start. So I turned, as one does these days, to Yelp. I found a visa services company in Burbank with a high rating and lots of good reviews, and upon the recommendation of a confident-sounding woman there named Stephanie, I applied

---

[†] This same friend later informed me that, according to a U.S. foreign service officer he knew, I should expect to be followed by Russian security agents during my trip. This seemed unlikely, but what did I know? I hadn't been to Russia in ten years.

for a multi-entry, three-year tourist visa. I submitted the paper-work in early July and crossed my fingers.

—m—

Meanwhile, I continued my preparation by going on a new shopping spree. I bought a multiport USB charger; a battery pack for recharging devices on long train trips; and a selfie stick, tripod, and trio of tiny clip-on lenses for my primary camera—my iPhone. All this equipment fit snugly into a backpack, with plenty of room left over for my laptop and iPad. Compared to the mountain of gear we'd taken on the first two trips, which included multiple cameras, a satellite phone, a BGAN satellite Internet communicator, and backups of every conceivable cord, cable, and software DVD, I'd be traveling light.

The technological differences among the three trips were nothing short of astounding. In 1995, Russian phone lines were notoriously poor, so Gary had made an arrangement with Sprint to connect directly, whenever possible, to the company's telecom nodes located across the country. We also carried phone cords and adapters, so in the rare city where we could dial up through the Russian Internet service Glasnet, we could connect our laptops to phone jacks. Either way, holding a connection long enough to upload our photos and text was a nerve-racking proposition.

To make the uploads go more quickly, Gary compressed the photos to a ridiculously tiny size. The digital camera (a Kodak DCS 420) took photos that were about 1.5 MB each, but Gary shrank them to a minuscule 25 KB. Even that tiny, the photos still took hours to send: on one memorable occasion, it took us eight hours to upload just 400 KB worth of photos. It was as if we were driving down the "Information Superhighway" with a horse and buggy.

Given the poor Internet connections, it would have been

impossible for Gary and me to update the website from the road. Fortunately, we had project partners in San Francisco, Tripp Mikich and Chuck Gathard, who worked with Gary to design and build the site and maintained it while we traveled. Every few days, we'd cross our fingers and attempt to send text and photos to Tripp and Chuck, and upon receipt—however long that took— they'd post our updates to the site.

In 1995, the World Wide Web was a new concept even in the United States; according to a Pew Research Center study, just 14 percent of Americans had ever used the Internet. In Russia, most people we spoke to outside of Moscow and St. Petersburg had never even heard of it. People would naturally ask who we were writing for, and I'd say, "Well, there's this thing called the Internet . . ." My attempts to explain sounded like a cross between Confucian sayings and schoolkids' brainteasers: "It's not printed out, but you can read it anywhere." Or, "Our partners in San Francisco put it on their computer, but it can be seen on anybody's computer if they know how to find it."

In Novosibirsk, I asked one woman whether she minded being identified by her real name. "It's not going to be published in Russia, right?" she asked.

"In theory, it can be read by anyone in the world," I told her. "They just have to plug their computer into a box called a 'modem,' then plug that box into a telephone line, then make the computer dial a specific number—"

"Stop, stop, stop," she said, waving a hand in the air. "Russians will never figure that out. Write what you want."

Against the odds, Gary and I were able to check our e-mail regularly on the 1995 trip, as long as we were in an apartment with a functioning telephone line (not always a given). But phone calls home were a different beast. Prepaid phone cards weren't yet widespread, so every couple of weeks, we'd stop by the local

Soviet-style Telephone and Telegraph office, where we'd stand in line, hand an employee a slip of paper with the phone number we wanted dialed, then race into one in a long row of phone booths when a flashing light signaled that the call had gone through.

By 2005, communications in Russia had leapt forward David and I were spoiled for choice: we could go online at ubiquitous Internet cafés, or by using prepaid Internet usage cards, or through services such as Russia Online, which had local dial-up numbers in all but two of the cities we visited. DSL, cable Internet, and Wi-Fi had also begun popping up, though this was rare outside Moscow and St. Petersburg. Phone cards made it easy for us to call home, usually for pennies a minute, and of course we had our satellite phone for more remote areas, such as when we were floating out on Lake Baikal or strolling through a field of cows in a Buryat village. Uploading photos still took time, though, especially since we were now sending multimegabyte pictures instead of the compacted 25 KB photos from the first trip.

On the third trip, communicating would be ridiculously easy. I'd be able to post photos and videos instantly with my iPhone to any social media site I liked. I could call home for free via Skype, and text friends and family for free using WhatsApp or Viber. Yet I was still curious how much it would cost to make calls, send texts, and upload photos through a regular cell phone connection, so I called my carrier, T-Mobile.

To my surprise, the customer service rep told me that under my existing cell phone plan, I could text, FaceTime, and use unlimited Internet data throughout Russia—no Wi-Fi needed. The only service that would cost extra was making and receiving cell phone calls, which would be charged at ten cents a minute. I couldn't believe my luck; how could all these international services be essentially free? Was there a catch? I asked the rep what their coverage was like in Russia, assuming that it must be pretty spotty to justify such a deal. "Hold on," she said, "I'll look at our map."

"Ah," she said after a moment. "Yeah, it's not great. There are whole big parts of Russia with no coverage at all."

Well, damn. "Can you tell me where, in general?" I asked. She gave me the URL so I could see the map for myself, and when I pulled up the image, I burst out laughing. Most of Russia wasn't covered, all right—because most of Russia is covered in permafrost, and nobody lives there. There was, however, a band of coverage all along the populated, southerly route of the Trans-Siberian, exactly where I'd be traveling. "I think I'm good," I told the woman. "Thanks."

As long as I was poking around online, I decided to check out places to stay in Vladivostok. The first two times there, we'd stayed in private homes—in 1995 with an American friend of a friend, and in 2005 with a Russian journalist who plied us with vodka and charged us a couple hundred dollars for our week-long stay. This time around I decided to just book a hotel, as I knew I'd be suffering from terrible jetlag and would sleep better if I had some privacy. Besides, the ruble was weak, and I was 48 years old now, so screw the foldout couch.

Before, arranging places to stay was one of the most time-consuming and stressful parts of the trip. Now, I actually giggled as I logged on to TripAdvisor to check out hotels. How about . . . the Vlad Motor Inn for $97 a night, or the Versailles Hotel, $119 a night, or maybe the more modest Hotel Teplo, $38 a night? I checked Google Maps to see where these hotels were located. And then I decided to mosey over to Airbnb, where I found a one-bedroom "sea & bridge view" for $42 a night, or a "cozy flat in the heart of Vladivostok" for $57 a night. I ended up booking a week at the Hotel Teplo, which didn't even require prepayment, and the confirmation appeared almost instantly in my in-box.

At last, I felt pretty much set. I had my gear, my hotel reservation, and my one-way Aeroflot ticket to Vladivostok. Now I just needed my visa.

On August 5, I got it. For all my fretting, the Russian consulate never asked any questions at all, and in fact they processed the visa more quickly than expected. Maybe I'd been unnecessarily paranoid, and there wasn't so much anti-American bias after all. For the first night in a while, I slept well, relieved that everything seemed to be going smoothly.

The next morning, I woke up to news of the Great Fromagicide.

The Russian government had publicly bulldozed or burned tons of imported food, primarily cheese, but also fruits, vegetables, and meat, that had been smuggled into the country in violation of its ban on Western agricultural products—a ban that was instituted a year earlier as a retaliatory slap to the countries that had imposed sanctions on Russia. Russian TV aired clips showing heavy machinery shoving mounds of Parmesan, Gouda, and other delicacies into dirty graves, while news anchors offered updates on such colorful developments as "an operation to liquidate dozens of tons of contraband pork," and the fact that "Dutch flowers will be examined with a microscope at the border."

It all felt rather silly, except that destroying tons of food during a severe economic downturn, especially in a country that had known too well the specter of hunger in its history, was serious business. By the end of the day, 200,000 people had signed an online petition asking the Russian government to stop the destruction. But as the *Guardian* reported, "Putin's spokesman, Dmitry Peskov, said the president had signed the law, and that meant discussion was over on the topic for now."

What the hell is going on in Russia? I thought. I couldn't wait to get back and find out.

Vladivostok:
The Lighthouse Keepers

On September 5, 1995, Gary and I wandered to a small clapboard house at the edge of Tokarevsky Cape, hoping to learn about the stark white lighthouse that stood nearby.

We had traveled an exceedingly long way to get here. From St. Petersburg, we'd flown to Vladivostok, 4,000 air miles, two herring-salad airplane meals, and seven time zones to the east. Then we took a taxi south of the city, to the top of a steep hill overlooking the windswept cape. The paved road ended, so we got out and hiked 20 minutes down a bumpy dirt road toward the water. Standing at the wooden picket fence outside the little house, we were less than 100 miles from the border of North Korea, and even closer to China. The only people we could see were a couple of old salts in the distance, fishing in tiny rubber dinghies; apart from those guys, we might as well have been standing alone at the edge of the earth.

Then we saw a third person, a man painting a shed just inside the wooden fence. "Excuse me," I called out in Russian, and he looked up, set down his paintbrush and ambled over. He was scarecrow thin, with the leathery skin and perpetual squint of a man who spends many hours outdoors. Without a word, he unlatched the gate and waved us in, as if he'd been expecting us.

"Hello!" I said brightly. "We're journalists from America! We're hoping to learn about the lighthouse."

"It was built in 1910," said the man, unsmiling and without preamble. "My father began running it in 1954, when I was ten years old. My brother and I grew up here, and now we run it like my father did." He told us his name was Vasily, and that he'd raised his own children here with his wife, Valentina. "Come meet her," he said, and abruptly turned to walk toward the house.

The yard was massive, with multiple wooden structures and a spectacular view of the bay and the lighthouse in the distance. It was a sunny September day, and as we walked across the grassy expanse I took deep breaths of the warm, salt-tinged air. We followed Vasily to the house, clomping up a small set of steps leading to a doorway hung with a lace curtain.

"Mother! We have guests!" he barked, and a petite brunette with wide cheekbones and dark eyes—clearly his wife, not his mother—peered out from the kitchen. She looked confused, then wary, as she instantly perceived by our clothes and goofy grins that we weren't Russians.

Upon hearing that we were Americans, she stiffened. "Does the government know you're here?" she asked. I told her we

Vasily at Tokarevsky lighthouse, 1995 (PHOTO BY GARY MATOSO)

hadn't made any special arrangements for our visit, adding that I wasn't aware any were required.

"Well, then, I'm not answering any questions," she snapped. "We are employees of the Ministry of Defense, and this is a military installation." She turned to glare at Gary. "Put away that camera."

Her husband waved his hand dismissively. "These are our guests," he told his wife. "Come on, let's have a drink." And he promptly disappeared from the room.

Valentina had been cooking when we arrived, and with obvious reluctance, she added two more plates to the kitchen table. Then she began loading it up with homemade dishes that made my mouth water: fried fish, pickled mushrooms, sliced tomatoes, stewed eggplant. Vasily reappeared with a bottle of vodka, and with a practiced hand he filled four shot glasses right to the rim.

We toasted to our meeting, and as I felt the alcohol warm my chest, I hoped that a couple of drinks might loosen Valentina up a bit too. We ate and drank, and I explained that Vladivostok was our first stop on a planned three-month trip across Russia. I told them we were hoping to show, through photos and stories, how people really lived here, and then Gary demonstrated the magic of his digital camera. Vasily refilled our glasses and offered another toast—to friendship!—and, in spite of herself, Valentina smiled. Then we toasted again. And again. And soon everyone was not only smiling, but laughing too. By the end of the meal, Valentina even agreed to let us come back later in the week and take a few photos.

The couple didn't have a phone, so two days later, we just showed up at dawn. No one seemed to be awake, so we meandered down the narrow gravel "cat's tail" path to the lighthouse, where Gary took pictures just as the sun's rays began to shimmer on the water. As we walked back, we saw Valentina scurrying into the generator room, a small separate structure that housed, among other equipment, a two-way radio. Vasily had shown us this room on the day we arrived, explaining that as part of the couple's duties, they were required to radio in weather data to the Vladivostok Meteorological Institute every three hours.

I wasn't sure how Valentina would react upon seeing us, but to my relief, she broke into a big smile and waved. Encouraged, Gary asked if he could take pictures while she called in her report. "Oh, no," she said, "Of course not." His face fell. Then she said, "Not in this," and gestured to the old housedress she was wearing. "Come back in a half hour."

We took another walk, and when we returned, Valentina was

Valentina (Valya) posing with the radio transceiver, 1995 (PHOTO BY
GARY MATOSO)

wearing a lacy dark blouse and pressed jeans, and she'd put on
eyeliner, blush, and coral-pink lipstick. She'd also wrapped her
hair in a kerchief-style scarf, giving her the look of an exceptionally stylish farm girl from an old Soviet poster. She posed
holding the radio transceiver in one hand and a pencil in the
other, and Gary took several lovely photos as sunlight streamed
in through a window, backlighting her face.

When the photo session finished, she led us back toward
the house as we surreptitiously high-fived behind her. We'd won
her over! We were good.

And so we were, until the soldiers showed up.

Valentina had reported our presence to the authorities the
day we arrived, as she was required to do. Now, to her apparent
shock, two men in uniform had come to check out the situation.
Seeing the men before they saw us, I heroically pulled Gary

behind a shed to hide. But it was soon clear that they had no intention of leaving, so reluctantly we slunk out. My God, were we really in trouble already? Would our grand adventure be over before it began? The men asked who we were, and whether we had the proper visas to visit Russia. When we answered that we did, they simply shrugged and headed back to their vehicle.

I hoped that passing muster with the soldiers would ease Valentina's fears, but she was spooked by their visit. She avoided us the rest of the day as we talked with Vasily and the couple's 18-year-old daughter Lusya, both of whom seemed to find the whole episode rather funny. As the afternoon light began to fade, Vasily once again invited us to stay for dinner, even breaking out a bottle of *samogon*—homemade berry-infused vodka.

Valentina eventually rejoined us, and as her husband and daughter teased her, she pooched out her lower lip. "I was just following the rules," she said peevishly. But as before, the alcohol and conversation loosened her up; it was obvious that she preferred being friends to being at odds. Soon, she revealed a mischievous smile and a disarming cackle, and when I showed her photos I'd brought from home, she *oohed* and *aahed* and even got a little teary-eyed at one of my young niece. At the end of the evening, she disappeared into her bedroom, and when she came back, she pressed a small object into my hand. It was a silver ring.

"I can't take this," I said, but she closed my hand over it with both of hers.

"I want you to have it," she told me. I couldn't believe how completely she had turned around; this Valentina was a different person from the scowling woman we'd met 48 hours earlier. By the end of dinner, as Gary and I finally wobbled drunkenly toward the dirt road, I found myself wishing we could have spent more time with her. Then we heard her voice pipe up behind us. "You know," she said to Vasily, "I'm actually kind of sorry to see them go."

—〰—

Ten years later, I came back. On September 3, 2005, I walked down that same steep dirt road, this time with David Hillegas, to find out how Valentina and Vasily were doing.

The lighthouse was still there, a slender white sentinel perched in the blue-black sea. But the narrow spit of land leading out to it, virtually untouched in 1995, was now packed with girls in bikinis and bronzed men chatting on flip phones. I could see a few dozen cars, a ferryboat, and even a small café situated on the shore nearby; the smell of sea air was now tinged with SUV fumes.

Tokarevsky Cape had morphed from edge-of-the-earth solitude to beach blanket bingo, but off to the side I could see the couple's house, looking much the same—though now it was surrounded by an imposing metal wall rather than the old wooden fence.

As we approached, I saw Vasily puttering about in the yard. "Hello!" I yelled, and he looked up. He motioned for us to walk to the door of the metal wall, and when he pulled it open I blurted, "It's me! The American journalist who came here ten years ago!" For an excruciating moment, he looked at me blankly, but at last his eyes glimmered with recognition. "Ahhh, yes, I remember you," he said, then cocked his head. "Was it really ten years ago?"

He waved us in and latched the door behind us. And as we followed him toward the house, he called out as before, "Mother! We have guests!"

Valentina was on the small patio at the rear of the house, vigorously stomping barefoot on sheets in a giant tub of soapy water. When she saw me, her eyes lit up. "Liza!" she said, using the Russianized version of my name.* "Is it really you?" She hopped out of the tub and came to give me a sweaty hug. Then she said, "Wait a minute, let me clean myself up," and disappeared into the house.

Now 61, Vasily was thinner and grayer, and he had a new mustache that helped camouflage the fact that he'd lost a few teeth. Valentina was aging well, her cheeks rosy and her hands and arms strong. I'd brought a gift of printed photos from the first trip, and as we sat down on the porch to reminisce, I asked what was new since I'd seen them last.

"For us, everything is the same as it was," Valentina chirped. "Oh, wait. Back then we had one grandchild. Now we have four."

She thought for a moment. "Some other things are different too. Before, when you came, I was afraid for some reason. I felt like I had to call my boss to report that you were here." She smiled. "But now it's more free. You can come and go as you like, take whatever photographs you like." At this, she waved her hand grandly toward the lighthouse, as though I'd just won it in a game show.

"What changed?" I asked.

She chuckled and said, "Democracy." And though she said it in a joking way, it did seem that whatever remnants of Soviet-era secrecy she'd felt burdened by back then were gone.

"Are you hungry?" she asked. "Let's eat." And as if by magic— did this woman always have delicious hot food lying about?— the table was suddenly laden with bowls of steaming beef stew, mayonnaise-drenched salads, and potatoes smothered in butter and fresh dill. Vasily cracked open a bottle of vodka—not *samo-*

---

*I'm fortunate to have a name that's easily Russianized, from Lisa to *Liza* (pronounced "Leeza"). My name is also mildly amusing to Russians, since the word *lisa* means "fox," and *dikii* means "wild." Hello, I am the wild fox. Nice to meet you.

gon this time, but store-bought vodka with a picture of a light-house on the label. Just as before, we toasted and drank . . . and drank . . . and drank, with Vasily refilling our glasses faster than we could drain them. Eventually, I slowed down as my brain got fuzzy. "Eh, weak American," Vasily observed, and Valentina shushed him. "They won't understand that you're joking!" she said, poking him in the arm.

David and I stayed for a couple of hours, talking and taking pictures, and I told Valentina we'd like to come back once more before leaving Vladivostok. "Call me on my cell phone tomor-row," she said.

"Ohhh!" I said. "You have a phone now! Fancy!"

"Yes!" she said. "But still no running water!"—which ex-plained the sheet-stomping laundry method.[†]

A couple of days later, David and I went out to the lighthouse for one more visit. This time, interspersed with the chitchat, Val-entina revealed that the couple's time at the lighthouse might be coming to an end. She'd heard rumors that the government was planning to build a bridge from their little peninsula to nearby Russian Island, an undeveloped military preserve. "They have three options for where it would go," she said, "and one of them is right over our piece of land. If they build it here, we will have to move, but they'll give us an apartment in town."

She seemed philosophical about this possibility, saying, "Of course I want to stay here until we're ready to leave, but if at some point we move to the city, that might not be so bad." I asked her if Vasily felt the same way. "No," she said. "He was born here, and he wants to die here."

As I prepared to visit the couple for a third time, I remembered

---

[†] Out of reach of Vladivostok's water supply system, Valentina and Vasily collected rainwater in a giant barrel for laundry and bathing. For drinking, they drew water from a large nearby cistern that was filled each week by the city.

Valentina's words. And I found myself hoping against hope that they hadn't come true yet.

—⁓—

On September 2, 2015, I took a taxi from the Hotel Teplo in central Vladivostok to the top of that same steep hill south of the city. But this time, the taxi kept on going, as the dirt road was now paved—not to mention lined with new, multistory houses.

I could see the lighthouse way out at the end of the cat's tail, but that was the only part of the view that looked the same. Scattered across the shorefront, I saw a giant white tent that housed a new café, a smaller restaurant called (in English) the Pit Stop, an outdoor dance floor, a kiosk selling Belgian waffles, several porta-potties, a row of bright green dumpsters, a few dozen yachts and boats in various states of repair, and so many cars and trucks it looked like I'd stumbled onto a used car lot.

The big metal wall was still there, surrounding the houses where Vasily and his brother and their families had lived. No one was in the yard, so I started to walk around the perimeter, looking for the door. I felt sure that, barring some catastrophe, Valentina would be OK. But I was worried about Vasily, who was a regular vodka drinker and heavy smoker and never seemed to eat much of anything. He'd be 71 now, well past the average life expectancy for Russian men, which was 65.

As I walked outside the wall, I couldn't find a bell to ring or a door to knock. Finally, I noticed a man painting a yacht nearby, so I called out to ask if Valentina and Vasily still lived here. "Yes, I just saw her this morning," he said. "Bang on the gate. The dog will bark, and they'll come to see who it is."

I did as he suggested, and sure enough, a dog started barking and yowling. After what felt like an eternity, the door swung open, and there stood Vasily. I was elated, but had the presence of mind not to shout, "You're alive!" Instead, I smiled goofily and started to laugh. "Ah, Liza," he said, and he smiled too.

"It's been ten more years," I told him. "So I thought I'd come back and see you."

"Come in," he said, and now I couldn't help myself—I gave him a hug, which seemed to take him by surprise. He chuckled, then turned and started loping toward the house. And then, as I'd dreamed of all summer, he called out, "Mother! We have a guest."

Valentina came to the door and broke into a grin. "Liza! I was just thinking of you yesterday!"

"Really?" I asked, and my face flushed with pleasure. "Did you realize it had been ten more years, and that I might show up again?"

"No," she said, "I just happened to think of you." Then, as if on cue, "Well, let me go get dressed." And off she went into the house to put on something more presentable.

When she emerged from her bedroom minutes later, wearing a bright pink blouse and olive-green Capri pants, she had a wicked little smile on her face. "Want something to drink?" she asked, then thumped the side of her neck, the traditional Russian signal for alcohol.

She'd been cooking, as usual, and started loading up the table with plates of rice, ground meat cutlets, pickles, and tomatoes. Then she went into another part of the house and came back with a squat little plastic bottle, which turned out, upon closer inspection, to be a shampoo bottle. When she noticed me peering at the label, she said, "We poured the vodka into this." She offered no further explanation, and I didn't ask. Then she took a tall can of beer out of the refrigerator—Yarpivo brand, with a brown bear pictured on the front. "I don't drink vodka anymore," she confided. "Beer is terrible for you, but I love it."

The three of us ate and drank, and this time it didn't simply feel like we were old friends—we *were* old friends. I started calling Valentina by her nickname, Valya, and we joked about how the "weak American" had, against the odds, managed to find her way back to Vladivostok. We talked about how scared Valya had been that first time, and she said, "Well, we didn't know who you were! We didn't know if you were . . ." She paused.

"*Spiiiies?*" I asked.

"Yes! Spies!" she said.

"Well, if I'm a spy, I'm obviously a bad one," I told her. "I've been visiting you for twenty years now and haven't done anything terrible yet."

There was a two-liter bottle of Coke on the table, which reminded me to ask about the Great Fromagicide. "I heard there weren't supposed to be any American foods in Russia now," I said. "But it looks like you can still get Coca-Cola, huh?"

Valya looked at me in shock. "Coca-Cola is American?" I confirmed that it was, and she shook her head in wonderment. Realizing that she probably wasn't the kind of person who cared a whole lot about imported cheeses, I instead asked her about Vladimir Putin.

"I adore Putin," she declared. She took my hand and led me into the living room, where a small portrait of the Russian president was nestled among the glassware in an open cabinet.[‡] Valya picked up the photo and kissed it, then gently placed it back in its spot.

Back at the table, Vasily, too, professed love for Putin. "He takes care of the homeland," he said. "He makes sure that other

---

[‡] This was a classic Russian *shkaf*, a large bookshelf/cabinet ubiquitous in Soviet homes. The shkaf was typically stocked with teapots and cups, tchotchkes, framed family photos, and pristine rows of the collected works of writers such as Gogol, Chekhov, and that perennial Russian favorite, Jack London.

people respect Russia." They both expressed sharp disdain for Barack Obama, with Vasily opining that he was "weak." I told them I didn't agree, to which Vasily said, "Well, you like your president and we like ours. It's not surprising." Then he poured our glasses full again, and we toasted to friendship between our countries. Because why spoil the mood with talk of politics?

"So, Liza," Valya said, leaning close. "Do you have a husband? Or children?"

"No," I said cheerily, then tried to think of some way to elaborate without elaborating. You could have driven a Mack truck through the ensuing silence, so as a follow-up, I blurted, "No husband! No boyfriend!" as if that explained everything. Valya cocked her head and smiled sweetly, but she seemed unsure what to say.

"Let's take some photos!" I said.

"Yes, let's," she replied. "Wait while I put on some lipstick!"

I followed her into the bedroom, and she perched in front of a small round mirror. She carefully traced the edge of her lips with a dark reddish-pink pencil, then colored in the rest with a lighter shade. "Do you want some?" she asked. Tipsy after four shots of vodka, I said, "Sure!" But after she finished with herself, she glanced at my makeup-free face and just put the lipstick away.

We took a few photos, and then Valya said, "Remember the pictures of me with the radio? All that old equipment is still there. Want to see it?" I told her I did, and she led me to the generator room.

I had forgotten how much equipment was in that room. There were multiple generators, the microwave-sized two-way radio, and a wall-sized metal box with so many knobs and dials that it looked like the Wayback Machine in the old *Mr. Peabody & Sherman* cartoons. Using my iPhone, I pulled up the 1995 photo of Valya in her kerchief at the radio, and she giggled and

Vasily and Valya in 2015, holding David's photo of them from 2005
(PHOTO BY LISA DICKEY)

tried to pose in that same position. I snapped a couple of pictures, and suddenly she blurted, "Wait! Wait!"

Her smile had vanished. "What if, when you get to the border, they look at these pictures and say, 'Why do you have all these photos of secret equipment?'" she asked. Just like that, she was as nervous as she'd been 20 years ago.

I was paranoid enough myself that I considered whether this could actually happen, even though the decades-old equipment was more appropriate for a museum than anything else. Then I realized that by the end of my trip, there'd be so many thousands of photos on my phone that anyone would give up before they scrolled all the way back to Vladivostok. "I think we're OK," I told Valya. "They're not going to look at these pictures at the border." But it was too late; she was spooked again.

"Let's walk to the lighthouse," she said.

We exited through the metal gate, then walked past cars and sunbathers as a couple of jet skis roared by, spraying water into the sky. We took a few photos with my selfie stick, then strolled back home. I asked if she wanted to see more of Gary's pictures from 1995, and she said yes. So I pulled my laptop out of my backpack and booted it up.

At least, I tried to. Nothing appeared on the screen except for a flashing question mark. What was this? I had no idea, but it certainly didn't look good. I shut the laptop. "It's not working," I said. "I'll fix it later."

Except that I couldn't. When I got back to my hotel that evening, I used my iPad to research "flashing question mark on laptop" and then followed the instructions, trying every possible way to get the thing to boot up. It was no use: my laptop's hard drive had died, on the very first day of my three-month trip. This was a horrific development, but fortunately, all I had to do was call Randi in L.A. and ask her to buy a new MacBook Air, load it with my data from our external hard drive at home, and ship it to me at the hotel. This, too, felt like a miracle of modern technology—that I could get a brand-new laptop, with all my documents and photos, delivered to me in Russia in just a matter of days.

Or so I hoped.

—⁓—

Two days later, Valya came to meet me at the big Lenin statue downtown, just steps from my hotel. This particular statue is of the "taxi-hailing" genre, with Lenin raising his right arm, gesturing toward the magnificent baroque train station perched on the waterfront of the Golden Horn Bay. Now, I was amused to see that Lenin appeared to be welcoming the massive *Diamond Princess* cruise ship docked just behind the station.

Tourism to Vladivostok is a relatively new phenomenon. As a high-security military port, this was a closed city during Soviet times, meaning no foreigners were allowed in. At the time of my 1995 visit, few Americans had ever been here—with the exception of Gerald Ford, who'd jetted over in 1974 for a quick visit to discuss arms control with Leonid Brezhnev. President Ford had been unimpressed, writing in his diary that the Okeanskaya Sanatorium, where the talks took place, looked like "an abandoned YMCA camp in the Catskills." The rest of Vladivostok didn't look much better, so even after the Russian government opened the city to foreigners in 1992, people kept right on not coming.

But now, everywhere I looked I saw souvenir stands, people in sun hats snapping photos, and guides with brightly colored flags leading groups of Asian tourists. Vladivostok's proximity to China, combined with relaxed visa restrictions for Chinese visitors, had led to a boom in tourism from that country. What was previously a run-down, sleepy, Soviet-feeling outpost had transformed into a gleaming, modern, thoroughly renovated city—including two brand-new, multimillion-dollar suspension bridges. The Russian government had been promising to build these bridges since the Khrushchev era, Valya had told me, but "Putin got it done." One of these was the bridge to Russian Island that she'd previously feared might obliterate their home.

With the opening of that bridge in 2012, the once-remote Russian Island had become a focal point of Vladivostok. The government built a sprawling new campus for the Far Eastern Federal University, with officials reportedly hoping to turn the area into a Silicon Valley of the East. This apparently entailed hosting numerous conferences, one of which, the Eastern

Economic Forum, was going on right now. In fact, at the very moment I was meeting Valya at the Lenin statue, President Putin himself was at the Forum, delivering a major speech about Ukraine. This followed an opening-day speech by Pamela Anderson, the star of *Baywatch* (or, as it's called in Russian, *Lifeguards of Malibu*) and a spokesperson for PETA, who spoke about climate change and endangered species.[§]

Valya was wearing a bright pink sun hat and a pink-and-white leopard-print blouse, part of what I was beginning to understand was an impressive collection of pink clothing. She'd brought a friend, a woman about her age named Katya, and as the three of us greeted each other, Valya smiled that wicked smile and said, "Look who's coming." She gestured behind me, and I turned, expecting to see Vasily. Instead, I saw a tall, striking brunette in a short dress and spiked heels heading our way. Was this who Valya meant?

"It's my daughter! Lusya!" Valya exclaimed, and I turned to look again. I'd spent an afternoon chatting with Lusya 20 years ago, when she was 18, and I had no recollection of what she looked like back then. But now she looked—like so many Russian women seemed to these days—like a model. "She's taking us to a place with a view," Valya said, and we set off in a little pack, two five-foot-tall Russian grandmothers and one bemused American, all trailing behind our Amazonian guide.

Lusya took us to a deserted rooftop atop a nearby hill, a place with a 365-degree view of Vladivostok. It was a perfect, sunny day, just a few puffy clouds floating by, and I marveled at the city's many new buildings, the suspension bridges, and the

---

[§] A headline the next day read, "Pamela Anderson Presented with White Tiger," which I initially took to mean she was going all Michael Jackson and starting an exotic petting zoo with the help of exuberant Russians. However, the white tiger turned out to be a small statuette, which she obligingly kissed for photographers.

shimmering water of Golden Horn Bay. With its many hills, coves, and scenic bays, Vladivostok is often compared to San Francisco, and from here the similarity was obvious.

As quickly as she'd come, Lusya said, "I have to get back to work," and she *clack-clacked* off in her high heels. Valya, Katya, and I meandered back down, and we set off toward the pedestrian mall, Admiral Fokin Street.

This was the stroll in which Katya informed me that "Americans think that in Russia, we have bears roaming in the streets." When I said I wasn't sure that was true, she waved her hand dismissively.

"A big part of the problem," she informed me, "is that President Obama doesn't like President Putin."

"Why?" I asked.

"Because three years ago, Putin was late for a meeting with him," she said. "It wasn't his fault; his plane was late. And because Putin is a well-mannered person, he apologized, but Obama took offense and he's never gotten over it." I'd never heard of this incident, but I knew better than to ask whether it had really happened. With her seen-it-all demeanor and deadpan proclamations, Katya was a woman who appeared never to have been troubled by uncertainty.

"You know," Katya went on, "President Putin is in Vladivostok right now. He's speaking at a conference on Russian Island."

"Katya!" hissed Valya under her breath. "Why do you tell her everything?"

"Everybody knows it!" Katya replied. "It's in the news. It's no secret." I was surprised at Valya's continuing nervousness; it was as if, after a brief respite in 2005, her old 1995 paranoia had swung right back around. Was this indicative of a change in Russian society generally, or just a personal quirk? Katya, in contrast, seemed willing to say whatever popped into her salt-and-pepper-haired head.

We kept walking. At the end of Admiral Fokin Street there was a mall-style fountain, and Katya paused there to scoop some water into her mouth.

"What are you doing?" Valya asked.

"Wanted to see if it was seawater or municipal," Katya announced. "Municipal. Tastes terrible."

We reached the Sportivnaya waterfront, where a jumble of outdoor cafés, children's theme park rides, and sculptures competed for attention, and in the distance we could hear music. It was coming from a stage set up for the "Days of Peace on the Pacific Ocean" festival: A group of pigtailed girls in matching white T-shirts and hair bows stood in front of a rather sparse audience, singing a song wishing happiness to the world.

"You're welcome," Katya said to me, gesturing grandly to the stage.

"Ooh, it's just starting," Valya chimed in. "Let's watch."

The festival turned out to be a celebration of the seventieth anniversary of the end of World War II in the Pacific. It was quite sweet, with groups of boys and girls taking turns singing and dancing on the stage, then exiting to rapturous applause, including ours. "You see?" Katya said. "Russians are friendly people. We just want peace."

Afterward, we ducked into a *stolovaya*, a Soviet-style cafeteria offering such classic Russian fare as borscht, carrot salad, and chicken cutlets. As we ordered soups from the paper-hatted woman behind the counter, she happened to hand me a chipped bowl. "Excuse me," Valya said. "Can we please have decent plates? We have a guest here *from America*." The woman looked at me, took back my bowl, and wordlessly filled another. I figured she was annoyed, but when I said, "Thank you," she actually smiled. I considered asking her how she felt about Barack Obama, but then thought better of it.

—∿—

In the afternoon, I received a text message on the little Russian Alcatel phone I'd bought.** The text asked if I wanted to go to Russian Island on Saturday, but I wasn't sure who it was from—this was a dirt-cheap, old-style pushbutton phone, and I couldn't figure out how to see the sender's name. When I finally deduced that it was from Valya's daughter Lusya, it took me another few minutes to work out how to reply. I managed to type the word "*da,*" and she texted back that I should meet them at the Lenin statue at 10 a.m. on Saturday, and bring a bathing suit.

It was 70 degrees that morning, another beautiful sunny day in what had so far been a very sunny trip. I walked down to the Lenin statue, and Lusya popped out of a giant maroon Toyota Land Cruiser parked nearby, waving me over. In the vehicle were her husband, Sergei, their daughters—11-year-old Karina and 14-year-old Diana—and Diana's classmate Nastya. I squeezed into the backseat with the girls, and as we headed out, Lusya told me that they were studying English in school and for the rest of the day were to speak only English with me. The girls all giggled.

As Sergei drove us across the new suspension bridge, the girls and I chatted in rudimentary English about their favorite singers, their favorite movies, whether they liked hamburgers. Arriving on Russian Island, I figured we'd head straight to a beach, as Lusya had told me to wear my swimsuit. Instead,

---

** Though I used my T-Mobile iPhone to communicate with people back home, it would have been very expensive for Russians to call me on it. So I bought a pay-as-you-go plan from the Russian carrier MTS. The rate was three rubles (one-half cent) for a one-minute call or a text message. Worth every kopek.

Sergei veered onto a muddy, unpaved path that plunged directly into the woods. The SUV started climbing as the road, such as it was, rose higher.

The SUV jolted and bounced on the rutted road, rocking like a carnival ride. Every few minutes, Lusya would shout, "Stop!" and Sergei would slam on the brakes. She'd open her door and dart out, charging into the woods to pluck tiny red berries or mushrooms she'd somehow seen peeking out from under the fallen leaves. She'd pass handfuls of berries to the backseat, and though they were sour, the girls and I popped them in our mouths like candy.

About 20 minutes after we'd turned off the main road, we finally arrived at the top of a hill. This was, Sergei informed us, the best view on Russian Island. Unfortunately, it was obscured by a foggy mist, so after a couple of quick photos, we got right back into the SUV for the hair-raising descent. After many more minutes of jouncing and bouncing, we finally got off that terrible road and back onto the paved one. Then, to my dismay, Sergei whipped the steering wheel around again, and we plunged back into the wilderness.

"It's a good thing I know you," I joked to Lusya. "Otherwise, I'd think you were taking me somewhere to kill me."

"Ha!" she replied. "This would be a good place to do it."

We bumped and slogged our way deeper into the woods, and just as I thought my brains would jolt out of my head, we reached a clearing. Sergei parked the SUV and we got out, stretched with relief, and started to walk.

If I'd thought this was the end of the journey, I was wrong. We walked . . . and walked . . . and walked. We tromped through fields of wild flowers and through copses of trees. We scrambled up cliff sides and paused at magnificent views of severe rock formations, sloping hills, and curving inlets. Finally, after several miles, we emerged onto a flatland of slate-colored rock and tide pools. We walked to the water's edge and put down our stuff.

The girls immediately changed into funny little yellow dresses. "What's this about?" I asked.

"They want to do a photo shoot," Lusya said. The girls scrambled over to a sheer cliff wall and proceeded to strike poses for the next hour, laughing and vamping. Lusya and I went for a swim, but the water was cold, so we didn't stay in long. After we got out and dried off, the two of us went for a walk.

Lusya and I had been chatting intermittently all day, getting to know each other. She exuded a no-nonsense vibe, though this wasn't off-putting; she just seemed like a woman who got things done. Her daughters obviously adored her, giving her flowers they plucked along the walk, asking for her help in fixing their hair for the photo shoot. She was constantly in motion, taking care of—well, whatever needed taking care of. Now, as we walked, she proved equally straightforward in conversation.

"Do you have a husband?" she asked. No, I said. "Have you ever?" I shook my head.

"Good for you," she said, and laughed. She told me she and Sergei had been married for nearly 20 years, since she was 19. "Ah," I said, nodding knowingly, at which point I suddenly realized that I could play this "no husband" card in a more empowering way. Rather than being the sad old American auntie who can't find a man, I could be the libertine who'd had countless lovers over the years and simply chose not to settle down. I made a mental note to practice saying, "Why *ever* would I want a husband?" with a knowing smirk.

After their photo shoot, the girls wanted to take a quick swim. Sergei, Lusya, and I poked around in the tide pools, looking for crabs and starfish, and the three of us marveled at a giant jellyfish that pulsated nearby. There were dozens of these monster jellyfish, though no one was afraid to touch them, as they didn't sting. Earlier in the day, I'd watched in awe as a woman swam through a cloud of them—another magical sight in a day that felt happily full of them.

Eventually the girls came ashore, dried off, and changed, and we began the long walk back to the car. Lusya asked if I wanted to join them for dinner, and I eagerly said yes—I really liked this family, and the girls reminded me of my nieces back home. Karina, the youngest, had told me earlier about her favorite restaurant in Vladivostok's Chinatown district, and that was where we were headed now.

—⁂—

On the drive, the girls asked me if I was on Facebook. "Of course!" I said, and Nastya handed me her iPhone. "Put your name," she said, in English—she wanted to friend me. I took her phone, then felt a pang of dread.

If she looked at my Facebook page, she'd see right away that I was married to a woman, as there were numerous of photos of Randi and me, including many from our wedding. Somehow, it hadn't occurred to me that this might be a problem on the trip, even though I'd known that Russians used Facebook. What to do? I assumed the girls would be shocked, and probably embarrassed, to find that I was gay. And I had to decide within the next 30 seconds what to do about it.

I handed her phone back. "I'll find you later," I said. "How do you spell your name?" It made absolutely no sense to do it this way, but Nastya spelled out her last name as I typed it into the memo app on my phone. "OK!" I said, a little too chipper, and put the device back in my pocket. *Maybe,* I thought, *I'll wait until I've left Vladivostok and friend the girls then. Or maybe I'll just never do it*—though the thought made me sad.

Arriving at Vladivostok's Chinatown, I was surprised to find it was small, dirty, and enclosed by a tall metal fence. The Chinese presence in the city had grown exponentially since I first came here in '95, when there were hardly any foreigners of any kind. By 2005, Chinese restaurants had opened up all over town, and one Russian woman informed me that most food products in the city were imported from there. "If it weren't for China, we'd die of hunger!" she'd told me then. Now, ten more years down the road, the Chinese influence on Vladivostok was even more widespread, with vendors, markets, and even tourists visible throughout the city—so this modest little Chinatown felt unexpectedly small.

When we walked into the Dobrynya i Anya restaurant, the staff greeted us warmly, as Lusya and her family were regulars. At the table, Sergei took the lead, ordering a half dozen dishes while the girls and I went to wash our hands. By the time we returned, a bottle wrapped in bright green paper had appeared on the table.

"What's this?" I asked.

"Chinese vodka," Lusya said. The waitress had put two shot glasses on the table, so Sergei waved her back over. "We need three," he told her.

"Yes," I said, gesturing to the girls. "One, two, three. For them." They giggled.

Lusya tore off the paper and cracked open the bottle. Thus began a series of toasts while waitresses brought out dish after dish of what I can only call Russo-Sino-themed food. There were a couple of garlicky beef dishes, chicken in some kind of tomato paste, a sweet slaw, and a mayo-drenched salad. Eleven-year-old Karina got soup, into which she enthusiastically poured several packets of sugar. And of course, there was the Chinese vodka, which was one of the strangest beverages I've ever tasted—sharp and highly alcoholic, with a decidedly petro-chemical edge.

We ate and drank until everyone was in a post-hike, post-prandial stupor. At this point, the owner—the eponymous Anya, though she was Chinese—came over to see how we had enjoyed our meal. We had a nice little chat, notable primarily because it was fascinating to hear someone speaking Russian with a strong Chinese accent. Then Anya gestured at me and asked Lusya, "So, is this your mother?"

I stared at her, mouth agape. *Really?* Did I really look old enough to be Lusya's mother—and, oh god, the *grandmother* of these children? Lusya, the fixer of all things, leapt in to say, "No, no. She's only ten years older than I am," to which Anya replied drily, "Aha. Maybe it's the haircut. She should get a different haircut."

I'm not especially vain about my looks, but as we got back in the car I was stewing. "You know," I said to Lusya, "my friend who I live with"—meaning Randi—"is your age, and occasionally people ask if she's my daughter. Strangely, it's usually Asian women who ask." This was true; when Randi and I had traveled in Thailand, we were asked several times if we were mother and daughter. I was horrified then, and horrified now, but I wanted to believe this was a cultural quirk rather than an accurate assessment of my appearance.

Lusya turned in her seat to look at me. "You live with her because you love each other, right?"

I stared at her. "Um . . . yes?" I said. Had she really just asked me that, so bluntly, in front of the girls? The conversation quickly turned in another direction, but I felt sure that Lusya knew, was inviting me to share, and didn't really care one way or another.

Sergei drove us through winding streets, up and up, until we arrived at a scenic overlook. We all piled out of the car, and spread out before us was the whole of Vladivostok, lights twinkling in the night, reflecting in the dark water of the bay. The Golden Bridge was a bright ribbon through the blackness, its V-shaped supports lit by red lights, and its slender cables branching outward like delicate spider webs.

As we walked to the overlook, I caught Lusya's arm. "When you asked me that, in the car . . . You understand, yes?"

"Yes," she said. She told me she'd guessed after our conversation on Russian Island. "And I don't mind at all. Neither do the girls. At their age no one cares." Just then, Sergei meandered over and asked what we were talking about. "Girl talk," she said, cutting him off, and she took my arm and walked me a few steps away.

I told her that people had advised me not to reveal this in Russia, but it was hard to pretend I was single and alone when I'm not. She nodded. Then I said, more as a clarification than a question, "You won't tell your mama, will you?"

"No," she said. "She's a different generation. Why upset her?"

But two days later, I told Valya myself, when the two of us went for a picnic. As we nibbled at deep-fried meat pastries and sipped from the cans of Yarpivo she'd brought, she said gently, "Liza. I was just thinking that while you know everything about us now, I still don't know anything about you." She seemed confused, even a little hurt, by my reticence to share. So I told her about my life, including Randi.

Her eyebrows flew up. "Ahhh. I've never known anyone like that before."

"Sure, you have," I said. "You've known one for 20 years, even if you didn't realize it. People don't always tell." She pondered this.

"Well," she replied, "the main thing is, you're happy. That's what counts. But . . . maybe don't tell a lot of other people."

Tokarevsky lighthouse, with jet ski buzzing nearby, 2015 (PHOTO BY LISA DICKEY)

I was relieved that my coming-out-in-Russia process seemed to be going smoothly so far,†† and this bonding with Valya seemed like the perfect way to end my time in Vladivostok. But, as I was just about to discover, my time here wasn't destined to end quite yet.

—⌒⌒—

I was in my hotel room, starting to pack, when a maid came by to say I had a phone call at the front desk. This was weird; why would someone call me at the hotel rather than on my cell phone? I walked to the lobby and a desk clerk handed me the

†† I should note that in general, coming out as a gay woman is far easier than doing so as a man. In Russia—and pretty much everywhere, really, except perhaps ancient Greece—the idea of two women together creates far less panic than that of two men together.

receiver. A woman at the other end of the line began speaking very quickly, and though I missed much of what she said, it gradually became clear that she was calling about the package with my new laptop: she was telling me it was undeliverable, and they were sending it back to the United States.

"No, no, no!" I said. "Why?" A string of impossible phrases followed: *There's a problem with the invoice, you can't receive a package at the hotel, the hotel isn't licensed to receive commercial goods, the value of the package is over the allowed amount, we're sending it back, there's nothing we can doooo* . . .

"You can't send it back!" I shrieked. Even if I could buy a new MacBook in Vladivostok, which I wasn't sure I could do, it would have none of my documents, passwords, data, and photos. I needed *this* laptop, and it had made it all the way here to Vladivostok, and now they were going to send it back? "Please, please, please," I said. "Is there anything I can do?" And then it was as if she were reciting Russian customs regulations in the voice of Charlie Brown's teacher—*wah wah wah waaaaaaah*. I took her number, begged her not to return the package just yet, and said I'd call back.

And then I called—who else?—Lusya. Not only was she the fix-it person, but she also, incredibly, happened to work for a shipping company, so she knew the ins and outs of Russian customs. I told her what had happened, and as I'd hoped, she immediately said, "Give me the number. I'll call her."

What followed was three nightmarish days of back and forth with DHL in Russia, DHL in Los Angeles, Russian customs, and the mom-and-pop store in downtown Los Angeles from where Randi had sent the package. We were instructed to write (and rewrite) letters declaring the package had been misaddressed, obtain new invoices indicating that I was the actual recipient rather than the hotel, fill out numerous customs forms, and be prepared to pay another $200 or so in tariffs.[‡‡] And it still wasn't clear whether they'd actually release the package. The USSR had been gone for nearly 25 years, but Soviet-style bureaucracy was clearly not dead yet.

I set my alarm to wake each night at 3 a.m. so I could talk with Randi in L.A. and tell her what we needed before she went to work. There was only a two-hour overlap when businesses in Vladivostok were open and those in L.A. hadn't yet closed, so that window—10 a.m. to noon Vladivostok time—was inevitably filled with frantic Skype calls and e-mails, as Lusya, Randi, and I tried to coordinate what the Russian side wanted with the American side. During these three days, I almost never left the hotel—though I did have to go to the train station to change my ticket to a later date. I'd brought a small stash of Xanax in case anything truly stressful happened on the trip, and as I started popping them, I wondered if I'd brought enough.

After yet another mad flurry of calls and e-mails, Lusya told me that it appeared customs would release the package. I was instructed to go to the Vladivostok DHL offices at 10 a.m. the next day, Friday, September 11, to start a multistep, multiple-destination process. I'd have to get everything done before the offices closed, or I'd be stuck in Vladivostok over the weekend—so when Lusya told me she'd take the day off work to drive me, I nearly wept with relief. That evening, she sent what became my favorite text message of all time: "Hello. 9 a.m. by Lenin. Bring your passport."

The next morning, I learned that Lusya drives like a bat out of hell. We raced to the DHL offices at the old Vladivostok airport—or at least, we thought we did, until Google Maps

---

[‡‡] At one point, the Russian DHL rep chastised me, saying, "You should simply have had the package sent to your name, in the city of Vladivostok. No street address." As if.

mistakenly sent us down a dirt road into a little village. We asked directions from a scruffy guy in a van, and he said, "Follow me," which in any other circumstance you couldn't have paid me to do. But he led us to the right road, and we finally parked and then hiked up four flights to the DHL office, where Oksana, the woman who'd called me at the hotel, gave us a stack of paperwork to fill out and then carry to the Russian customs office—which was at our second destination, the new airport.

This was like the classic Soviet purchasing system: you stand in one line to point out what you want, in another line to pay the cashier, and in a third line to hand the receipt to a saleslady and get your item. But these lines, unfortunately, were miles apart. Lusya and I sped to the airport, parked, and hurried in, and when we managed to locate a uniformed customs official, the woman walked us up to a sliding-glass door leading into a secure area.

I expected her to whip out a magnetic keycard, but instead she wedged her fingers between the doors and forcibly pried them open, in a pose reminiscent of Samson knocking down the temple columns. This was twenty-first-century Russian airport security? We followed her in, and I filled out another ream of paperwork while the official declared that I needed to pay "Fourteen thousand, two hundred twenty-nine rubles and thirty-six kopeks. No credit cards. Exact change, please." Fortunately, Lusya had warned me this might happen, so I'd brought a stack of bills and a pocketful of change, from which I now carefully counted out the exact amount.

We raced back to the DHL office, and finally—*finally!*—I had my new laptop. I told Lusya I wanted to take her and her family out for dinner as a thank-you, and also as a farewell, as this would be my last night in Vladivostok. But I had one more task to complete before then.

There was no point in lugging the broken laptop all the way across Russia, so I decided to destroy it. One rarely gets such an opportunity, so I thought it would be fun to get creative—throw it off the top of a building, or toss it into the bay, or pour a cup of coffee over it, filming everything in slow motion. Back at my hotel room, I opened it up and pressed the "on" button. I wanted to photograph that infuriating flashing question mark for posterity before the orgy of destruction began.

Except . . . the laptop booted right up.

I sank onto the bed, dumbfounded. How could this be? I stared at the screen, then started clicking on documents and web pages. Yep, everything worked perfectly.

I never told Lusya; how could I? We went back to Anya i Dobrynya that night and toasted with that rocket-fuel Chinese vodka, and I just kept saying, "Thank you, thank you, thank you," my gratitude mixed with a terrible twinge of guilt for what I'd put her through.[§§]

The next morning, Lusya, Valya, and Katya came to the train station to see me off, each bearing gifts: from Valya, a plastic container of home-picked plants for potpourri; from Katya, a giant 3-D refrigerator magnet with tigers, and a whistle made out of a conch shell ("in case a man tries to mess with you on the train"); and from Lusya, a plastic bottle filled with *samogon*. I hugged each of them, unable to believe it might be ten more years before we saw each other again. But the Great Laptop Debacle had put me behind schedule, so it was already past time to get to my next, very different destination: the "Jewish Homeland" of Birobidzhan.

[§§] Later that night, still racked with guilt, I called an L.A. computer-guru friend to ask if I was a complete idiot. She said that even though my old laptop booted up, it was unstable and probably would have conked out again on the trip. I still felt dumb.

—ᴍ—

Birobidzhan:
Stalin's Jewish Homeland

AT ONE-THIRTY IN THE MORNING, 15 HOURS AFTER leaving Vladivostok, my train pulled into Birobidzhan. Lugging my bags onto the platform, I looked up at the sight that had so surprised me back in 1995: on the station building, the word BIROBIDZHAN was written not only in Russian, but in Yiddish too.

I glanced for just a moment, as I was nervous to be arriving alone in the dead of night. Fortunately, a few other people had straggled off the train, so I followed them toward a parking lot where, to my relief, there were a couple of waiting taxis. I climbed into one and told the young driver, "Hotel Vostok."

"You have a reservation there?" he asked, eyeing me in his rearview mirror. "That hotel is expensive." And it was, in fact, one of the most expensive in Birobidzhan, at 1,250 rubles a night. Which, at the current exchange rate, was about 20 U.S. dollars. Which tells you everything you need know about how fancy the town is.

The boxy, six-story Vostok sits in the center of Birobidzhan, just a few blocks from the train station. I carried my bags up the front steps and into the lobby, and an older woman seated behind the front desk took my passport. Then she looked at her computer and said, "You booked your room for the twelfth. But today is the thirteenth." She *tsk-tsked*, shaking her head. "You should have booked for the thirteenth, saved yourself some money."

"But it's two a.m. on the thirteenth," I told her. "Check-in time is noon. I wouldn't have wanted to wait that long to get into my room."

"Oh, no," she said. "We put people in rooms as they arrive. It's the thirteenth today, so you should have booked for the thirteenth. Very simple. That's your mistake."

Now I was irritated, but it made no sense to argue. As she fiddled with papers behind the desk, I looked to the side and saw a freestanding rack labeled "Souvenir Shop." The only items displayed were a dozen small, framed paintings of black-hatted Jewish men in various poses—carrying menorahs, playing poker, playing clarinet while floating in a flock of birds, staring a giant fish in the face. They were bizarre, bordering on anti-Semitic, and I wondered idly why the hotel didn't just carry postcards instead. Then, the woman interrupted my reverie by asking how I wanted to pay for my room.

I handed her a credit card. "Ohhh," she said, and pinched it between her forefinger and thumb as though handling a rare document. She fished around under the desk, pulled out a hand-held credit card reader, and said, "I never do this. I hope I don't mess it up." She ran the card through the slot very, very slowly. Not surprisingly, it didn't register. "You have to do it a little faster," I told her. "Don't be afraid." She tried a couple more times, and finally the card registered.

She peered again at her computer. "It says to type in the last four numbers on the card," she said. "And then press oak." Press oak? She was speaking Russian, but she said this last word in English, like the tree. I leaned over the counter to look, and on her computer screen was a prompt with the word "OK." This was becoming a very entertaining hotel check-in.

After some hesitation, the woman managed to type in the four numbers and press "oak." Then she told me my room number and wished me a good night.

"And the key?" I asked.

"There's a *dezhurnaya* upstairs," she told me. A *dezhurnaya*! In the Soviet era, hotels always had dezhurnayas—ladies stationed on each floor who kept the room keys and monitored comings and goings—but I hadn't encountered such a system in years. Birobidzhan truly did seem to be stuck in a time warp, which was perhaps not surprising, considering the odd history of the place.

———

In the late 1920s, more than two decades before the State of Israel was established, Joseph Stalin decided to create a Jewish homeland in Russia. But not just anywhere in Russia: the government's decree designated land "near the Amur River in the Far East"—a desolate, swampy outpost 4,000 miles away from Moscow. If the map of Russia were a dartboard with Moscow at the bull's-eye, Birobidzhan, nestled above the northeast corner of China, would be the spot where a drunk guy accidentally chucked his dart into the wall.

To convince Jews to move there, the government offered free railroad passage, free meals along the way, and 600 rubles to each settler. Soviet propaganda organs produced pictures of smiling workers hauling grain and driving tractors, all of them tanned and happy under the perpetually sunny skies of Stalin's promised land. Thousands of Jews took up the government's offer, coming from not only Russia but all over the world— Argentina, the United States, even Palestine—to settle in the new Jewish region.

Some came to escape anti-Semitism. Many came because they had nothing, and therefore nothing to lose. And even more came in the early 1930s to escape starvation, as tens of thousands of Soviets began suffering and dying under Stalin's brutal collectivization policies in Ukraine. As waves of migrants continued to flow here, the Soviet government in 1934 designated the area as the Jewish Autonomous Region, with Birobidzhan as its capital.

This sounded pretty, but the reality was less so. The defining characteristics of the Jewish Autonomous Region were freezing winters and blisteringly hot summers with clouds of ravenous mosquitoes. So, even though 41,000 Jews arrived during that first decade, 28,000 of them turned around and left by the end of 1938. Yet new migrants kept on coming, and by 1948 the region's Jewish population had swelled to 30,000. Then came a sudden, brutal wave of anti-Jewish repression, as the Soviet government closed schools and synagogues, arrested writers, and drove Jewish cultural and religious life underground. From that point on, the Jewish population here began a slow decline.

A visitor to Birobidzhan during the Brezhnev era might hear older men speaking Yiddish in the park, but apart from that, not much marked this place as a onetime Jewish homeland.

Glasnost led to a modest revival of Jewish culture in the 1980s, but it also led to a new, possibly final, exodus, as thousands of Jews took advantage of newly relaxed travel laws to leave the country. Following the collapse of the Soviet Union in 1991, the floodgates truly opened, and thousands more streamed out, including most of the remaining Jews of Birobidzhan. By the end of 1992, fewer than 5,000 Jews were left here.

So, when Gary and I arrived in Birobidzhan in September 1995, we weren't sure how much—if any—Jewish culture we'd find. I asked around to see if there was a synagogue in town, but nobody seemed to know. A taxi driver agreed to take us on a search, and after driving in circles, we managed to find a small wooden building with wrought-iron Stars of David in the windows. I knocked on the door, and a short, white-bearded man wearing a yarmulke answered.

This was Boris Kaufman, the self-appointed keeper of what turned out to be Birobidzhan's only synagogue. There was no rabbi in Birobidzhan, Boris told us, so there were no official prayer services here. But twice a week, he led services for a small group of mostly elderly women. "Please join us for the next one, if you'd like," he said. We eagerly accepted, excited to witness a service in this historic remnant of the once-thriving Jewish Autonomous Region.

When Gary and I arrived at the appointed time, Boris asked me to put on a headscarf. I wasn't familiar with Jewish rituals, so I didn't think anything of it, but once the service started it quickly became clear that Boris was making up his own rules. Because what we ended up witnessing was more evangelical tent revival than Jewish service.

Boris read from a Hebrew prayer book, shuddering and rocking back and forth in apparent religious ecstasy, while the old women, weeping and waving their hands, called out verses from

Boris Kaufman at the old synagogue, 1995
(PHOTO BY GARY MATOSO)

the New Testament. "Jesus said, 'I am the way, the truth and life!' " one shouted, as Boris rocked in his chair, a little smile on his lips. It was a jarring scene, as Boris later acknowledged. "Perhaps it bothers some people that we worship Jesus here; I don't know. I've never asked them," he told me. "But it's not as though we took over the synagogue from Jews who wanted to hold services. The generation of older Jews who used to come gradually died out, and no one else came to fill the void."

Yet Boris, who was ethnically Jewish, also told us he wanted to see Birobidzhan's Jewish culture preserved. Every morning before the sun rose, he and his mentor, a twenty-something former Yeshiva student named Oleg Shavulski, sang Jewish prayers. A slender, sad-eyed man with a neatly trimmed beard, Oleg taught Boris how to wear the tefillin and translated Hebrew words the older man didn't know. When we asked about the Jesus-worshiping gatherings in the synagogue, he sighed heavily. "Boris is confused," he said. "But he will come around eventually. One does not come to the truth in one day or two days. It takes many days."

Oleg was one of the most vocal proponents of revitalizing Jewish culture in Birobidzhan. He told us there were promising signs: Sunday school classes (taught by Oleg) had started up again, a new cultural center had opened, and School No. 2 was not only offering Yiddish classes again, they were also putting on a Rosh Hashanah pageant the following week.

Yet it was hard to avoid the feeling that this was too little, too late. With no rabbi, no functioning synagogue, and no prospects for getting either anytime soon, how much longer could the city's Jewish community survive?

For that matter, how long could Birobidzhan itself survive in the face of its shattered economy? In the four years since the collapse of the USSR, factories had closed down, thousands of people had lost their jobs, and many who were still working hadn't been paid in months. With its tree-lined streets and small-town feel, Birobidzhan wasn't without its charms, but the lack of employment and a persistent sense of malaise were like a cloud hovering just overhead.

This place was dirt poor, and what little money did trickle in went straight to Sokhnut, an organization whose main purpose here was to help Jews get out. "No one wants to invest any money in this city," Oleg said bitterly. "The easiest thing in the world is to leave, to quit. But there will always be Jews in Birobidzhan, and we must make it possible for them to have a normal spiritual life. Someone must be here to take care of those who stay."

This, we discovered, was the central question for Birobidzhan's Jews in 1995: Stay, and work to revive the city? Or call it a day, and move to Israel (or Europe, or North America)?

Sokhnut director Mikhail Diment, a weary-looking man of 60 whose office was decorated with a large Israeli flag, spent every day working to help people leave. "We are the one race that knows exactly where it came from," he told me. "We are linked by faith, by the Torah. And Israel is our homeland." Those who wanted to leave, he said, should feel no guilt for doing so.

Author David Waiserman, who was born and raised in Birobidzhan, was dismayed by the mass exodus. "The Jews who are leaving this city are leaving for one reason: economics," he told me. "They got a call from somebody in Israel who said, 'Hey, Moishe! Get over here and have a look at this place! They got nice cars here, and great food!' So the people go." He paused. "But my parents built this city. They are lying in its graveyard. How can I just pick up and go? This is where my roots are."

Maria Shokhtova, a Yiddish teacher at School No. 2, told me that during her childhood in Ukraine, her father prayed "every morning and every night. He knew all the rituals, and we used to go to the synagogue." But these days, she didn't do any of those things—and she didn't know anyone else who did, either. "I live in a little village called Waldheim with my daughter now," she told me. "When we first came to Waldheim, it was all Jewish. Now you can hardly find any Jews there."*

Alexander Yakubson, a 48-year-old lawyer, was truly torn

---

* *Valdgeym*, as it's called in Russian, was the site of the Jewish Autonomous Region's first collective farm (*kolkhoz*), founded in 1928.

Birobidzhan train station sign, written in Russian and Yiddish, 1995
(PHOTO BY GARY MATOSO)

about what to do. He and his family had emigrated to Israel in 1991, then returned to Birobidzhan three years later to find it a changed place. "When we left Russia in 1991, the economy was more stable, the factories were still working. There was almost no crime," he said. "When we returned last year, the picture was totally different. There are so many unemployed here now, so many people are poor. Now the Russians envy the Jews in this country, because the Jews can leave."

"My wife wants to go back to Israel," he said. "I'm not sure what I want."

Hearing the anguish in his voice, I couldn't help but think that perhaps when you have two homelands, you really have none. Because you never know where you truly belong.

—⚬⚬—

I titled my 1995 story "The Last Jews of Birobidzhan," and as the 2005 trip drew near, I expected to find little more than a ghost town here, at least in terms of Jewish culture.

On the day David and I arrived, we took a taxi to the little synagogue to see if it was still standing. It was—and Boris Kaufman was there too, looking the same in his long white beard and yarmulke. Boris told us that he still held services, though he no longer allowed the worship of Jesus Christ. "There were several women who wanted to do that," he said, shrugging. "But in 1996 or so, I told them we had to keep to Jewish religious traditions here. So they left."

But the bigger news, by far, was that Birobidzhan had a new synagogue. And for the first time in decades, it had a rabbi—an energetic young Israeli named Mordechai Scheiner, who'd arrived in 2002.

This was truly surprising. And the new synagogue complex was even more so: not only was there a beautiful new sanctuary, there were also Sunday school classrooms, a small museum, administrative offices, and a library. The synagogue had a Torah and specially designed ceiling lights that formed a Star of David, and the Sunday school had a computer classroom outfitted with ten brand-new computers. All of this was funded by government and private sources, including the American Jewish Joint Distribution Committee in addition to Russian organizations—and enough money had been earmarked to keep it open a long time. It seemed that the Jewish Autonomous Region had been saved.

And yet . . . and yet . . . a different reality emerged when I tried to track down the people I'd spoken with in 1995. Boris's mentor, Oleg Shavulski, who'd railed bitterly against those who left Birobidzhan, had moved to Germany. Maria Shokhtova, the Yiddish teacher, had moved to Israel. David Waiserman, who'd told me, "This is where my roots are," had left too, emigrating to Israel. And Alexander Yakubson, the lawyer who'd moved to Israel, then back to Birobidzhan, had returned once again to Israel.

In fact, only three people I'd spoken to in 1995 *hadn't* left: Boris Kaufman; union leader Yakov Sherman, who had unfortunately suffered a debilitating stroke; and—most surprisingly—Mikhail Diment, the Sokhnut director who'd spent the whole of the 1990s trying to get his fellow Jews out.

Judging from my admittedly small sample size, it seemed that the exodus from Birobidzhan never really stopped. Yet at School No. 2, a whopping 600 students were now enrolled to study "the languages and culture of the Jewish people"—up from just 100 in 1995. Not all these students were Jewish, but many were. The school's director, Liliya Komissarenko, told me that this was one of the most telling signs that Jewish culture in Birobidzhan was experiencing a true resurgence.

"But how is that possible, with so many Jews still leaving?" I asked her.

"The more Jews that leave, the more that are left here," she replied. I looked at her blankly. Was this a riddle?

"Now, many more people here are discovering and embracing their Jewish roots," she explained. "These are people who, before, had no interest in their Jewish heritage. But now they're acknowledging who they are." In other words, Jewish families who'd gone underground during the Soviet era were now, finally, coming back out.

Many others confirmed this. Albina Sergeyeva, director of the Freud Center, told me, "Ten years ago, many of those who left didn't want to proclaim themselves Jewish. Now, people call themselves Jewish, and they talk about how their grandmothers and great-grandmothers practiced the Jewish faith." Lev

Toytman, who'd come to Birobidzhan as a boy in 1934, said, "After 1917, people forgot who they were. Especially those born after the 1930s and '40s, they were Pioneers and Communists. The synagogues were closed. But now people will say they're Jewish. Things have changed."

Not everybody believed that Birobidzhan's Jewish population had grown; official estimates put the number at fewer than 4,000. But Vasily Gurevich, deputy chairman of the Jewish Autonomous Region, opined that ultimately "numbers don't matter. It's the spiritual life of the town that matters. There may be fewer Jews, but we've created better conditions for those who've remained.

"Now the young people know what a menorah is," he concluded. "They didn't before."

And if anyone still didn't know, all they had to do was stroll down to Birobidzhan's train station, which now boasted a giant menorah out front—one of many Jewish landmarks in the city, including a statue of writer Sholem Aleichem, as well as one of a fiddler in front of the Philharmonic Hall. Yes, Birobidzhan was still a small, swampy, economically challenged outpost, but it did seem in 2005 that the Jewish Autonomous Region would survive.

Ten years later, it was time to find out for sure.

—⁘—

The morning after my late-night check-in at the Hotel Vostok, I found a different woman seated behind the front desk. "Can you tell me how to get to the synagogue?" I asked her. I remembered that it was in the city center, which was small enough that I hadn't thought it necessary in 2005 to write down the street address.

"Synagogue?" the woman asked.

"Yes," I said. "The Jewish . . . church?" She looked at me quiz-zically. "It was built in 2004," I said, "not far from here . . ." I assumed that she wasn't Jewish, as the vast majority of Birobid-zhan residents weren't, but did she really not even know what I was talking about?

"Ah, I think I know the place you mean," she said at last. "Walk out of the hotel and turn left. Go past the Rodina movie theater and the World War II memorial. You'll start to see some Jewish stars. It's probably around there."

I thanked her, then headed out into the early autumn sun-shine. The street in front of the hotel had been turned into a pedestrian mall, though the first couple of blocks were bleak, littered with abandoned kiosks and flashing electronic billboards. Once I got past those, however, the city's sidewalks were spa-cious and tree-lined, very pleasant for a morning stroll. With its sleepy pace and modest storefronts, Birobidzhan seemed to have changed little since I was here last.

Unlike Vladivostok, with its miles of waterfront, rolling hills, and winding streets, Birobidzhan was a flat grid. The center of town was a rectangle, bounded by the train station to the north, the Vostok hotel to the east, the Bira River and Philharmonic Hall to the south, and School No. 23 to the west. Within that rectangle were most of the local landmarks: the House of Cul-ture, the World War II monument, the Regional Museum, and the synagogue.

Ten minutes into the walk, I turned onto Lenin Street and started seeing menorahs—not "Jewish stars," but close enough. A long wrought-iron fence was decorated with them, and in front of that stood a silver statue of a Hasid blowing a shofar.

This marked the entrance to the synagogue complex, which was dominated by two large buildings: the synagogue and the Freud Jewish Community Center. The grounds were beautifully tended, with colorful flowers providing a backdrop to a stark black granite stone, a monument to victims of the Holocaust.

I walked into the synagogue's lobby, but the inner door leading to the sanctuary was closed. Should I knock, or just go in? This was the start of Rosh Hashanah; were there religious reasons why I, a non-Jewish woman, shouldn't enter? I walked back outside, momentarily stymied. Then it occurred to me that I could text Randi in Los Angeles to ask—she was Jewish; she'd know what to do. She texted back one word—"knock"— and at that moment, I looked up to see a little boy peering out the synagogue window.

I waved, and he waved back. Then a man appeared in the window, and he beckoned me in. "Rabbi Riss is arriving from Khabarovsk today," he told me. "Come back in two hours." So Mordechai Scheiner had moved on, but Birobidzhan had a new rabbi. This was a good sign.

With two free hours, I took a taxi to the old synagogue. Not only was the little building still standing, it also had a fresh coat of electric blue paint, clean white trim, and decorative iron Stars of David. Moving closer, I saw signs in the windows announcing that the grounds were protected by video cameras. No one answered my knock, though a plaque out front indicated that it should have been open since 10 a.m. I was disappointed no one was there, but happy to see that the place seemed well kept.

That afternoon, I returned to the new synagogue to meet Rabbi Riss, and to my surprise and delight he spoke English. "I lived in Brooklyn for a couple of years," he said. "So that helped." I asked him how he managed to go from bustling New York City to sleepy Birobidzhan, and he replied, "Actually, I was born here."

Eliyahu Riss was born in Birobidzhan in 1990, and no, that

is not a typo: two years into his tenure as the spiritual leader of the Jewish Autonomous Region, the rabbi was all of 25 years old. When he was still a baby, his family—like so many in Birobidzhan at that time—moved to Israel. They spent the next thirteen years there, but in 2004, Eliyahu's father decided to bring his family back for a visit. Upon seeing the new synagogue and the flowering of cultural life here, he decided to return for good. So at age 14, Eliyahu found himself living once again in the city of his birth.

He left at age 16, moving to Moscow to study at yeshiva. At 20, he went to New York City for two more years of study; at 21 he got married, and at 23 he agreed to become Birobidzhan's rabbi. "People told me I was crazy to do it," he said with a wide smile. "But I consider this a mission." He told me that Boris Kaufman had moved to Israel, and the old synagogue was essentially a museum now.

"We're having a youth dinner this evening, if you'd like to come," Rabbi Riss said. "You are still a youth, yes?" he added, smiling again. In fact, he never really stopped smiling: this rabbi radiated bonhomie. "We also have prayer services tomorrow, and the blowing of the shofar. It will be a big day!" I thanked him, and told him I'd see him that evening.

As I walked back to the Vostok, I felt exhausted. My nose had been running all day, and my head felt stuffed with cotton. At the end of my time in Vladivostok, Lusya had been suffering from a cold, and now, as I started sneezing, I knew I'd caught it. I took the elevator to the fourth floor and asked the dezhurnaya for my key, eager to collapse into bed.

"I must inform you that there is no hot water in your room," she said. "There won't be any all week. However, there is another room with its own water heater." *Ah, good,* I thought. *They're moving me into that one.* "Just let us know when you want to bathe," she said. "And we will let you in to do so." Apparently everyone on my floor would be using that one bathroom to shower, a revelation that was both irritating and, considering the state of the hotel's customer service so far, not terribly surprising.

—⚬—

The young people's dinner that night was eye-opening. About 15 people, most of whom appeared to be in their twenties, sat at a long table laden with plastic plates of salads, stews, and sliced meat. In honor of Rosh Hashanah, the Jewish New Year traditionally celebrated with apples and honey, the rabbi had brought Jim Beam Honey whiskey. He sat at the head of the table, smiling, making jokes, and talking about how we should feel gratitude for everything God has given us. Down at my end of the table, however, the mood was different.

The rabbi hadn't introduced me to the group, so no one seemed to know who I was. After sitting silently for the first part of the meal, I decided to make small talk with the guy to my left, a dark-haired, broodingly handsome young man. "So, were you born in Birobidzhan?" I asked.

"Yes, unfortunately," he answered, then added that he was eager to leave and didn't care where he ended up, as long as it was anywhere but here. "Where do you live?" he asked. When I told him California, his eyes widened. "That must be nice," he said, then cocked his head to look at me more closely. "How did you travel all the way here? Do you have money?" I shrugged, unsure where the conversation was going. "It's expensive to go to America. Maybe you can help me?" I smiled and sipped my Jim Beam Honey. This might turn into a long night.

Once word got out that I was American, the conversation at the table shifted. A guy sitting to my right said, "I was there once. New York. Actually, it was Brooklyn." He took a bite of beet salad. "There weren't many Americans in Brooklyn. Just Chinese and black people."

"Ah," I said. "Well . . . those people are actually Americans too."

"Yeah, maybe," he said. "But not like the Americans in the center of Manhattan. That's where they all are." To say that he was speaking in code would be an insult to the notion of code. For him, "American" equaled "white," and at this moment, I wasn't inclined to argue the point.

The talk turned to Ukraine, and the guy on my left got into a disagreement with the guy on my right as to how much the press —both Russian and American—manipulates public opinion. The mood in the room felt prickly, but I wasn't sure if this was real, or just an unfortunate combination of difficult conversation, feeling out of place, and the ongoing stuffiness in my head. I was glad when the dinner finally ended.

The next morning, I showed up at the synagogue for the prayer service. A half dozen men were in the sanctuary, and one guided me into a small partitioned area with chairs and a coat rack. Ah, yes—I'd forgotten that in Orthodox Jewish services, men and women are segregated. This was disappointing, not only because I'm an agnostic who dislikes random segregation of any kind, but also because I couldn't see anything beyond the partition walls.

Eventually, both the sanctuary and the women's area filled up. Rabbi Riss started singing prayers in Hebrew in a strong, resonant voice, and I closed my eyes to let the sound wash over me. Despite the headaches of my visit so far, there was something thrilling about hearing these ancient prayers, especially in a place where people had fought so hard to preserve their Jewish faith.

During a short break, Rabbi Riss gave the congregation, most of whom were elderly, a spiritual pep talk. "Rejoice!" he told them. "Rejoice that you have your health, you can pray, you can move about. You don't have the life of an invalid. You have everything—yet you say this isn't life?" He seemed to be speaking to the same malaise I'd sensed at the youth dinner the night before, and I wondered how pervasive it might be in the community these days.

Back at the hotel, my room was stuffy and hot. Mid-September in this part of the world can be quite warm, and the high this week was expected to be in the mid-80s. I lay down on the bed, then noticed an air-conditioning unit embedded high in the wall. Hooray! I found the remote control, turned it on, and sank into my pillow for a quick nap.

When I woke up, my eyes were itching like hell. I went into the bathroom and washed my face—in cold water, since that's all there was—then went out for an evening walk. I felt the need for some fresh air, both physically and figuratively.

—⚹—

The next morning, I could hardly get out of bed. I spent the whole day in the hotel, AC blasting, and midafternoon I carried my toiletries down the hallway to use the now-communal shower. The rest of the time, I slept, sniffled, sneezed, and rubbed my eyes. The room had a vague odor of cigarettes and seemed coated in an ancient layer of Soviet dust, but I forced myself to stay in and rest, hoping that by the following morning I'd be well.

I wasn't. At 7:30 a.m., shuffling into the bathroom, I was in for a shock. My eyes were puffy and bloodshot, and one was tearing up. *Oh, my god,* I thought. *I have pinkeye!* I'd had it twice in my life, and both times I'd gone straight to a doctor. But that was the last thing I wanted to do here. My one experience with Russian doctors, in St. Petersburg in 1995, had involved a scalpel sterilized with a Bunsen burner, so I felt a wee bit skittish about them.[†] I quickly dressed and left the hotel.

As I ate breakfast at the nearby California Café, my eyes started feeling a bit better. I finished up my fried eggs and coffee, and headed back to the hotel to prepare for the day. But the minute I got up to my room, my eyes started itching again. This wasn't pinkeye; it was an allergy. I hurried back out again, more annoyed than ever.

My first stop was at School No. 23, where I had an appointment with the director, whom I'd also interviewed ten years earlier. In her tailored suit, with a confident bearing and two cell phones always within reach, Liliya Komissarenko was the kind of put-together, no-nonsense administrator you want running your school. She invited me into her office, but when I asked if she remembered me from 2005, she smiled sweetly and said, "You know, I meet a lot of people."

I told her I'd visited her at School No. 2 back then, and asked why she was no longer there.

"School No. 2 was destroyed," she replied. "The building was old and unsafe, so the government knocked it down. We merged with School No. 3, and to make sure nobody felt offended, they decided to name it School No. 23."

The new school was now the center of Jewish education for Birobidzhan's children. One thousand students were enrolled— up from 600 at School No. 2 in 2005—and all of them took classes in Jewish culture and history, including a mandatory tenth-grade course on the Holocaust. Around 200 kids were

---

[†] I'd caught ringworm from petting a rescued street cat. To my surprise and dismay, Skin Clinic No. 1 not only sterilized their tools with Bunsen burners, they also had a resident cat that wandered around the waiting room rubbing up against the patients.

Students learning Yiddish at School No. 23, September 2015 (PHOTO BY LISA DICKEY)

studying Yiddish, which the director called the "native language of our territory."

"In the nineties, people studied Hebrew when they wanted to leave," she told me. "Those who were staying studied Yiddish, the language of the settlers—of my parents, my grandparents." This explained why the train station name and street names in Birobidzhan were written in Yiddish, rather than Hebrew. "We have two Hebrew classes left," she went on, "but we're phasing them out. We don't need to prepare our students to emigrate. We live in Russia!"

I asked how many of the students at School No. 23 were Jewish. "We don't analyze the population of students by nationality," she said, with a brusque shake of her head. "It's not even possible to sort out which nationality they all are.[‡] But we study Jewish tradition, which is important to all, regardless. And we follow the Jewish calendar and holidays—Hanukkah, Pesach, Purim, Shavuot. And all the dates that are connected to tragedies of European Jews: Babi Yar, Holocaust Remembrance Day, and so forth. This differentiates our school from others.

"Yesterday was our Rosh Hashanah pageant," she told me, smiling proudly. "The whole hall was full of students. It's too bad you didn't come!" I instantly regretted the day I'd spent resting: it would have been fantastic to see hundreds of students gathered in celebration of the Jewish New Year, rather than lying about miserably in the Hotel Sneezalot.

I thanked the director for her time, then headed off once more to the synagogue. Rabbi Riss had promised a tour of the complex, and I was eager to finish this last bit of research in Birobidzhan, if for no other reason than to get out of that hotel and on to the next destination. Birobidzhan was a fascinating place, but something always seemed to go wrong here.[§]

At the synagogue, I was surprised to see dozens of people milling about the grounds. There was a class of uniformed

---

[‡] The director's use of the word "nationality" might sound odd to Western ears, but in this context it's understood to mean "ethnicity." In Soviet times, and even for several years after the collapse of the USSR, passports here identified citizens by the "nationality": Russian, Georgian, Armenian, Jewish, etc. The practice was discontinued in 1997, but a 2013 poll revealed that 54 percent of Russians would like to see it reinstated.

[§] In 1995, what went wrong was that Gary and I had to flee the local police, who came poking around our apartment after neighbors tipped them off that Americans were staying there. (We hadn't registered our visas locally, which was either an ironclad requirement or not a requirement at all, depending on whom you asked.) We went on the lam, racing to the only safe place we could think of: the home of an American missionary couple we'd happened to meet at a restaurant two days earlier. They graciously allowed us to stay the night, taking care to put us in separate rooms because we weren't married.

kindergarteners, a group of students from the nearby Sholem Aleichem University**, and a couple of Americans with an interpreter. Rabbi Riss was giving a tour, alternately describing esoteric elements of Jewish faith with more quotidian information about how the community here survives.

"The government pays for School No. 23, and it pays for Sholem Aleichem University," he told the group. "It pays for our Sunday school, where we teach Jewish traditions, history, and Hebrew. And every two years, we have a big Jewish festival here, and many international artists come. The government pays for that too."

"Today, Birobidzhan is a political place, not just cultural," he went on. "They're trying to show that we have a big Jewish life here." This was an unusually honest assessment. With official figures showing just 1,700 Jews living here now, the amount of money pouring in to support the synagogue and various activities was, per capita, quite high. It was obvious that the Russian government wanted this place to survive.

With anti-Semitism a perennial problem in Russia, this was a good public relations move. In the Soviet era, Jews were repressed as a matter of course—denied entrance to universities, denied housing and jobs, decried publicly as enemies of the USSR. As the Soviet Union creaked toward its end in the late 1980s, record numbers of Jews fled; in 1989 alone, more than 70,000 left the country. As of 2010, just 159,000 Jews remained in Russia, a fraction of the 1930s peak of nearly 900,000. Of the Jews still here, the vast majority are in Moscow, many others are in St. Petersburg, a handful are in Birobidzhan, and the rest are scattered in tiny pockets elsewhere.

** Founded in 1984 as the "Birobidzhan State Pedagogical Institute," renamed in 2005 as the uninspiring "Far Eastern State Socio-Humanitarian Academy," and renamed again, in 2011, as the "Amur State University named after Sholem Aleichem."

Yet even if the government's support here seemed like a PR move, Rabbi Riss seemed sincere in his desire to provide spiritual support for the Jewish community. In this, he admitted facing a fair number of obstacles. For one thing, he'd relinquished his Russian citizenship when his family left Birobidzhan back in 1991, and so far he'd been unable to get it back. "I've been trying to get a Russian passport for 11 years," he told me, "but every time, they say, 'You did something wrong with the paperwork.'" His wife and children all had Russian passports, but as an Israeli citizen, Rabbi Riss was forced to repeatedly apply for temporary work visas, adding an extra layer of complication to his commitment to stay.

There were other problems. "My wife doesn't like it in Birobidzhan," he said. "The first year was very difficult—there's no place to get kosher food, and it's so far away from everything." His wife wasn't alone in her aversion to the place: after Mordechai Scheiner left in 2008, Rabbi Riss said, they couldn't find another rabbi willing to move here. So for three years, Birobidzhan had a beautiful new synagogue, but no rabbi.

"We would have a better life in Israel or Moscow," Rabbi Riss admitted. "But this is my mission. I will stay here as long as I can." True to form, he broke into a big grin. "On the bright side, there's no anti-Semitism here. When I walk around, everyone says 'Shalom!' even if they're not Jewish. In Moscow, I felt like people would say bad stuff, or sometimes curse. But here, it's like in Israel."

That seemed a bit of a stretch. Yet once again, thanks to government funding, the new wave of students at School No. 23, and this determined young rabbi, it seemed the Jewish Autonomous Region would continue to survive.

—᠊ᢁᠣ᠊—

I was starting to think Birobidzhan might be the end of me, though. As soon as I got back to the hotel room, my eyes started to burn again. Now I was angry: I charged down the hallway to ask the dezhurnaya if I could switch rooms. "Do you have any nonsmoking rooms in this hotel?" I asked.

"They're all nonsmoking," she said.

"Then why is there an ashtray in my room?"

"Eh, it's empty!" she said, with a flick of her hand.

I considered changing hotels but was convinced the others would be no better, and at least the Vostok was right in the center of town. More important, leaving a prepaid hotel room seemed like an unnecessary extravagance that only a wasteful American would consider. I didn't want to be that person.

The other option was to leave Birobidzhan altogether. I was actually ready to leave, but because the town isn't directly on the Trans-Siberian line, fewer trains came through, and there were none to my next destination, Chita, until two nights hence. I booked a ticket, then consoled myself by thinking, *just 48 more hours in that damn room*. My eyes hadn't begun itching until I'd turned on the air-conditioner, so I resolved to leave it off, no matter how hot the room got.

The next morning, though, I woke up as itchy-eyed as ever. I called Rada, a young Russian interpreter who'd struck up a conversation with me at the synagogue. She'd given me her number, and though I hadn't planned on using it, now I felt desperate. "Do you know of any apartments I could rent just for one day?" I asked. "I'm leaving on the train late tomorrow, but need a place for tonight." Rada leapt into action, making a few calls, and she even joined me to look at a couple of apartments. But they all seemed just as dusty as the Vostok, so after a couple of hours, we gave up. Grateful for the help, I invited Rada to dinner that evening. Just 36 hours to go.

I couldn't stand the thought of going back into the hotel, so I went to a café and had a cup of tea. Then I sat outside on a park bench, until a swarm of tiny mosquitoes attacked. I started walking, wandering first past the train station, then to the Philharmonic Hall, then down by the river. At one point, I looked up and saw a jet contrail, which startled me as much as if I'd seen a UFO—that's how off the beaten track Birobidzhan felt.[††]

Finally, with the sun setting, I came back and sat on a bench across from the hotel. A big electronic billboard was blaring the same advertisements over and over, and I started to memorize them. My favorite one was for a window supply company called Okna Etalon (Standard Windows), because their jingle was set to the melody of the Passover song "Let My People Go." I sat waiting for their ad to cycle back around, so I could sing along: "Ok-naaa E-taaaaaa-LON!"[‡‡] At long last, 27 Okna Etalons later, it was time to meet Rada for dinner.

I took her to the nicest restaurant I'd found in Birobidzhan, an Italian place one block from the synagogue. Over plates of pasta and pizza, we chatted in English, and gradually I started to feel good again. My cold was abating, my eyes were no longer itching, and tomorrow night I'd finally be moving on to a new city.

When I got back to the hotel—for my final night there!—I sent Randi an e-mail. "I'm so ready to get to the next destination, I can't even tell you," I wrote. "I am really hopeful that these random irritations will stop happening and I can just settle into the trip."

I hit "send," shut my laptop, and lay back on my pillow. Within minutes, I was asleep.

[††] The nearest airport is in Khabarovsk, more than 100 miles away. It's surprising how strange an airplane in the sky looks when you haven't seen one for a few days.

[‡‡] My second favorite was for a business called Klatch. I thought this was another Jewish reference (*klatsch*), perhaps for a coffee shop. Then I looked up the store online, and it sells purses. Klatch=clutch.

—w—

In the black of night, my eyes popped open. *The bed is wet. The bed is wet!*

Where was it coming from? Was it coming from . . . me? I staggered out of the bed and felt my way to the bathroom, banging into the dresser and my suitcase along the way. I switched on the light and looked down, but I couldn't figure out what had happened. Was that water on my legs? *Oh, god. No, no, no.* It wasn't water. It was pale, watery diarrhea.

My stomach lurched. How did this happen? I hadn't even felt anything until it was too late. I started cleaning myself up, then realized in a flash of horror that it might be all over the bed too. I hurried out and pulled back the blanket: the sheets were stained. I yanked them off the bed and carried them into the shower stall, where I began trying, unsuccessfully, to scrub them clean using tiny travel packets of Woolite a friend had given me for the trip. As I hunched over them, with tears in my eyes and my guts rumbling, I began to wonder if I'd made a mistake coming back for this third journey.

The worst thing about getting sick while traveling is that you never know how much worse it might get before it gets better. And if this was food poisoning, which I suspected it was, it could get much, much worse. Fear was making my heart race, so I left the sheets in a heap and began pacing up and down the room, trying to calm myself. I finally remembered I had Imodium in my medicine bag, and I choked down one of those. Then I kept pacing, pacing, pacing for another half hour, until I was too exhausted to continue.

I lay gingerly on the bed. After a while, the gurgling finally subsided, and I dared to think the crisis might have passed. I closed my eyes, and eventually managed to fall asleep.

That's when the fire alarm went off.

It was a high-pitched shrieking sound, with a recorded voice intoning, "Respected guests! This is the fire alarm!" over and over and over. I lay in the bed, fantasizing about murder, determined that I would not get up unless I smelled smoke or heard people stampeding down the hallway. About ten minutes later, the alarm finally, mercifully, stopped.

The next morning, I woke early and packed my bags. My train didn't leave until after midnight, but I couldn't stay in this hotel another millisecond. I knew I'd have to tell the dezhurnaya about the soiled sheets, and I absolutely dreaded it. I felt like a schoolchild who'd wet her pants in front of the class.

At the desk, I could barely get the words out. "I'm very sorry to tell you this, but I was sick, and the sheets are dirty . . ."

"Oh, you poor thing! Don't worry!" she instantly cooed. "It's all right."

"Thank you," I said. I couldn't look at her, but just went to the elevator, pressed the button, and stood there willing the doors to open. I walked straight out through the lobby, and caught a taxi to the Nika Hotel, outside the city center.

There was only one room left at the Nika, and it was huge, comfortable, and—incredibly—spotless. I couldn't believe how stupid I'd been not to check in here days ago. I sank into the bed and turned on the TV, and for the next 15 hours I sipped juice, nibbled on crackers, and channel-surfed, mostly watching what was apparently the world's longest karate tournament on some sports channel. At this point, I was halfway convinced that coming on this journey again had been a mistake.

Finally, at midnight, it was time to head to the train station. I was facing a 37-hour trip to Chita, in a coupé shared with three strangers and a communal toilet shared by dozens, but even that seemed a relief compared with risking another day here.

FOUR

Chita: There Will Be Disneyland

"IT WAS TWO YEARS BEFORE I REALIZED THAT RICHARD Gere was a girl!" exclaimed Sasha, my host in Chita. I laughed, partly because this was absurd, but mostly because I was finally healthy, rested, and ensconced in the apartment of this delightfully cheerful woman.

Willowy, dark-eyed Sasha—a friend of a friend of a friend— had generously invited me into her home despite knowing virtually nothing about me. This was how it always seemed to go in Chita, a quaint city on the eastern fringe of Siberia. In 1995, Gary and I stayed with a couple named Natasha and Sergei, who met us at 3 a.m. at the train station waving an American flag. By 2005, they'd moved away, so David and I stayed with a couple named

Pasha and Vika, who invited us to share a two-bedroom apartment with the five people already living there. I couldn't face the
prospect of that cramped arrangement this time around, so I did
a little networking before the trip. That's how I ended up with
Sasha in her spacious, sunny, lemon-yellow-painted apartment.

Richard Gere was Sasha's cockatiel. "I got him sixteen years
ago, when I was twelve," she told me. "My mom and I were in
China, and I saw him at a pet market. We brought him back
home—and then, two years later, he surprised me by laying little
eggs!" I asked why she'd named it Richard Gere, and she said,
"You know, the name just seemed to fit."

Looking at the little white bird with its red-feathered cheeks
and bright yellow crest, I didn't see the resemblance. But sitting
at the kitchen table with Sasha and Richard, I couldn't have been
happier than if the real Richard Gere had walked in and chir-
ruped at me.

It wasn't until Sasha met me at the Chita train station with
her big smile and chatty good humor that I realized how lonely
I'd been. I had spent a lot of time by myself in Birobidzhan, and
though the two-day train trip to Chita was restful, I'd hardly
spoken a word to anyone. Traveling on the Trans-Siberian Railway is as solitary or as social as you want to make it; there's
usually no shortage of people happy to talk and share their stash
of bread, sausage, cheese, and beer. But I'd spent most of this
trip in my bunk, just reading, sleeping, and recovering.

In the three decades that I'd been traveling on Russian
trains, the essentials had changed very little. The cheapest tickets
are for *platskart*, or third class, in which the bunks are out in the
open throughout the length of the car. I traveled in second-class
cars, which are divided into a dozen or so *kupes*—little private
rooms with four bunks and a small shared table. The one or two
toilets per car are communal; they flush directly onto the tracks

and usually smell like some combination of pee, oil, and metal. Showers are nonexistent, which means that passengers traveling long distances over multiple days—and there are many of these—also tend to smell, shall we say, not so fresh.

Each car has its own conductor, a uniformed man (*provodnik*) or woman (*provodnitsa*) who keeps an eye on things. The conductor gives you sheets for your bunk, keeps the car clean, and provides a glass with a metal holder (*podstakannik*) for tea and coffee, which you can make yourself with the help of a tank of hot water at one end of the car. He or she also sells snacks (Snickers bars appear to be a perennial favorite) and raps smartly on the door of your kupe a half hour before you reach your destination. Some conductors run their cars as tightly as a drill sergeant; others seem as though they'd rather be anywhere else than looking at your sorry face as you ask them to please replenish the toilet paper.

Boarding the train carries the thrill of the lottery: When traveling with complete strangers in such close quarters, the quality of your trip depends largely on who else is in your kupe. Some passengers, particularly middle-aged males, spend their entire journeys wearing the same clothes and maintaining a steady state of inebriation. In these cases, the kupe often takes on its own special scent, a uniquely Slavic blend of cheap tobacco, damp wool, alcohol, and loamy sweat. Many travelers dress as though they're relaxing at home, wearing sweatpants and the ubiquitous house slippers known as *tapochki*.

If you're stuck with a chatty neighbor, a screaming child, a snorer, a partier, or some dreadful combination thereof, these long train journeys can feel like a trip through hell. Fortunately, my sole kupe-mate on this particular journey slept a heroic 20 hours per day and said very little when he was awake, so my 37 hours to Chita were quiet and restorative. Getting picked up at the train station by Sasha, who spoke perfect English and was eager to show me around, was a pure bonus.

—⁓—

In 1995, Gary and I decided to do a story about Chita's main thoroughfare, Lenin Street. The street was a study in contrasts: dour gray buildings towering over one-story Siberian wood cottages. Shuttered storefronts flanked sidewalks packed with street vendors selling everything imaginable—cigarettes, mittens, boots, medicines, sweaters, children's toys. And the main part of Lenin Street ran from a prison, where we watched young girls shout over the walls to their loved ones inside, to a park commemorating heroes of the Revolution.

Chita had the air of a once-beautiful garden gone to seed. Stately pre-Revolutionary buildings were afflicted with crumbling plaster. Old women in fur hats perched along the sidewalk, selling jars of yellow berries and pails of potatoes. A row of Soviet-era seltzer water machines, their communal glasses long gone, sat unused and neglected.* With a population of just under 400,000 people, a sizable percentage of which seemed constantly to be cramming itself into the city's decrepit buses, Chita exuded not so much a mellow vibe as a weary one.

The main attraction on Lenin Street was Lenin himself. Unlike most statues commemorating the Soviet leader, Chita's was made of pink granite, which took on a warm glow as the sun rose. He presided over a massive square—Lenin Square, naturally—which was bounded on all sides by boxy government buildings. As Gary and I wandered across it, I had the thought

---

*In Soviet times, these were all over the country. People would drop in kopek coins, wait while the water poured into the glass, drink it, then leave the glass for the next customer. Many thousands of people drank from the same unwashed glasses, in a bold display of either boundless societal trust or unhygienic madness. Or both.

Chita's pink granite Lenin statue, 1995 (PHOTO BY GARY MATOSO)

that, save for that unexpected splash of pink, this could be any square in any Russian city in practically any decade of the twentieth century.

And then I discovered the Panama City Motel.

Our host on that first trip, Natasha, mentioned it offhandedly one evening. A wealthy oil executive named Valery Bukhner had just opened a hotel just outside the city, she told us, and "all the materials were shipped from the U.S. Everything. Even the toilet paper." Panama City, Florida, was a mere two-hour drive from my hometown of Pensacola. Was this the namesake of Bukhner's motel? If so . . . why? I decided I needed to meet this Bukhner fellow and find out.

The next morning, I took a taxi to the outskirts of Chita. As I gazed out the window at passing rows of Soviet-era apartment blocks, a tall yellow and white sign popped into view. MOTEL PANAMA CITY RESTAURANT AND LOUNGE, it said, in both English and Russian. When I stepped out, I found myself surrounded by pert gray bungalows. It was as if an entire development had been lifted by tornado from the Florida Panhandle and deposited intact onto the Russian steppe.

Bukhner couldn't meet me that day, but an employee let me poke around in one of the rooms. Sure enough, it was equipped entirely with American products—Astroturf welcome mats, pastel motel art, light switches with ON-OFF written in English, and Kenmore refrigerators. There were even Honeywell thermostats graded in Fahrenheit, rather than the Celsius system used in Russia. The motel's advertising slogan was "a small piece of faraway America," and it truly felt like that, right down to the New Testament nestled in the bedside table drawer.

I interviewed Bukhner by phone later that day, and he told me he'd decided to build the motel during a 1992 business trip to the United States. "I traveled through seven states by car in two weeks," he said—including a stop in Panama City, Florida— "so I saw a lot of motels along the way."

He told me that the motel's grand opening, appropriately enough, had been on the Fourth of July. By coincidence, U.S. Ambassador Thomas Pickering was in Chita at the time, and he came by to give a short speech, after which he presented Bukhner with an autographed dollar bill. "I had the dollar framed," Bukhner said proudly. "And I have a whole album of photos from the ambassador's visit, as well as a videotape we made. He really liked the hotel."

Yet the Panama City Motel paled in comparison to Bukhner's next planned project.

"I want to build a Disneyland in Chita," he told me. "It's my own quirky little dream. I want the children of the Chita Region to have the same wonderful amusement parks that children of other countries have." I held my tongue, not sure whether this very enthusiastic businessman knew just how unlikely it would be for the Disney behemoth to choose little, unknown Chita, 125 miles north of the Mongolian border, for its next theme park.

"I have been to Disneyland in the U.S. and France," Bukhner told me, "and I love it. It will cost a lot of money to build one here—Disneylands are not cheap. But I'm raising the money for it now. There will be a Disneyland in Chita."

When I returned to Chita in 2005, there was—spoiler alert—no Disneyland. But the Panama City Motel was still there—only now, it boasted a Chinese restaurant and a couple of yurts in addition to its bungalows. For good measure, the complex had also added a bowling alley, casino, and a few neon-lit palm trees.

David and I spent an afternoon meandering around the motel's grounds with Pasha, our host in Chita this time around. An energetic 39-year-old, Pasha was an amateur photographer who worked at the city's Drama Theater. Trim and blond, with a lock of hair that flopped charmingly over his forehead, Pasha would have made a winning Hermey if the theater were ever to mount a production of *Rudolph the Red-Nosed Reindeer*.

We were sharing the two-bedroom apartment with Pasha, his common-law wife Vika, her daughter Dasha and brother Edik, a family friend whose name I never caught, and a dog and a cat. Hosting us at all was an act of astonishing selflessness, but Pasha and Vika also insisted that David and I take their bedroom. We were grateful but embarrassed, so we spent a lot of time outside the apartment, to give the family some space. As

Pasha in front of Panama City Motel bungalows, with Soviet-era apartment blocks looming behind, 2005 (PHOTO BY LISA DICKEY)

we wandered up and down Lenin Street, the sights, sounds, and smells at first seemed very familiar. Gradually, however, I started noticing a few subtle differences.

The pink granite Lenin statue still hailed the rising sun each morning, and the old ladies still sold jars of berries on the sidewalk. There was still an intriguing mix of Siberian cottages, boxy government buildings, and pre-Revolutionary mansions lining the streets. But now there were more stores, and the quality of goods for sale was higher. Lenin Street even boasted a few high-end arts and crafts stores, one of which sold fancy picnic baskets for the unheard-of sum of 4,600 rubles—about $165, or what some Russians earned in a month. There were numerous new computer stores and Internet cafés, and the city's sidewalks and building fronts had been repaired and renovated.

The people looked different, too—better dressed and healthier than they had ten years before. When I suggested this to Pasha, he said, "Even four years ago, the mood of the people used to be, 'How can I get through this? What do I need to do to live?' People would get tired just thinking about things as simple as how to get food. But now, I've noticed that people's faces are brighter.

"Young people—and people in general—are lighter in spirit, because it's possible to relax more," he concluded. "You can see it in people's faces."

Chita in 2005 felt like a city on the rise. Next to the Soviet-era Udokan movie theater, with its hand-painted movie posters,[†] was the bright new Seeds gardening store. Near the old women selling their produce, the Solarium tanning salon had opened for business. And looming over a tiny Siberian cottage that had been turned into a beer bar was a huge new building housing a "luxe" dentist and the Philosophy of Beauty aesthetic center. Some people clearly had money to spend, and they weren't afraid to spend it on luxuries.

Ten years later, as I prepared to walk down Lenin Street once more, I wondered what it would look like now, in the midst of the ruble's current collapse—or, as Russians called it, the *krizis*.

—∞—

Sasha and I strolled from her apartment to Lenin Street, and one of the first stores I saw had a familiar green awning with white and yellow lettering: a SUBVEI SENDVICH shop. This was my first time seeing a Subway in Russia, though I'd seen a couple other

---

[†] The main attraction in September 2005 was a film called *Unknown Guests*—or, as it was called in the United States, *Wedding Crashers*.

American fast-food joints—Burger King and Cinnabon—in Vladivostok. Despite the Great Fromagicide and ongoing official antipathy toward Western food products, American fast food was still available and, judging from the lines, still popular in Russia.

A block or so away, on the other side of the street, a row of old women was selling jars of berries, just as they'd been doing when I first came here 20 years ago. But behind them was another new sight: a sign for something called the "Zaibaikal Business Incubator." This was part of a new trend I'd been seeing, the rise of business development and education. The day before, across from Chita's train station, I'd noticed a red banner strung atop one building—the kind of banner that in the Soviet era might have said "Power to the people!" or "Citizens have the right to vacation!"[‡] But this one read, "Take a step toward a successful career!"

There were also numerous signs advertising English and Chinese language classes, for everyone from young children to adults. In 1995, practically no one I encountered outside of Moscow and St. Petersburg spoke English. In 2005, a few did—mostly people who were studying for some very specific purpose. Now, many more people seemed to be studying these languages as a matter of course, simply because they were useful to know.

Sasha and I soon found ourselves at the *Dom Ofitserov* (Officers' House), a beautifully restored, apricot-colored mansion decorated with a huge banner marking the seventieth anniversary of the end of World War II. I'd always loved this building, with its statues of heroic fighters out front and collection of Soviet tanks in the rear courtyard. Following the lead of a

---

[‡] I saw a banner with this phrase in the resort town of Yalta in 1989. It remains my favorite Soviet slogan of all time.

young boy, and with Sasha's encouragement, I climbed atop a World War II–era IS-2 tank emblazoned with the slogan "For our Soviet Homeland!" while she snapped photos.

The city-block-sized park behind the Officers' House had been significantly spruced up since I'd last seen it. Large billboards displayed black-and-white photos of old Chita, including images of turn-of-the-century Buddhist monasteries, called *datsans*.[§] A pair of historic wooden gazebos, long destroyed, had been re-created to their exact original measurements. A new "love park" featured a statue of a courting couple and a bench that sloped whimsically toward the middle, so that two people sitting on it would end up cuddled together. And the crowning glory of the park, the attraction that reminded me of Valery Bukhner, was a new "Kingdom of Shrek and Fiona" amusement park, with a Ferris wheel, miniature train, and a children's swing ride with seats shaped like watermelons.

Thinking of Bukhner reminded me that I needed to head back out to the Panama City Motel, to see how it was faring. But first, I wanted to track down Pasha. I hadn't had a good "ten years later" moment since showing up at the lighthouse on my first day in Vladivostok.

The next morning, I walked down to the Drama Theater, where Pasha had worked in 2005. "I have a strange question," I told the woman at the one open ticket window. "I'm looking for a guy named Pasha, blond hair, who works here." Incredibly, I'd realized just that morning that I either hadn't written down, or possibly never knew, Pasha's last name. She said nothing, so I babbled on. "I'm from America. I met him ten years ago, when I was in Chita," I told her. "Do you know how I might reach him?"

[§] Chita is located just over 30 miles from the Republic of Buryatia, which has a sizeable Buddhist population. More to come about this in chapter 5.

Now she smiled, ever so slightly. "Short guy?" she asked.

"Yes!" I said.

"He doesn't work here anymore." I exhaled with disappointment. "But hold on, I can get his phone number for you."

She made a call, and as she did so, she fiddled on her computer keyboard. Then she turned the screen to me and mouthed, "Is this him?" The photo was of a jowly, middle-aged man wearing a uniform of some sort, possibly a costume for a play.

"No," I said. "Not him." Pasha was young and spry, and this fellow looked like an aged bureaucrat from a nineteenth-century Russian novel. The woman raised her eyebrows in surprise, and the thought suddenly flashed into my head that ten years had passed, so Pasha *was* middle-aged now. He wasn't going to look the same as he did in 2005. Hell, I didn't look the same as in 2005—I'd already been mistaken for a grandmother of teenagers. I peered at the photo again. Yes . . . I guess . . . it could be him.

The woman handed me a piece of paper with two numbers, and I thanked her and stepped outside. I dialed them both, but no one answered and there was no way to leave a message. But just knowing that I had a way to reach him put a spring in my step as I walked back to the apartment.

That night, I called again, and this time Pasha picked up. "Hello, Pasha? It's me, Liza, from America," I blurted. "Do you remember me?"

He burst out laughing. "Liza! Of course I remember you!" he said. "Are you here in Chita?" I told him I was. "Woooowww, really? You came back? I can't believe it!" He laughed again. "Vika is right here, she says hi!" I could hear Vika shouting excitedly in the background. We made a plan for me to come to their apartment—the same one David and I had stayed in ten years earlier—the next evening for dinner.

Pasha came outside to greet me wearing a T-shirt and red basketball shorts. "Liza!" he cried, and scooped me into a big hug. He'd gained some weight and was sporting a new mustache, but apart from that he looked pretty much like the Pasha I remembered—that photo I'd seen hadn't done him any favors. With his arm still around me, he walked me into the building and up to the door of the apartment.

Ten years earlier, the place had been a bit of a mess, with clothes and toys strewn about and cat and dog hair blanketing the floors. The main bedroom had been crammed with a bunk bed, two desks, a foldout sofa, and, oddly, a refrigerator. While I'd truly enjoyed spending time with Pasha and Vika, life in the cramped apartment had been stressful for David and me.** As I walked into the apartment now, it looked to be in terrible disrepair, with the wallpaper torn and peeling. But Pasha waved his hand and said, "We're renovating! Just haven't quite finished."

We went into the kitchen, and there was Vika, looking absolutely unchanged since the last time I saw her. Wearing a yellow blouse and bright pink hoodie, and with her dark hair dyed fuchsia on top, she was a riot of color. We hugged, screaming "Vika!" and "Liza!" and then settled in to chat as Pasha started making blini for dinner.

"Liza, you look exactly the same," Pasha said. He then patted his stomach with one hand. "I've gained weight, but it's for a good cause! I stopped smoking three years ago." I congratulated

---

** In fact, we endured one of the most stressful moments of the 2005 trip here, when David's laptop got knocked off a wobbly stool—the only free spot he could find to put it on—and refused to boot back up. I was on the brink of panic when David managed to pop the thing open, fiddle around with a tiny screwdriver, and get it working again. "How did you do that?" I asked him. "I have no idea," he said.

him, and he said, "I actually gained a lot more weight, but then I lost some." That helped to explain the photo I'd seen, where he'd looked so much heavier. He told me he wasn't drinking as much either, but because I'd brought along a bottle of vodka, tonight would be an exception.

Pasha patiently ladled batter out of a red plastic bowl, spooning it onto a hot cast-iron pan and smoothing it into thin pancakes, while Vika put out plates of cheese, pink sausage, white pork fat, and sliced cucumbers. "So, how is everyone?" I asked. "How's Edik?" Pasha replied that he had a six-year-old daughter now and was no longer living with them. The friend who'd lived here had moved out too, leaving just Pasha, Vika, and Dasha— an impish, pigtailed girl in 2005 who was now, somehow, seventeen.

Once Pasha finished making a stack of blini, he said, "Come on, I'll show you the renovation." We went into the living room, where he proudly pointed out the cheery new wallpaper and curtains. The bedroom, too, had been transformed, with the bunk bed, old sofa, and refrigerator replaced by a double bed and a tidy sewing desk. But one odd decoration remained: a massive gray stuffed animal of an indeterminate species, which hung incongruously in the door leading to the bedroom. I remembered having been perplexed by this creature ten years earlier—was it a mouse? A cat? A bear?—and it was no less confusing for having apparently continued to hang there for a full decade.

Back in the kitchen, Pasha opened the vodka and poured shots for himself and Vika. For me, he offered a special nut-based liqueur that tasted vaguely of Amaretto. "Here's to friendship!" he said, and we drank. "Have some *salo*," Vika said, pushing the plate of pork fat toward me. This was a Russian delicacy, but I demurred. It would take a few more toasts before I'd be ready to devour a slab of pure gleaming fat.

Pasha told me he'd lost his job at the Drama Theater when the leadership there changed a few years back. He then took a job at a TV station, working as a camera operator, but after two years he decided it wasn't for him. After that he drove a taxi for a while, and these days he cobbled together an income from a variety of jobs, working as a photographer, a driver, a DJ, an emcee, and occasionally pitching in at his son Misha's company.

"Misha has his own company?" I asked. I'd met Misha only briefly in 2005, because for most of the time I was in Chita, he'd been in the hospital recovering from foot surgery. He was just 15 then, and so eager to meet David and me that he'd asked the doctors to let him leave the hospital early so he could come to the apartment for dinner on our last night in town.

Pasha told me that now-25-year-old Misha had started an events planning company called Avantazh. He was also married, and he and his wife were hoping to start a family soon. "You wouldn't believe how serious young people are these days," Pasha said. "They don't drink, they don't smoke—it's not fashionable anymore. Although, Dasha does smoke," he said with a shrug. "But mostly, they try to be healthy. They exercise, and watch what they eat."

I had already noticed that everywhere I went, it seemed as if Russians were talking about how healthy, or not healthy, their food was. Terms like *natural*, *organic*, *GMOs*, and *hormone-free* were sprinkled into conversations, as people—especially young people—seemed fixated on their diets in a way I hadn't seen here before. In my three days with Sasha, she'd cooked me six delicious meals made with organic produce from her parents' garden, explaining each time how wholesome and nourishing everything was. And Vika was in on the movement too, making her living selling a product called Energy Diet, which billed itself as a "fast, helpful, safe food" for a "balanced diet."

Was this shift toward a healthier lifestyle part of a natural cycle, or were young people particularly influenced by the choices of Vladimir Putin, who famously didn't smoke, didn't drink, and exercised vigorously (and frequently shirtlessly)? I wasn't sure, but when I asked Pasha and Vika what they thought of Putin, they responded the same way the lighthouse keepers, Vasily and Valya, had: they loved him.

"I know Americans don't really like Putin," Pasha told me, "and that your government blames Russia for what's happening in Ukraine. But really, America is behind it. Why is America funneling arms to Ukraine? Why is your government always stirring things up in faraway parts of the world?" I didn't agree with his black-and-white assessment of Ukraine, but I didn't have a good answer for his final question, either. It's difficult to defend the notion of "American exceptionalism"— assuming I'd even want to—in a way that doesn't sound ridiculously self-important. I'm neither an expert on Ukraine, nor am I as well versed in twenty-first-century international relations as I'd like to be. So, for purposes of this trip, I decided that it was smarter simply to listen to what Russians had to say, rather than leaping into arguments.

"The problem," Vika interjected, "is that America doesn't respect Russia. They think we're backward—like we have bears wandering around in the streets here."

I laughed. Really? This again? "You're not the first person I've heard that from," I told her.

Russians were obviously tired of not being taken seriously. The Soviet Union had been a superpower, respected and feared, but post-Soviet Russia was a weakened country that, particularly under the unpredictable Boris Yeltsin, struggled to be taken seriously on the world stage. Russian pride had taken a beating, and it was only in recent years that it had started to recover.

Part of Putin's appeal to Russians was, clearly, that he was making their country matter again. His actions, words, and very bearing conveyed the message that Russia was strong, and his provocative political moves guaranteed that the rest of the world had to pay attention. The effect Putin had on Russians' sense of pride reminded me of the effect Ronald Reagan had on America in the early 1980s: Reagan followed the pervasive national malaise of the Carter era with a relentless message that the USA could be great again. Similarly, Putin followed the economic turmoil and drunken escapades of Boris Yeltsin with an unyielding message of Russian unity and strength. He rekindled the Russians' pride in themselves; it wasn't surprising people loved him for it.

In fact, they loved him enough that his approval ratings were still sky-high, even in the midst of the current economic turmoil. Western observers often questioned whether polls in Russia reflected public opinion or were fixed; in my admittedly small sample size, I was finding that yes, people truly did love Putin, even as they were very worried about the state of the nation.

"The ruble *krizis* is creating hardship for everyone," Pasha told me. "Everyone has to take out loans at some point, and 22 percent interest is about the best rate you can get." This tracked with what I'd heard in conversations with people in Vladivostok and Birobidzhan: credit cards and loans were available, but the interest rates ranged from 22 percent to 40-plus. I'd heard one horror story about a man who'd bought a new Mercedes for his wife, taking out a dollar-based loan. When the ruble plummeted over the next 15 months to half its value, he suddenly owed twice as much money. Imagine buying a $40,000 car, then having to cough up $80,000 to pay it off. This was the type of scenario many Russians faced upon the collapse of the ruble.

Pasha and Vika were fortunate in that they owned their apartment and didn't require much money to live. Pasha's van, which he still used commercially as a driver, was a beat-up relic with a cracked windshield, but it ran. And the money he and Vika earned, through their combination of odd jobs and sales, was enough to live on. "We do fine," Pasha said. "And I enjoy my work."

"Do you want to see what one of my other jobs is?" he asked. He brought me into the living room, to his computer. "Wait . . . wait," he said, clicking through a series of desktop folders. I took the opportunity to glance again at the indeterminate gray animal hanging in the bedroom door; what *was* that thing? "OK!" he finally exclaimed. "Have a look."

On the screen was a black-and-white photo of a goateed Vladimir Lenin, wearing a newsboy cap, with one eyebrow quizzically cocked. The quality of the photo was unusually sharp, and as I peered closer, I heard Pasha snickering quietly. Wait . . . was this . . . *Pasha*?

"How do I look?" he asked. The truth was, he looked amazingly like Vladimir Lenin. "I dress up as him sometimes, for events," he said, then clicked through more photos: Lenin at a bar, Lenin hoisting a massive beer stein, Lenin crooning into a microphone. Pasha's Lenin truly was—wait for it—the life of the party. "I do it sometimes for Misha's events too."

Ah, yes, Misha, the young entrepreneur. "Can I see him?" I asked Pasha.

"Sure!" he replied. "I'll call him."

"Thank you, Comrade," I said.

—⚏—

Misha and I met for lunch the next afternoon. Whippet thin and sporting a blond crew cut, he was dressed in the business-casual

Pasha posing with a photo of himself as Vladimir Lenin, 2015
(PHOTO BY LISA DICKEY)

garb of the entrepreneur: dark suit jacket, patterned button-down shirt, and faded blue jeans. He was a young man now, and he carried himself, and his black leather briefcase, with confidence—but when he smiled I still saw that charmingly gawky 15-year-old I'd met a decade earlier.

We sat down in a booth at the Traveler's Coffee restaurant, and instead of giving us paper menus, the server handed us each an iPad. "Wow," I said. "High tech." Then I noticed a large circular device affixed to the banquette, just over Misha's left shoulder. "What's that?" I asked.

"You push the button to call the server," he said. I looked closely, and there were actually three buttons: one with a picture of a bell, for calling the server; one with a line through the bell, in case you need to cancel your call to the server; and one with a dollar sign, for when you're ready for your bill. I hadn't expected to see the next wave of restaurant technology in far eastern Siberia, but this place—which was actually part of a national chain—had a good system going.

Misha and I ordered club sandwiches and cappuccinos, and I asked him about Avantazh. He explained that the company created parties and events for clients. "I started it two years ago," he said, "and all this time, I've been investing money into the business, to keep it going. Now, it's finally starting to turn a profit." Where did he get the money to invest? "By working at other jobs," he told me. "I've worked as a sound person and DJ at a restaurant, and I also buy old cars, refurbish and resell them."

This was gutsy, I told him, especially since he was doing it in the midst of a severe economic downturn. "Yes, the *krizis* has affected everything," he said. "People won't allow themselves to spend money right now, which makes it hard for a business like this to survive." But while he planned to keep working at his other jobs, Avantazh was his main focus. He was utterly determined to make it succeed.

When I asked how it felt to have his father work for him, he laughed. "That didn't go so well," he said. "We couldn't sort out the relationship."

He explained, diplomatically, that Pasha's work ethic wasn't the same as his own. Pasha was a free spirit, he said, and some tension arose from their different approaches to the job. Further complicating matters was the fact that father reported to son. "I told him, 'At work, you have to call me Mikhail Pavlovich'"— the use of the patronymic "Pavlovich" (which, of course, came from Pasha's own given name, Pavel) denoting respect—"but at home we could just be father and son." But Pasha couldn't get used to that idea, and the work relationship soon fizzled out.

I observed that young people seemed more serious about their jobs, their health, and their lives in general. Did he think that was true?

"Yes," he said. "Young people are eating healthier—more fish, less meat. It's fashionable to exercise now, and it wasn't before." He told me that he exercised almost daily, didn't drink, and didn't smoke. "It's not cool to smoke anymore," he said. "In my circle, if there's a group of ten people, maybe one will go out to have a smoke."

We finished up our sandwiches, and just as I was about to reach over to press the dollar-sign button, Pasha suddenly appeared, plopping down beside me in the booth. I asked if he was checking up on me, and he laughed. "I'm checking up on you both!" he said. When I told him how impressed I was with his son, he beamed.

"OK, I should get back to work," said Misha. His father then turned to me. "You need a ride somewhere? I don't have anything going on this afternoon." *And that about sums it up*, I thought. I hugged Misha goodbye, then climbed into the van for a ride back to Sasha's place. She and I had a date to go to the Panama City Motel.

—❧—

The same yellow and white sign towered over the motel, and as Sasha pulled into the parking lot I saw the gray bungalows, looking much as they had before. But the complex had even more new additions, most notably a karaoke bar and a strip club. And while there were splashes of color from a few flowerbeds, the grounds were a bit unkempt, with overgrown grass, chipped paint, and hastily patched roofs.

We walked through the bungalows and into a newer section of the complex, where a more traditional hotel building stood.

At the front desk, a blonde woman in a blue and white uniform sat in front of three wall clocks, which showed the time in Chita, Moscow, and Beijing. I explained that I was an American writer who'd first come here twenty years ago, and that, if she didn't mind, I'd really love to look into one of the rooms to see if they still had American furnishings and equipment.

"Of course," she said, and walked us down the hallway. She showed us a room, and while it was perfectly nice, I didn't care at all about the rooms in this newer building. "Would it be possible to see a bungalow?" I asked, enjoying the sound of the word in Russian: *boongalo*. To my surprise, she simply handed us the key to number 18, sending us off to explore on our own.

The welcome mat in front of bungalow 18 was exactly that: a mat with WELCOME in English. This was a good sign. I turned the key, and we walked inside to find an ordinary-looking hotel room with two double beds, a small table with chairs, and a long, low dresser with a TV and phone. Then I started looking more closely.

The light switch was an American stem-style switch, with ON and OFF written in English. "Look at this!" I called to Sasha, then went to peer at the air-conditioning and heating unit under the window. Sure enough, it was a Carrier brand unit, with all the controls in English. I started bouncing around the room like I was on a treasure hunt: there was an old GE "13-memory" phone, a Briggs toilet, a gray fuse box with instructions in English, an English-language TV remote. Sasha and I looked at each other and burst out laughing.

At that moment, the door opened. A hotel employee walked in, and Sasha and I clammed up as if we'd been caught defacing a monument.

"I need to replace the water bottles," the woman said, and busied herself doing that—though Sasha and I both knew the

Motel soaps bearing the Panama City Motel logo, 2015 (PHOTO BY LISA DICKEY)

real reason she was there was to check up on us. Either the woman at the front desk had gotten skittish about having given us the room key, or possibly someone had heard and reported the two weirdos who were cackling in boongalo 18.

We walked out with the employee and returned the key to the front desk. Sasha had to get back to work, but I stayed to explore the rest of the complex. There was a Chinese restaurant, as well as a sauna, a steakhouse, and even a Panama City brewpub that made its own beer. I asked a woman working in the pub whether business was good, and she told me, "We mostly get Chinese tourists now, though occasionally American motorcyclists come through." This explained the clock showing Beijing time, and the fact that the motel's business card had information printed in Chinese, Russian, and English. (It didn't, however, explain the fact that American motorcyclists were now riding across Siberia—the first I'd heard of such a feat.)

So, the Panama City Motel had survived. Sadly, its founder had not; Valery Bukhner had died of cancer a few years earlier. Just before leaving the motel complex, I noticed a small plaque next to a rusty flagpole, right in the center of the bungalows. The message was brief:

"DUTY, HONOR, FREEDOM"
MOTEL "PANAMA CITY"
BUILT 07.08.95
THE CREATION OF
THE GENERAL DIRECTOR
OF OAO NEFTEMARKET
BUKHNER, V. R.

Unexpectedly, the plaque left me a little choked up. No matter how crazy his goal of bringing Disneyland to Chita might have been, Valery Bukhner was, at the very least, a fantastic dreamer who'd succeeded in bringing a touch of whimsy to deepest Siberia. I suspect that if I'd seen such a plaque twenty years earlier, I'd have laughed at it. Now, pushing into middle age myself, I saw the poignancy in leaving one's mark, however frivolous it might seem, on the world.

—⟋⟍—

FIVE

Ulan-Ude: Byoorn and Tyoorn

IT WAS LATE EVENING WHEN I BOARDED THE TRAIN TO my next stop, Ulan-Ude. I entered my *kupe*, and to my dismay, the only other passenger in it was a young man.

Of all the possible passenger combinations in a four-person kupe, I disliked this one the most. When you're the only passenger, you can just lock the door and reasonably assume nobody will try to break in during the night. When there are multiple passengers—especially if they don't know each other—it's less likely that any one person will seriously act out. But when it's just one man and you, locking the door from the inside won't help you if he becomes aggressive. And whenever you have to go down the hall to the toilet, he is, unavoidably, alone for a while with your bags.

I knew the chances were slim that this guy would cause me any serious trouble, but he looked rather red-faced, as if he'd been drinking. He said hello, and I nodded, unwilling to speak and reveal by my accent that I wasn't Russian. As the train began inching out of Chita station, he suddenly stood up, unbuttoned his pants, and pulled them off to reveal boxer briefs. It wasn't unusual for people to change into sleepwear for the night—but normally, they'll ask the other people in the kupe, especially those of the opposite sex, to step out first. The fact that this guy had drunkenly yanked his pants down, with me sitting right there, wasn't a good sign.

He sat across from me in his underwear while I silently made my bunk. Just then, his cell phone rang. "Hello, darling," he said in a low voice. "I miss you. Yes, yes, my little sun, my heart." He paused. "My *solnyshko*, I love you so much. My angel, I miss you. Yes, my darling. I love you, my princess." He spoke these words in a kind of monotone, barely above a whisper.

I lay down in my bunk and started to read, while across from me, the man continued his litany of endearments as he pulled on sweatpants. If I was worried earlier that he might act inappropriately, now I was worried that I might be crushed by the weight of his affection for his girlfriend. It felt like a parody, this unending slew of sweet nothings, as if the man had memorized a list from a pamphlet, *What Women Like to Be Called*.

He stayed on the phone for another ten minutes, never once saying anything of consequence, but just reciting every endearment I'd ever heard one person call another. When he finally finished, he asked me politely, "Is it OK if my friend comes in and we drink some beer together?" I nodded. Maybe I was being naïve, but strangely enough, this guy had won me over with his absurd fountain of telephonic sweetness. Within minutes, a male friend of his entered the kupe, and the two of them chatted quietly, drinking beer. I wasn't sure why, if they knew each other, they hadn't booked the same kupe, but it wasn't a great enough mystery to keep me from drifting off to sleep.

In the months leading up to the trip, I'd been nervous about traveling by myself. I had done a lot of solitary traveling in my early twenties, backpacking alone through Pakistan, India, and Malaysia, but back then I was filled with the optimism—and ignorance—of youth; it either never occurred to me that bad things could happen, or I simply chose not to think about it. At age 48, I felt more wary. I'd elected to do this trip alone, unwilling to face the emotional and financial responsibility of bringing along another person. But part of me feared that this had been a shortsighted decision.

During the first few weeks of the trip I locked my valuables into my backpack, then chained the pack to the bed, every time I left my hotel room. There were six items I couldn't afford to lose—laptop, iPad, iPhone, Russian cell phone, wallet, and passport—and I obsessively checked and rechecked where they were, taking care to touch each one as though afflicted with a special kind of Traveler's OCD. When walking down the street, I wore my "don't fuck with me" face: eyes forward, jaw set, stern expression. Of course, this is how Russians generally walk around; they don't smile, or greet strangers, or even make eye contact. People here mind their own business on the streets, so I aimed to do the same.

This is not a natural attitude for me. I'm one of those people who smiles and says hello to strangers. Walking around with a dour look on my face was wearying, and even a little depressing, but it felt necessary. And then I got to Chita.

Walking down Lenin Street with Sasha was a revelation. We joked and laughed, chattering loudly in English as we strolled along. It was a huge relief not to be alone anymore, and Sasha's cheery exuberance loosened something I'd been holding tight inside. Her example made me realize that I'd been a bit tightly wound these first few weeks. It also reminded me that, while staying in hotels had the advantage of privacy, staying with Russians in their homes felt safer and more welcoming.

Now, as my train hurtled toward Ulan-Ude, I was looking forward to another warm train station greeting—this time from a couple I'd known now for 20 years, Oleg and Sveta.

—∽m∽—

By the time Gary and I arrived in Ulan-Ude in early October of 1995, we were not only weary from the trip, we were tired of each other. Traveling with a friend or loved one for weeks on end is difficult enough. Traveling with someone you've only just met, while working frantically to find story subjects, write, photograph, edit, and translate everything from Russian to English (and vice versa), was utterly exhausting. We were together every minute of every day, even sharing a bed in most of our Russian hosts' homes, and our patience with each other had begun to fray.

Oleg and Sveta's apartment provided a desperately needed respite. Lanky, balding Oleg was a journalist, so he understood the demands and stresses of our project. Sveta, a blonde bank manager with a baby-doll voice and incongruously raucous laugh, was a fantastic cook. The couple had a 12-year-old son, Alyosha, who spent hours playing with his adorable new puppy. And Oleg had a vast collection of jazz albums, a rarity in Russia, so on our first night we were treated not only to Sveta's homemade *pelmeni* (traditional Siberian meat dumplings) and as many vodka shots as we cared to consume, but to Frank Sinatra, Ella Fitzgerald, and Billie Holiday crooning in the background.

*Oleg and Sveta in
their kitchen, 1995*
(PHOTO BY GARY
MATOSO)

Ulan-Ude is the capital of the Republic of Buryatia, a
crescent-shaped area east of Lake Baikal that's home to a million
people, roughly a quarter of whom are Buryat.* Ethnically,
Buryats are related to Mongolians, with similar physical characteristics of broad, high cheekbones and epicanthic folds, and
their languages are close enough that some linguists consider
Buryat a dialect of Mongolian. The majority of Buryats are Bud-
dhists, and one of Ulan-Ude's two claims to fame is the Ivolgin-
sky Datsan, the spiritual center of Buddhism in Russia, which is
located about 20 miles outside the city. (The other is the largest
Lenin head in the world, a 25-foot-tall bronze behemoth looming over the central square in Ulan-Ude.†)

---

*Russia has 22 autonomous republics, mostly in regions having large non-Russian
ethnic groups, such as Tuva, Chechnya, and Dagestan. Republics have their own
constitutions and can declare their own official languages.
† Unveiled in 1970 in celebration of Lenin's one hundredth birthday, the head has been
described in various printed reports as cross-eyed; Buryat in its features; and Jewish,
because the snow that collects on its head resembles a yarmulke.

Gary and I wanted to explore Buryat culture; in particular, we hoped to find a farmer to profile. Though he was Russian, Oleg was the editor of the *Buryat Youth* newspaper, and he invited us to come to his office one morning to meet a few of his Buryat colleagues. That's how we met the poet and journalist Tsyren-Dulma Dondagoy.

With her snow-white hair and regal bearing, 63-year-old Tsyren-Dulma was a striking figure. She spoke Russian in a lilting cadence, telling us about what it was like to grow up Buryat. "I was five years old the first time I rode a horse," she said. "My father just lifted me up and put me on, then gave the horse a slap and off I went. That's the way a Buryat learns to ride."

Under Soviet rule, she told us, Buryats suffered discrimination. "During the Brezhnev era, our culture was suppressed," she said. "People kept their beliefs hidden; that was the only way. I was a Communist Party member then, but even so, I was always a Buddhist. We didn't have temples or lamas, but all the same, people never stopped believing." Her words called to mind the Jews of Birobidzhan, who had also seen their culture and religion pushed underground during Soviet rule. But unlike the Jewish community, Buryats had no other homeland to which they could flee. If Buryat culture was to survive, it would have to survive here.

I explained that we were hoping to meet a Buryat farmer, to learn about the region's culture and see the countryside. Tsyren-Dulma thought for a moment, then reached for a piece of paper and pen. She wrote a few sentences in the Buryat language, then folded the paper and handed it to me.

"Take this letter to the village of Khoshun-Uzur," she said. "It's about three hours away, by bus. When you get there, give it to Baldama Shagdanovna." I asked if she had the woman's address. "No," she replied. "But everyone there knows her. You will have no trouble finding her."

I asked if she would translate the letter into Russian for me, and she happily complied. It said:

Dear Baldama Shagdanovna,

    I'm sending these young guests from abroad to you for help. They would like to become acquainted with the life of a Buryat family, and spend the night with them. Try to show them the village of the poet Gombozhoray, or maybe take them to Galtai. Take them to a place where the influence of the city is not so strong. Help them if you can—maybe they can stay with you?

                With warm greetings,

                Tsyren-Dulma

                3.10.95

Now, *this* was an adventure. Gary and I were excited to head into the hinterlands, but the idea of it made Oleg nervous. He didn't particularly like sending his American guests on a one-way bus trip into the remote countryside, but what other option was there? He couldn't take us himself, as he had to work. So, early the next morning, he drove us to the station, watched us board the bus, and implored us to call when we arrived, assuming we could find a phone. We promised we would.

It had snowed overnight, and as Gary and I took our seats on the freezing, decrepit bus, all I could think was, *Let's get this show on the road!* I was eager for the driver to rev up and turn on the heat, but unfortunately, the posted bus schedule appeared to be merely a suggestion. We sat shivering in the parking lot for an hour and a half before the driver even started the vehicle. Then, not long after we got under way, the bus conked out—the first of three times this would happen. Somehow, the driver managed to fix it each time, and after five hours we finally made it to Khoshun-Uzur, which turned out to be little more than a collection of wooden houses and vegetable gardens.

Gary and I lumbered off the bus, and to my relief a young man happened to be walking nearby. "Excuse me," I said in Russian. "Do you know where I can find Baldama Shagdanovna?"

"This way," he said, and led us down a narrow dirt road. After a hundred yards or so, he pointed at a small log cabin surrounded, like many of the houses, by a tall fence.

As we approached, a cacophony of barking erupted inside the fence. The noise startled me, and I stood rooted, unsure what to do. Through the slats, I could see an old Buryat man standing on the porch. "What do you want?" he called out over the yapping of the dogs.

"We have a letter for you!" I shouted back.

"Well, come on, then!" He stepped off the porch and walked toward us, grabbing the dogs' collars before opening the gate. He gestured for us to walk up to the house, where a tiny older woman with extremely bowed legs met us at the door.

"Come in!" she said, beckoning us into the house. "Take off your coats, sit down." She beamed at us, even though she had no earthly idea who we were. We handed her the letter and told her we were visiting from America, and she giggled and clapped her hands. "You are the first foreigners I have ever met," she exclaimed, then quickly corrected herself: "Well, except for Mongolians, but they don't count."

She ambled stiffly around the room in search of reading glasses, and when she finally found a pair, she put them on and sank into a chair. Reading Tsyren-Dulma's letter, she raised a hand to her mouth and giggled again. "Of course I will help you," she told us. "But first, let's have something to eat."

Baldama Shagdanovna reads the letter, 1995. "You are the first foreigners I have ever met!" she exclaimed. (PHOTO BY GARY MATOSO)

Baldama laid out a feast of beef soup, sliced vegetables, pickles, bread, sour cream, jam, and honey. "Everything on this table, we made with our own hands," she said with evident pride, explaining that she and her husband felt lucky to live in the countryside, where they could grow their own produce. As we ate, she and her husband spoke quietly to each other in Buryat, apparently discussing what to do with us. "Ah, I know," she finally said to me. "I'll send you to Buyanto, in Galtai."

That was how we met the gentleman farmer Buyanto Tsydypov. Buyanto deserves his own chapter, which will come next; for now, the main thing to know is that his house was the only one in the village of Galtai with a phone, so once we got there, I was able to call Oleg and reassure him that Gary and I were safe. Even so, when we returned to Ulan-Ude a few days later, Oleg greeted us with relief, as though we'd come home from a war.

—⟨⟩—

When I returned to Ulan-Ude in 2005, I was happy to see that Oleg and Sveta had changed very little. Oleg had grown a beard, and Sveta had gotten a wee bit plump, but their apartment was still the same haven of delicious home-cooked meals, lavish vodka toasts, and endless jazz. Just as Gary and I had done in 1995, David and I stayed with them for a couple of relaxing days before heading back out to Galtai to see the farmer.

Sveta and Oleg were smart, well-read, professional people. They were also endearingly goofy. Oleg loved to tell the Russian jokes called *anekdoty*, and he was forever exclaiming, "Oh, have you heard this one?" before launching into some long, convoluted story, filled with slang, that invariably ended in a punch line I didn't get.

He'd talk and talk, then stop abruptly, staring at me in futile anticipation of a laugh. This happened a few times, and his disappointment was so profound that I decided next time to laugh regardless of whether or not I got the joke. Soon enough, Oleg launched into yet another anecdote, and when he was done, I burst out laughing like I'd never heard anything so funny. "I'm not finished!" he said, sounding hurt. *Whoops.* To my frustration, and Oleg's confusion, I never could seem to correctly guess when to laugh at his jokes.

Sveta was goofy in a different way. With her carefully curled blonde hair, thinly plucked eyebrows, and closet full of business suits, she looked the part of a put-together bank executive. But at home, she threw on a housedress and drank like a pro. She was forever cocking her head and offering wry asides to whatever Oleg was saying, often while elbows-deep in whatever she was making for dinner. I felt so comfortable with her that, in 2005, she was one of the few Russians I told that I was gay.

Sveta was a devotee of cupping therapy, which involves placing small bell-shaped glass cups on the skin, then using a vacuum to create suction and pull blood to the surface. In theory, this treatment—which humans have practiced for thousands of years—relieves pain and muscle discomfort. It can also result in bright, round bruises. On David's and my last night with the couple, Sveta, fueled by numerous shots of vodka, merrily vacuumed the little glass cups to her forehead and cheeks, dancing around and laughing uproariously while Oleg shrieked for her to take them off so her face wouldn't bruise.

—⚬⚬⚬—

Arriving in Ulan-Ude for my third visit, I was ready once again for smooth jazz and silly good fun. Sveta and Oleg did not disappoint.

Oleg picked me up at the train station, and when we arrived at the apartment, Sveta was in the kitchen, wearing a blue housedress and with curlers in her hair. She was making *chebureki*, a Caucasian staple of meat fried in homemade pastry dough.

"Liza!" she exclaimed, and pulled me into a hug. "I'm so happy to see you!" I embraced her tightly, touched by this heartfelt greeting, but characteristically, Sveta then threw a curveball. "I'm really glad you're here," she said, "because we need you to teach us how to play poker."

Well, this was a non sequitur. Perhaps Russians assume that all Americans know how to play poker, just as Americans supposedly assume that bears wander the streets here. But though Sveta couldn't have known it, I'm actually an avid poker player, and not having played in a month, I was hankering for a game. Oh, yes, this was going to be fun.

Oleg went into the living room and retrieved a slender silver briefcase. "We have the poker chips," he told me, "and we've tried to learn by reading books, but we don't really get it."

"Don't worry," I said. "It's easy. I'll teach you."

As I soon learned, Oleg and Sveta were total gamers. They'd spent most of their free time over the last five years playing billiards, eventually getting so serious that they were playing up to eight hours a day on weekends. "We even bought our own cue sticks," Oleg said. "We had to go all the way to Irkutsk to get good ones." They'd spent hundreds of dollars on their custom-made sticks, he told me, which they left locked up at their local pool hall, the Kovboi.[‡] Sveta had set a goal of playing in competitions, but after so many hours spent practicing, her back started giving her trouble. They wanted to learn poker in part because they could play at home, sitting down, which would be less taxing on Sveta's back. We agreed to have our first lesson after dinner that night, with their son Alyosha, who was now 32, joining as our fourth player.

Sveta spent the afternoon cooking, preparing a feast of roast chicken, lamb bouillon, eggplant layered with tomato and cheese, sliced smoked fish, and chebureki. As the dinner hour neared, Oleg broke out a bottle of *samogon*, homemade vodka made in a nearby Old Believers village.[§] We drank toast after toast, and although I'd been drinking pretty steadily since arriving in Russia a month earlier, this was threatening to turn into a night of epic consumption. I knew I should slow down, but Oleg kept on pouring shots, so I kept drinking them.

[‡] The Kovboi, or "Cowboy," is decorated with American-style touches, such as big black-and-white photographs of Clark Gable and Jayne Mansfield, and a giant statue of a cowboy in a checked shirt, wraparound shades, and a ten-gallon hat.

[§] The Old Believers are a religious sect that splintered off from Russian Orthodoxy in the seventeenth century. There are numerous Old Believers villages scattered throughout Buryatia, including the village of Tarbagatay, which offers tourist excursions and, oddly for a religious sect, homemade liquor for sale.

Oleg, Sveta, and me in their living room, 2015 (PHOTO BY ALEXEI LEBEDEV)

I asked the couple how their lives had changed since we'd last seen each other. "Well, we fell in love with Thailand," Sveta purred. They'd gone four times in a three-year span, mostly beach vacations in the wintertime, when Ulan-Ude's temperatures plunge below zero Fahrenheit. "It's where I got this dress," she said, pointing at her blue shift that, I now noticed, was decorated with elephants. They'd also gone to China recently, she said, to buy new furniture for the apartment; everything is so cheap there, the savings made up for the cost of the travel. I recalled that Sasha had purchased Richard Gere in China, and I marveled again at how common it was now for Russians to go on shopping sprees there.

The couple wouldn't be taking any trips abroad for a while, Oleg said, because of the ruble crisis. "It's hard to make ends meet," he told me. "Our salaries are the same, but prices are higher." And the newspaper business, in which he'd worked for decades, was in particularly bad shape; as the head editor of *Buryat Youth*, he now spent as much time worrying about the paper's finances as its editorial content. Sveta was still working at the bank, and even if she wanted to leave, she couldn't, "because I'd be afraid to lose my pension money," she said. I asked how her situation now compared to that of 1995 and 2005, and she didn't hesitate. "Now is better than 20 years ago," she told me, "but Soviet times were better than now, because you always knew what was what."

"Meaning?" I asked.

"Back then, you knew the price of everything, what would happen at work, exactly when you could retire, and what your pension would be," she replied. "Now, everything is more difficult. There are unknowns. There weren't before." Of all the complaints I'd ever heard Russians make about the post-Soviet era, this was the most prevalent: people missed the certainty of the USSR years, when the basic necessities—salary, education, health care, pension—were (for the most part) guaranteed. This was understandable, especially in the midst of the *krizis*, when each new day might bring a sickening drop in the value of your savings and your salary.

We reflected on that thought for a moment, but neither Oleg nor Sveta could stand being melancholy for long. "Do you want to hear a funny story?" Oleg said, breaking into a grin. I feared another incomprehensible joke was coming, but instead he started telling the story of how the couple got together, back in the early 1980s.

They'd been introduced through friends, and when Oleg went to Sveta's apartment for the first time, he was surprised to see that she had a Billie Holiday record. Few Soviets knew much about American jazz, and fewer still owned any jazz records, so he was impressed.

"Wow," I said, and turned to Sveta. "You were a jazz fan? You two were obviously meant to be together."

"Ha!" she said. "I had been looking around at the record store, and when I saw Billie Holiday, I thought, *Ooh! Black American lady singer. It must be disco!* When I got home and put it on, I was so disappointed."

"But you didn't know that," I teased Oleg. "You thought you'd found the perfect woman."

"Not exactly," he replied. "What I really thought was, *If I marry her, that record will be mine.*"

We eventually cleared the dishes away, and I counted out stacks of brightly colored poker chips for everyone. I started shuffling the cards, and everyone *oohed* and *aahed* over my ability to do the bridge shuffle, a skill that would impress exactly no one back home. I explained the rules of Texas Hold'em, and within minutes, the cards were flying. Sveta especially liked one quirk of the game, the part where the dealer must "burn" a card, placing it facedown before turning up the next one—in theory, a protection against cheating. "Burn and turn" is a phrase one often hears at poker tables, but in Sveta's rendering, it became *Byoooorn . . . and tyoooorn!*

The next three hours went by in a drunken blur, and by the end, Sveta had a mountain of chips and the rest of us had none. This wasn't entirely beginner's luck: she was impossible to read and unpredictable in her play, two great traits for a poker player to have. "Next stop, the World Series of Poker!" I said, and she gave a pert little nod.

"Liza, can we play tomorrow?" she asked. "I want to win again."

—⟊—

The next morning, I had a hangover—my first of the trip, a minor miracle considering how much drinking I'd done so far. I slept until 10 a.m. on the foldout couch in the living room, while Oleg and Sveta tiptoed around; it was Sunday, so neither of them had to work. Every so often, Oleg would squeeze past my bed to get to the balcony, where he smoked one of the multitude of cigarettes he went through daily. In the sober light of morning, he reverted to the nervous energy I remembered from earlier visits.

"Are you planning to go back to the farmer, in the village?" he asked me. I told him I was. "Are they expecting you?" I said no, that my preference was just to show up, as I'd done at the lighthouse in Vladivostok, as that made for a better story. Oleg shook his head. "I think you should call them," he told me. "I don't like the idea of you going out there alone, with no one to meet you."

I tried to convince Oleg that there was nothing to worry about. The farmer, who would be in his early fifties now, was undoubtedly still living with his wife in the house they owned in Galtai. And if by some strange chance he wasn't there, his siblings and cousins also lived in Galtai. I knew the idea of my going off alone made Oleg nervous, but I was reluctant to change my plans for the sake of assuaging what felt like an overblown fear.

But that afternoon, when we checked the bus schedule, we learned that the only public transportation to Galtai was a minivan that arrived in the village at 6 p.m.—and there were no return minivans to Ulan-Ude until the next morning. So, not only would I be arriving unannounced at dinnertime, I'd also be stranded for the night if for some reason the farmer wasn't there. I realized that Oleg was right: I needed to get in touch with the farmer.

Though Buyanto had a telephone in his house, I'd never bothered to get the number. I did have contact information for his son Beligto, though. In 2005, Beligto was a 20-year-old college student in Ulan-Ude, and he'd given me his cell phone number and e-mail address. But when I dialed the number, the man who answered wasn't Beligto. And the e-mail I sent to his address instantly bounced back.

Now what? Ten years ago, I'd have been out of options. But now, I realized I could search for Beligto on Facebook. Within minutes, I found him, though judging from his page he was an infrequent user of the site. I sent him a friend request and private message, including my cell phone number, and then Oleg, Sveta, Alyosha, and I settled in for dinner and another night of poker.**

All day long, Oleg and Sveta had been talking about how excited they were to drink beer tonight. I couldn't figure out why this was such a special event; what was so extraordinary about having beer? And for that matter, why was I the only person who seemed to have suffered any ill effects from the rivers of vodka we'd consumed the night before? These people really loved to get their drink on, which in Russia was saying something.

Sveta laid the table with homemade pizza, leftover chicken, and sliced smoked fish, an ideal array of salty foods to accompany this greatly anticipated beer. Oleg put five liter-sized bottles on the table: four Heinekens, and one bottle of something called "Red Dragon rice beer." This was his favorite, though apparently nobody else liked it.

Then, Oleg fetched two of the largest beer steins I have ever seen. They were from Germany, in the shape of boots, and each one held enough beer to drown a good-sized squirrel. He poured a bottle of Heineken into the first, and the liquid came up to

---

** I wasn't keen on having the farmer's son stumble across photos of my big gay wedding, but it was too late to worry about that. Also, for as nervous as I'd been at the beginning of the trip, now I pretty much expected everyone in Russia to parrot some variation of the line, "I'm OK with it, but don't tell anybody else."

about the boot's ankle. He emptied another bottle into the second boot and gave it to Sveta, and when we toasted and started to drink, the curve in the steins caused a loud sloshing sound to emanate from the toe: *sploosh-sploosh-sploosh*.

"Let's eat!" Sveta said. "I want to play poker." We quickly wolfed down some pizza, then moved the plates to the side so we could get to the game. The next hour was a riot of clattering poker chips, *sploosh-sploosh-sploosh*, and *byoorn and tyoorn!* But as the evening wore on, with no word from Beligto, I could see Oleg's brow starting to furrow. We began talking about what other options we had for finding him.

"How about *vKontakte*?" Alyosha asked. Of course! This was the most popular Russian social media site—the Russian Facebook, as it were. Alyosha was active on the site, so we paused the poker game so he could search for Beligto. After a moment, he turned the laptop screen toward me. "Is this him?" he asked, showing me a photo of a square-jawed young Buryat man with close-cropped hair. "Yes!" I said. Alyosha sent him a private message that included my cell phone number—and about an hour later, my phone rang. It was Beligto. He gave me his father's cell phone number, and that's how I was able to let the farmer know I was coming.

I couldn't help but compare this to our adventure 20 years ago, when Gary and I had ventured into the countryside with nothing more than that letter handwritten in Buryat. Social media and cell phones had truly changed everything, even in the most remote places on earth—places like the tiny village of Galtai.

—⁊⁊⁊—

SIX

Galtai: Slaughter and Feast

Buyanto Tsydypov was in his white Volga se-dan, driving along a dirt road outside Galtai on a bright September morning in 1995, when he suddenly whipped the steering wheel to the right. In the backseat, I flopped over onto Gary, and as we bumped along through a grassy field, I wondered where we were headed.

The field was vast and rolling, the sky an endless canopy of blue. Although the grass we were racing over was more scrubby than lush, there was a rough beauty to the untouched landscape. In the distance, sheep grazed on a hillside, and as we approached, Buyanto coasted to a stop and turned off the engine to avoid scaring them away. "Let's go," he said to the man in the passenger seat, his brother-in-law Zhinat-Dorgo. The two of them got out of the car and began walking slowly toward the flock.

Suddenly, they broke into a run. Buyanto charged toward a young sheep as Zhinat-Dorgo skirted the edge of the flock, trying to keep it from scattering. For a few exhilarating minutes, Gary and I watched the men maneuver and dodge among the animals, finally corralling the one they wanted. Buyanto, a sturdily built 33-year-old, grabbed the sheep around its neck and wrestled it to the ground, while Zhinat-Dorgo hustled over with a rope. Working as one, the men tied the sheep's feet, immobilizing it. Then Zhinat-Dorgo lifted it up and carried it to the car, as Buyanto popped the trunk. I watched with mouth agape as he tossed the animal in the trunk and slammed it shut. "Let's go!" Buyanto said, for the second time in ten minutes—but this time, he was smiling proudly.

As we drove back to Galtai, I could hear the animal kicking and bucking in the trunk. "He's a healthy young sheep," Buyanto said. "It's good to prepare a young sheep for guests." In the backseat, Gary and I looked at each other. We'd been excited when Baldama Shagdanovna told us she'd found a farmer for us to profile—but we never expected this.

After a short drive, we arrived at the village, which was little more than a long dirt road lined with a couple dozen wooden houses. Buyanto's wife Tsypelma opened their gate, and he eased the Volga into the yard. Their home was a sturdy wood structure with bright blue trim and lace curtains in the windows, but that wasn't where we were heading. Buyanto hoisted the sheep out of the trunk, then carried it into a small room that stood apart from the main house. I hurried to follow, but not before noticing with dismay that the frightened animal had left pellets of feces in the trunk.

Buyanto laid the sheep on its back, with its forelegs stretched above its head and back legs still tied. His ten-year-old son, Beligto, held the forelegs tight while his father bent over the animal's midsection with a large knife. With a few quick strokes, he cleared the wool from the sheep's belly. I held my breath as Buyanto raised the knife again, but he stopped short, peering at it. He put the knife back down, then walked out of the room as the animal still lay stretched on the floor, its eyes wide open. When he returned, he was carrying a flint; the knife was, apparently, too dull for the task at hand.

Slowly, with precision, Buyanto scraped the flint a half dozen times along the blade. Then he bent once again over the sheep. As I watched, and Gary photographed, he cut a long vertical incision down the animal's belly, then plunged his hand into the bloody opening, nearly up to his elbow. He fiddled around briefly inside the sheep's body, then stopped, his hand still deep inside the body cavity. Both he and the sheep were completely still as the animal's eyes turned glassy and its mouth slack; it died without a single kick or buck.

"This is how Genghis Khan taught us to kill sheep," Buyanto said, at last withdrawing his bloody arm from the animal's body. "By pinching shut the artery that runs along the spine." He washed his hands, then dried them with a rag.

The sheep had barely breathed its last before the preparation of its carcass began. Buyanto first cut into the skin around its legs, then sliced upward toward its belly. Punching at fatty tissue with his fists and the knife, he began slowly to separate the animal's skin from its body, exposing the still-twitching muscles of its thighs. Steam rose in the dimly lit room, and the air became thick with the dusky smell of mutton. Beligto and his eight-year-old sister Bayarma watched placidly as their father worked the sheepskin free.

"I was 15 years old when I killed my first sheep," Buyanto

said. "My father stood by me, telling me what I needed to do. I had seen him kill many sheep before that, and helped him like Beligto is helping me. We pass the tradition on," he said, slicing at the fatty tissue with his knife. "It's in the Buryat blood."

Once the sheepskin was fully removed, Buyanto cut into the body cavity. He reached in and removed the stomach, intestines, liver, kidneys, and heart. Then he lifted out organs I didn't recognize; looking closer, I saw that they weren't organs at all, but enormous clots of congealed blood. Finally, with a ladle, he scooped liquid blood out of the cavity and poured it, thick and steaming, into a metal bowl. All of this would be cooked and served to the guests. The only internal parts of the sheep not eaten were the contents of the stomach and intestines, which Tsypelma was now squeezing out into a pail on the floor.

When it was time for the feast, Tsypelma brought out white china dishes loaded with boiled sheep parts. One dish held bones, mostly enormous flat ribs fringed with meat and chunks of gleaming white fat. Another held intestines, which had been emptied, cleaned, turned inside out, and wrapped tightly with narrower intestinal tubes. Others had been stuffed with gristle and fat, then sliced like roulettes. Buyanto poured everyone a shot of vodka, then raised his glass high.

"You came to us like thunder out of a clear blue sky," he said. "Welcome." We toasted, and he invited us to dig in. He offered us a taste of everything, remarking on the ribs, "You may be tempted to take the jawbone first,* but the ribs are more tasty. Clean them off as best you can. The Buryats have a saying: the cleaner the bones, the prettier your children will be."

For the second course, Tsypelma brought out the sheep's boiled stomach, swollen nearly to bursting with a mixture of

---

*I was not.

blood and spices. Buyanto sliced it open, then passed it around so everyone could take spoonfuls of the congealed purplish-brown mixture inside. I reluctantly took my share, quickly stuffing it into my mouth and then washing it down with clear mutton bouillon. And the dishes kept coming: slices of tongue, of heart. I was simultaneously touched by Buyanto's generosity and horrified at the volume and variety of guts I was eating.

Then, Buyanto's elder brother remarked that in traditional Buryat culture, I would never even have been at this feast. "The women never sit at the same table with the men," he said. "They come in only to serve the food, then they must back out of the room the way they came, so as never to turn their backsides to the men." It was true—as hard as the Buryat women had worked to prepare the feast, I was the only woman who sat at the table that night.

—⁓—

With its rutted dirt roads and rustic wooden houses, Galtai seemed untouched by time. As they had for centuries, Buryat families tended small patches of land, growing cabbages, potatoes, onions, and beets in the dark earth. They milked their own cows, made butter and sour cream, and raised pigs and sheep for slaughter. The village had electricity, but there was no running water in any of the houses, so each had its own outhouse set apart from the main dwelling. Horses pulled carts down the uneven dirt roads and through the village's single intersection.

The nearby Banner of Lenin collective farm (*kolkhoz*) had been the area's main employer for decades, and Buyanto had worked there as an agronomist, organizing the planting and harvesting. He'd grown up in Galtai, one of eight brothers and two sisters, most of whom still lived nearby.

"Two and a half years ago, I had nothing," Buyanto told me.

Buyanto the maverick farmer with his wife Tsypelma, son Beligto, and daughter Bayarma, 1995 (PHOTO BY GARY MATOSO)

"But when privatization of government lands began in the early 1990s, I had an opportunity to receive hundreds of hectares of land for free. Then in 1992, President Yeltsin signed a decree stating that start-up private farms could operate tax-free for a period of five years. So I decided to start my own farm. Now we have six hundred sixty-seven hectares of land, one hundred twenty cows, and three hundred sheep, and four of my brothers and their families also work on the farm.

"I am like the 'gentleman farmers' in English books," he said with a laugh. His farm, which sold wheat, meat, and freshly baked bread, was already profitable, thanks in large part to Yeltsin's tax break.

The land where Buyanto's sheep and cattle grazed was typical of the countryside of Buryatia, with low, rolling hills and flat lands that seemed to stretch forever. In late September, Buyanto's wheat fields were still tall with grain, even though the first snow had fallen. He and his brothers split the duties of the farm: one brother, a veterinarian, cared for the animals, another managed the wheat harvest, and another was in charge of building new structures on the farm, such as a *banya* (sauna) for the families and storage sheds for equipment. Buyanto managed the farm, researched the local markets, and handled all official business with the local government, which he said was very much opposed to private farming.

"The government of the Buryat Autonomous Republic would rather see everyone still working on the kolkhoz," he told me. "The idea of private farming frightens them. They will do everything they can to make things more difficult for us, but one thing they can't take away is the tax law that made all this possible."

Risk-takers were few in this tiny village, and by local standards Buyanto was already a legend. I spoke with a few of his neighbors, and they described him in glowing terms, praising the honesty and uprightness of his family, his abstinence from smoking, his relative sobriety compared with many men in the village, and his courage in starting his own private farm. But no one expressed the desire to follow in his footsteps.

"People are afraid to do what I have done," Buyanto said as we drove out to the wheat fields to inspect the combines. "They are afraid for tomorrow. What if the Communists come back into power after the next elections? Then all of this could be suddenly taken away.

"I went from office to office for a solid year to work everything out so I could have this land," he said. "This is my land. I am not afraid of what the future will bring."

But he was also taking no chances. "Come with me," he said. "I want to show you a sacred place." Gary and I piled into the

Volga with six other people, including Tsypelma and a few relatives, and we set out again across the fields. Buyanto sang Buryat folk songs in a strong, clear baritone as we bounced along through the countryside.

Twenty minutes later, he pulled the Volga to a stop high on a hillside, where a yellow wooden frame stood silhouetted against the afternoon sky. The frame held a row of tall, narrow sticks, and on the end of each stick, a Buddhist prayer cloth fluttered in the biting autumn wind.

In times of trouble and thanks, Buryats came from nearby villages to tie their prayer cloths—called *khimorin*—to these sticks and make their offerings to the gods. A blackened spot on the hill marked the place where people lit offering fires, and a solitary bench stood a few steps beyond. The rest of the hill was rocky and bare, with only a few tufts of brown grass sprouting insistently through the dirt.

"I went to the datsan yesterday, and the lama told me that things were not right on my farm," said Buyanto, placing a bottle of vodka and plates of mutton and bread on the bench. "He said that my horse had fallen, and that I needed to pray to get things back in order. He looked at the astrological charts, and told me to come here."

Buyanto built a small fire from sticks and paper, then poured a shot glass of vodka in the center to purify the flame. As the smoke curled skyward from the holy fire, he removed an aqua-blue khimorin from his jacket, unfolding it to reveal the drawings and Tibetan script within.

"Here in the middle is the spiritual horse, and all around are the Buddhist gods," he said, pointing out the figures on the top of the cloth. "Below that is a Tibetan prayer, and at the bottom we have written our names and the names of others we are praying for."

He grasped the corners of the khimorin and fanned the flames slowly, purifying the cloth with sacred smoke. After a time he moved to the top of the hill, where he tied the khimorin to one of the sticks. The wind was harsh on the hillside, snapping the multicolored cloths with each gust.

Tsypelma gathered dried wisps of pungent grass and added them to the fire, while Buyanto took the bottle of vodka to begin the offering. He poured a shot glass full, murmured a prayer, then tossed the liquid into the wind, where it separated into glistening drops. He began walking in a clockwise direction around the frame, continuing to toss vodka offerings in the air. "Vodka is a pure drink, and so it is good to offer to the gods," he said.

Once Buyanto completed the circle, he poured each person a glass of vodka in turn. Before drinking, the Buryats dipped their ring fingers into the liquid four times, and scattered four drops onto the ground, to the gods of wind, fire, water, and earth. Even when drinking at home, they follow this ritual; wisps of grass added to a holy fire, a handful of pine nuts placed under a prayer wheel—all offerings, no matter how small, are believed pleasing to the gods, Buyanto told me.

When everyone had consumed vodka and a slice of bread and butter, the Buryats pressed their hands together in prayer and began to move around the frame clockwise at a half trot. They circled the top of the hill several times, then stopped by the fire. Buyanto fell to his knees, bending low to touch his forehead to the ground.

Tsypelma watched her husband with a mixture of admiration and bemusement. "He's giving you the whole treatment," she told me in a whisper. "He knows he's on stage."

Buyanto stood and wiped the dirt from his knees. "*That,*" he said, grinning, "is the way a Buryat prays."

The three days Gary and I spent with Buyanto, Tsypelma,

and their children were a true highlight of the 1995 trip. I felt overwhelmed by their generosity, their warmth of spirit, and the beauty of the Buryat land and culture. As we prepared to leave, Buyanto had just one request. "Please, send me a photograph of my family," he asked Gary. "Let's shake on it, like men." As they shook hands, Gary promised he would. I hugged Buyanto and Tsypelma, feeling incredibly grateful to have met them, and hoping that one day I might see them again.

—⁂—

Gary never sent the photo. So, when I was preparing for the 2005 trip, I asked him to print out a few that I could hand-deliver to Buyanto when I saw him. Feeling guilty, Gary printed out photos for everyone we'd met on our trip, and I had been presenting them as gifts, to people's evident delight. He'd printed four for Buyanto, and asked me to convey his apologies along with them.

Remembering the gravity of Buyanto's expression as he'd shaken hands with Gary, I feared this might be too little, too late. Buyanto had slaughtered a sheep in our honor, for goodness' sake, and we'd failed to fulfill the one promise we'd made—how would he respond to my showing up again at his home? I was nervous enough that the night before David and I set out for Galtai, I had a dream that when I presented the photos to Buyanto, he looked at me and said, "Well, what am I supposed to do with these? Put them up on my wall?"

We headed to Galtai on a Sunday morning, riding in a clean new minivan rather than the rickety old municipal buses that used to run the route. When we arrived in the village, it looked exactly as it had ten years earlier: a lone intersection, and a small cluster of wooden houses with brightly painted shutters. All around, the land stretched on for miles, gentle hills rising to meet blue skies at the horizon.

I pounded on the gate of Buyanto's house, but no one answered. Peering over the fence of the house next door, I could see a woman inside, cleaning. "Hello!" I shouted in Russian. "Do you know where Buyanto Tsydypov is?"

She came outside and opened the gate. "I'm his sister-in-law," she said. "He's at the farm, and his wife is in Ulan-Ude today." She invited us to sit in the kitchen, and she put on a kettle for tea. I didn't recognize her, but I figured she must have been living here in 1995. "Do you remember the Americans who came to visit ten years ago?" I asked her.

"Oh, yes!" she said. "They were supposed to send a photograph, but never did."

Argh. I attempted to choke down a sip of tea as I felt my face flush deep red. Now I was desperate to see Buyanto, so I could prostrate myself at his feet in apology. I asked the woman how long it would take to walk to the farm, and she told me about an hour, then gave me directions.

David and I set off across a wide expanse of cow-pied pasture. The sun was high in the sky, and all around we could hear the buzzing of crickets. After about 45 minutes of walking, we got to a house surrounded by rusting farm machinery. When we asked for Buyanto, a young woman invited us in to wait, saying, "He's not here, but he'll be back soon."

An hour later, Buyanto finally arrived. As he approached the house, I heard the woman say, "You have guests. Two Americans." I walked toward him and held out my hand. "Do you remember me?" I asked. "I was here ten years ago, with a photographer named Gary."

There was no hint of recognition on his face. He simply

looked at me as I stood there wearing a dopey grin, dying inside. After approximately ten thousand years, he said, "Aha. I remember." He did not smile. "So, what are you doing here?"

I babbled something about wanting to see him again, to find out how he and his family and his farm were doing, and I thrust the four photos into his hand. "I'm so sorry we didn't send these," I told him. "But I'm glad to be able to give them to you now."

He looked at the photos, and at last, he smiled. "I woke up early this morning," he said, "and when I looked out the window I saw a magpie. For us, that's a sign that you'll have guests. I thought to myself, *Who's coming to visit today?* I would never have thought it would be guests from America.

"Let's go," he said, and for the next hour, we rode around the farm and adjoining lands in his beloved white Volga sedan—the same car he'd had ten years earlier. He told me that nearly all the private farmers in Buryatia had gone out of business. "There were more than two hundred private farms in this region," he said. "Now there are only five or six left. There used to be an official association of Buryat farmers. Not anymore. Agriculture is in a bad state right now."

Buyanto's farm had survived, but only because he'd made a deal with a boarding school that had opened in 2000 in Galtai. The school, called an *internat*, served 180 students, and Buyanto's farm provided beef, mutton, and wheat in exchange for a monthly fee. "Without the school, we wouldn't have been able to keep the farm going," he told me.

The decline of the farming industry wasn't the only hardship Buyanto's family was facing. Tsypelma had been diagnosed with skin cancer, and over the summer, she'd been undergoing treatment. She was tired all the time, he said, and her hair had started to fall out. Tsypelma had won me over ten years ago with her

Buyanto stands amid the rolling hills and endless sky of Buryatia,
2005 (PHOTO BY DAVID HILLEGAS)

subtle humor and warmth, not to mention the Zen-like calm she radiated. I hated the thought of her being ill, and I could see on Buyanto's face the anguish it was causing him.

The drive ended at Buyanto's house, which looked exactly the same as it had in 1995. We clomped up the front steps, and there was Tsypelma, who'd just returned from running errands in Ulan-Ude. She was a little thinner than she'd been, and she looked tired, but I was so excited to see her, I greeted her with a big hug.

But Tsypelma didn't remember me. "It's the treatment," Buyanto said. "It affects her memory." She smiled shyly, seeming a little embarrassed. Yet later that day, she had a flash of memory at an unexpected moment. I sat on the couch in their living room, and as is my habit, I tucked one leg under the other. "I remember you sitting like that before," she suddenly said. "Now I can picture you."

David and I had brought a bottle of vodka as a gift, and that night over dinner, we drank the whole thing. The evening ended as evenings often did at Buyanto's—with him singing Buryat folk songs at the top of his voice. I can't remember how or why, but David and I followed this with a vigorous rendition of "We Shall Overcome," with Buyanto joining in. The last thing I remember was Buyanto declaring, "Tomorrow, I will cut a sheep for you! When a Buryat has an honored guest, he must kill a sheep!"

—⁓—

The next morning, Buyanto drove David and me to a rocky hillside not far from Galtai. We hiked up a few hundred feet to a cave, and Buyanto pointed out ancient drawings of people, cows, and sheep. "I had never seen these," he told us, "until two Swiss tourists came to Galtai with a map not long ago and showed me where it was."

The wind whistled down the hillside, through a lone tree with bright yellow leaves, and a crow suddenly flew by, the flapping of its wings echoing against the rocks. As I watched Buyanto surveying the land, squinting against the morning sun, my heart felt full. He'd had a rough ten years—the first person I'd found on the 2005 trip who was worse off financially than he'd been before. His children were both doing well, which was a relief: 20-year-old Beligto and 19-year-old Bayarma were now students at the East Siberia State University of Technology and Management in Ulan-Ude. But there was a heaviness to Buyanto that hadn't been there before.

He'd promised to kill a sheep, so off we went in the Volga to find a flock. Just as he'd done ten years before, he chased down

"This is how Genghis Khan taught us to kill sheep." Buyanto, 2005
(PHOTO BY DAVID HILLEGAS)

a healthy young sheep, tackled it and tied its legs together, then hoisted it into the trunk. Then, instead of driving to his house, he took us to one of his brother's houses, where his niece would help him prepare it.

This time, the slaughter did not go as smoothly. Buyanto cut a slit down the sheep's abdomen, but as he plunged his hand in, the animal started struggling. As it bucked about, some of its internal organs began spilling out and it began to panic. As man and beast wrestled, other animals nearby—chickens and dogs—began to fret and squawk too, in a scene that became increasingly difficult to watch. Finally, mercifully, the sheep succumbed.

At the feast that night, Buyanto offered heartfelt toasts to our friendship and to seeing each other again. For as unexpressive as he'd been when David and I first arrived, now he seemed almost overcome. I told him I felt silly for having worried that he'd hold a grudge about the unsent photograph, as he's not that kind of man.

"Do you think I've changed?" he asked me.

I told him no.

"But I have, inside," he said. "I don't trust people anymore. People have changed. They only think about money and how they can help themselves."

I felt surprised, and saddened, by his words. He went on. "I've been deceived by people I thought were friends. I've even been deceived by my relatives. When you were here ten years ago, people were different. It's sad."

For a moment, the table was silent. Then, as if he couldn't stand the gloom that had descended over his feast, Buyanto smiled once again. He lifted his glass to offer another toast. "Come again to Galtai," he said. "But don't wait ten more years to do it."

The next morning, David and I once again piled into the back of the Volga, this time to return to Ulan-Ude. Buyanto and Tsypelma were going into the city to help their son and daughter settle into their dormitory rooms, so they gave us a lift. Bayarma, who was a pigtailed nine-year-old in 1995, was now a student of dairy technology, and Beligto, now a strapping young man of 20, was studying economics. We had a snack of tea and leftover mutton in Beligto's dorm room, and then it was time for David and me to go.

Buyanto and Tsypelma walked us to a nearby bus stop, so we could catch a bus back to Oleg and Sveta's. I found it difficult to say goodbye—especially to Tsypelma, as she seemed weary and sad, and not fully recovered from her cancer treatments. She began to cry as our bus approached, and I hugged her tightly, reluctant to let go.

—ᴡ—

As the third trip approached, one of my biggest fears was that Tsypelma had not survived her bout with cancer. I dreaded the thought of traveling back out to the village and finding Buyanto living there alone, without her. Their ease with each other, and Tsypelma's gentle teasing when Buyanto took himself too seriously, seemed like the hallmarks of a strong and enviable marriage, and I desperately hoped to find them still together, happy and healthy.

The night before I headed out to Galtai—the night of poker and *sploosh-sploosh-sploosh* beer at Oleg and Sveta's—was when we found Beligto through the vKontakte social media site. On Beligto's page, I'd noticed a photo, posted just a month earlier, of Tsypelma smiling and looking radiant. I had burst into tears, relieved beyond measure that she was OK. And although they'd never met her, Oleg, Sveta, and Alyosha joined me in toasting to Tsypelma's health that night with a special *sploosh-sploosh-sploosh*.

The next morning, I boarded a minivan to head into the Buryat countryside. The driver called out names of villages, to see where passengers needed to be dropped off, and when he called out "Galtai," I raised my hand, as did the woman next to me. She looked at me in surprise, no doubt wondering what business was bringing me to her tiny village.

"I'm visiting Buyanto and Tsypelma," I told her. "Do you know them?" She said she did; in fact, she worked with Tsypelma at the internat—the school in town. I explained that I'd met them 20 years ago and had a strange habit of dropping in on them every ten years. The woman shook her head and smiled. Then she turned away, dialed a number on her cell phone and started chatting in Buryat.

When she hung up, she turned back to me. "Tsypelma will be waiting for you when we arrive." I laughed—I'd had no idea that's who she was calling. But I liked the notion that I was getting personalized pickup service, even in a village so small that I could have somersaulted from its bus stop to any house without even getting dizzy.

The trip took an hour and a half, and we went through Khoshun-Uzur, the village where, 20 years earlier, Gary and I had carried the handwritten letter to Baldama Shagdanovna. Feeling nostalgic, I mentioned this to my seatmate, and she said, "Ah, yes. Baldama Shagdanovna is no longer living, but her daughter is the director of the *internat*." Now I was the one shaking my head in wonder. If I kept coming out here, I'd know everybody in the whole region before long.

When we pulled into Galtai, Tsypelma was there waiting for me. I wasn't even off the van before we both started laughing, marveling at the sheer absurdity that I was back in her tiny village again. We hugged, and I said, "I can't believe I'm here!" She and I walked to the house, arms around each other, and if it didn't sound so thoroughly ridiculous, I'd have said I felt like I was coming home.

Once again, Galtai was unchanged, as was Buyanto and Tsypelma's house, right down to the bright blue trim and lace curtains. Buyanto was waiting for us on the front steps, a big smile on his face. We hugged, and as we walked inside, I saw that the table was already laid with dishes of food, including several salads and the traditional Buryat meat dumplings known as *pozi*. I presented a box of chocolates and a bottle of vodka to the couple, and that's when I learned the first of many changes.

"I don't drink anymore," Buyanto said. "Five years now." This came as a surprise, because although we drank plenty when I'd been here before, other people I'd spoken to had praised him for his moderation—a rarity among men here, it seemed. "My mother died five years ago," Buyanto explained. "And on her deathbed, she said, 'Son, please stop drinking.' So I did."

His brother Bayarto had quit too, he said—but his sobriety had only lasted six months. He'd started drinking again, and eventually it spiraled out of control. "Last year, in December, he drank for three days straight," Buyanto told me. "At the end, he drank bad vodka, and he died." I asked if he'd been close to his brother. He nodded. "I was heartbroken when he died," he said.

Buyanto had always been a merry drinker, telling stories and singing songs, and he was eager for the merriment to continue even if his drinking had ceased. He poured shot glasses full for all three of us, and offered lavish toasts as he had before. He and Tsypelma followed the Buryat tradition of dipping their ring fingers into the vodka four times, scattering four drops for fire, earth, wind, and water, and I did the same. We all three raised our glasses to our lips, but only Tsypelma and I drank.

As we started to eat, I thanked them for once again taking me into their home. "Genghis Khan had one law, which people still follow," Buyanto told me. "'If a traveler comes, invite him into the house, feed him, give him something to drink. Only then should you ask him why he has come.' Buryats always offer hospitality to their guests."

With trepidation, I asked how the farm was doing. "I don't work on the farm anymore," Buyanto told me. "I quit seven years ago, and one of my brothers took over. They do some business selling meat, but it's not like it was before." The deal with the internat had ended, he said, and eventually he got tired of the struggle to keep the farm afloat. "I had to take out a lot of loans," he told me. "In the end, it was too much stress."

He'd taken a job at Buryatzoloto, the gold-mining company where his son, Beligto, was working as an economist. "I worked as a carpenter and a welder," he told me. "I traveled to many places—Magadan, Yakutsk, Batagay, Deputatsky." The job was physically demanding and the conditions uncomfortable, he said, and he also didn't like being so far away from home. So he quit.

Buyanto was fortunate enough to then find a local job, driving a school bus. It didn't pay much—just 7,500 rubles a month (about $115 at the current exchange rate). Yet even that was apparently too much for the local government to cover once the ruble crisis hit. "I haven't been paid for a few months," Buyanto told me. "There's just no money. So I stopped driving." He wanted to work, but "there are no paying jobs," he said with a shrug. And even if there were jobs, "I'm fifty-three years old. No one will hire me."

So it was that the "gentleman farmer," the maverick entrepreneur who'd been the toast of the village in 1995, was now unemployed. Buyanto was a proud man, so I could only imagine how he felt revealing this to me. But he seemed accepting of his situation, raising his hands as if to say, "What can I do?" The couple's needs were few, and Tsypelma was making 16,000 rubles a month (about $245) at the internat. They had their home and their health, and food on the table, and that was enough.

The only thing that seemed to truly gall Buyanto was the fact that he was still waiting to be paid for farming equipment he'd sold three years earlier. "I sold my combine for two hundred thousand rubles to a farming concern," he said. "They paid me one hundred thousand rubles, but never paid the rest." He'd given most of his equipment, and the livestock, to the brother who was now running what was left of the farm, though he'd kept one big tractor, which sat in the yard with the white Volga, which he rarely drove anymore. Now he drove a Toyota Fielder station wagon, which his son Beligto had helped him to buy.

Tsypelma and Buyanto in their living room in 2015, holding photos from 1995 and 2005 (PHOTO BY LISA DICKEY)

Beligto lived with his wife in Ulan-Ude. "And our daughter, Bayarma, lives with us," Buyanto said. She was 29 now, recently divorced, and had a four-year-old daughter named Saryona. They would be home soon, he said.

"You have a granddaughter?" I asked, delighted. "Yes," Buyanto beamed. "She is our light. We are so happy to have her and Bayarma with us." She gave him something to look forward to during these long days without work, he said.

When Bayarma and Saryona arrived, midway through dinner, I was struck by how much the little girl looked like her mother as a child. In 1995, Gary had taken one of my favorite photos of the trip—a shot of nine-year-old, pigtailed Bayarma squatting in front of the house, playing a dice-type game with sheep vertebrae left over from the feast. I brought that photo up on my laptop to show it to little Saryona, and as she peered at the photo, the resemblance between her and her mother was uncanny.

Everyone was tired after the excitement of the day, so after several cups of milky tea we started to get ready for bed. Tsypelma walked me to the outhouse; the night was pitch black, so she carried an industrial-sized flashlight to illuminate the path. Later that night, I would regret all those cups of tea, as I had no idea where the flashlight was and didn't want to stumble around outside, where several dogs were on long chains and the path would be shrouded in darkness. I gritted my teeth and willed the morning to come.

—ᵐ—

Tsypelma took the following day off work—a request made easier by the fact that her boss turned out to be the woman I'd sat next to on the minivan. With Buyanto not working, we three would have the whole day to spend together.

We did what we always did: we went for a drive, with Buyanto at the wheel. But instead of the Volga, we went in the Toyota. And to my surprise, Tsypelma got into the backseat with me, so that Buyanto was alone in the front, like a chauffeur.

Our first destination was the place with the ancient wall paintings. As we drove along, Buyanto hummed, and every once in a while, he'd tap the car horn a couple of times. We were often on single-track dirt roads that cut through grassy fields, so I wasn't sure if these beeps were meant to warn oncoming drivers, or an accompaniment to Buyanto's humming, or just a tic he had. Then, Tsypelma pulled out a little plastic bag of rice, and everything soon became clear.

Every few minutes or so, she'd pluck a few grains of rice out of the bag, roll down her window a crack, and toss them outside.

She'd then gently wave her hand in the air, palm up, and bow her head. These few grains were an offering, and I began to notice that whenever Buyanto would tap his horn, she'd reach into the bag and give her rice offering. Neither of them spoke of this small ritual; it was clearly not for show. It was just a periodic expression of their gratitude. There was something about seeing Tsypelma gazing placidly out the window, the little plastic bag on her lap, taking a moment to present this most elemental and humble offering to the gods, that moved me.

"In the days of the Soviet Union, these fields were tall with wheat," Buyanto said. "But there are almost no farmers left now, because there's no government support." Even the Banner of Lenin collective farm had closed, throwing scores of local people out of work. "People are growing marijuana in these fields now," he told me. "They say it's really good marijuana, because the growing conditions are good. I don't know."

When we arrived at the place of the paintings, we walked a short distance up a hill, to a tree fluttering with strips of cloth. Buyanto reached into his jacket, handed one to me and one to Tsypelma, and said, "Make a wish." Each of us took a moment to make a wish, then we tied our cloth strips to the tree. We hiked farther up the hill, higher and higher as the wind whipped at our faces, and finally, we reached a big cave. People had left coins as offerings at the entrance, but there were no paintings inside. Buyanto couldn't remember exactly where they were, so the three of us began wandering around, peering at the cliff-side walls, and suddenly we started seeing them everywhere: faded red drawings of birds, people, horses, and constellations of dots. We'd call out to one other, "Come look at this one!" and Buyanto galloped ahead, looking for bigger and better paintings to show us.

The second spot we went to was an ancient burial site, called a *khereksur*, which Buyanto told me dated back to the first century. Without Buyanto, I'd have never even noticed it was there, but he pointed out a small pile of stones set in the earth, with larger circles of rocks radiating outward. "It has been looted," he said; for centuries, the site had remained intact and undisturbed, but now it was a mishmash of tossed-aside rocks and piles of debris. Surrounded on all sides by vast fields, under an overcast sky with occasional beams of sunlight dramatically piercing the clouds, the burial site felt like a place out of time.

Buyanto then took us to Five Fingers, a giant stone that happened to have eroded into the shape of an upturned hand. Buyanto had brought me here ten years ago, when Five Fingers stood unadorned. Now, I could see that someone had tied together a half dozen or so blue silk scarves, wrapping them around the hand. There was also a ceramic plate on the palm, where people could leave coins or other offerings. Buyanto and Tsypelma touched the stone with their foreheads, and Tsypelma raised her own hand in the same gesture I'd seen her make in the car—a gesture of thanks. I watched as the couple walked around the stone several times, their hands pressed together in prayerful poses.

—⟳—

Back at the house, our focus turned to more earthly concerns. Vladimir Putin was in New York to make a speech at the United Nations, and there had been much speculation about how he and Barack Obama would interact. It was no secret that the two leaders didn't like each other, and tensions were flaring over the recent upheaval in Syria. As Buyanto and I sat on the couch, watching Russian news on TV, I found myself truly nervous about how the meeting had gone. Relations between the United States and Russia were already so poor, I dreaded the possibil-

Tsypelma at Five Fingers, 2015 (PHOTO BY LISA DICKEY)

ity that they could plummet even lower—and not only because it might make my travels uncomfortable.

As Buyanto and I watched, the newscast cut to a clip of Putin and Obama shaking hands. "Heyyy," Buyanto exclaimed with a grin, raising his arms in celebration. He turned and offered his hand to me. "They shook, so now we can shake." He vigorously pumped my hand up and down. "Now we can keep seeing each other!"

"Every ten years!" I said, laughing.

Like almost everyone else I had asked so far, Buyanto was a big fan of Putin. A couple of years earlier, when Putin had been in the area opening up a new school, Buyanto had somehow made his way right up to him as he was greeting the crowds. On the *shkaf*, the open bookshelf in the living room, there was a photograph of Buyanto standing next to the Russian leader. "My friends can't believe I got so close!" he told me, beaming. The photo was clearly a prized possession.

The other big news of the day was the continuing plight of Syrian refugees, who had begun streaming into Europe that fall. Russian news showed clips of desperate-looking people hurrying across fields, carrying almost nothing with them, as a commentator described what kind of assistance various countries were providing. Buyanto turned to me. "How much do refugees get in America?" he asked. I told him I wasn't sure. "Maybe I can become a refugee?" he joked. "An economic refugee." He gestured outside and said, "The streetlights have been turned off in Galtai. There's no money for electricity. Sometimes they turn off the electricity everywhere for a day or two, if people in the village don't pay their bills."

I already knew that Buyanto and Tsypelma were living on her salary of roughly $245 a month, so I'd been dreading the question he asked next. "How much do you earn in a month?" he asked me. How could I answer this question? I earned an ungodly amount compared to anyone in Galtai, though not enough to buy a house in West Hollywood. The vast majority of people on the globe would consider me rich, and compared to them, I was. I certainly didn't feel rich, but that just showed how perverse my expectations were as a high-income person living in a major Western city.

I felt queasy at the idea of answering Buyanto's question truthfully, but I also didn't want to lie. "I make a lot," I told him. "But our cost of living is higher than in Buryatia." I told him that my "roommate" and I paid $3,200 a month in rent, and his eyes widened. I felt guilty, as if this revelation were an affront, and at that moment I realized that I hadn't felt so comparatively rich on my first two trips here. In 1995, I'd been living on savings and paying $100 a month for my St. Petersburg apartment. In 2005,

I was making decent money as a ghostwriter, but my then-partner and I paid just $1,500 a month for the mortgage on our small house. Answering Buyanto's question not only made me profoundly uncomfortable, it was making me question my life choices.

Mercifully, Tsypelma called us in for dinner. Bayarma and her daughter were home, so the five of us sat down for a meal of chicken stew, cucumber salad, and rice. There would be no sheep feast this time around, and there was never even a mention of it. I was happy to enjoy this simpler meal, and as the evening wore on, Buyanto once again started singing his beloved folk songs, his voice echoing off the whitewashed walls and wooden floors of the kitchen. He closed his eyes, drawing out the notes as Tsypelma squatted by the fireplace, nudging the coals with a long iron poker.

Upon finishing one particularly heartrending ballad, Buyanto told me, "We used to sit and sing these songs, peaceful, plaintive, never in a hurry." Then he burst out laughing. No matter how difficult things got for him, there was an essential cheerfulness in the man that always managed to find its way out.

—⁂—

The next morning, Buyanto and Tsypelma drove me into Ulan-Ude. They planned to drop me off at Oleg and Sveta's, but before that, they wanted to show me one more special place: The Rinpoche Bagsha Datsan, a Buddhist temple where they often came to worship. Buyanto wanted me to meet the lama there, a Tibetan named Lopsang Nonzho.

The datsan was an unremarkable two-story brick building, but because it had been built atop of the highest hill in the city, the views on all sides were spectacular. We could see for miles in every direction, past the homes and buildings of

Ulan-Ude, to the gently curving Selenga River, to the Khamar-Daban mountain range in the distance. The sky was a brilliant blue, streaked with dramatic cirrus cloud formations, and on either side of the datsan were two giant gold-domed *stupae*, domed structures that stood like otherworldly sentinels against the endless sky.

Buyanto led us into the datsan, where a 20-foot-tall gold Buddha peered out peacefully over the sanctuary. The walls were covered with brightly colored paintings and elaborately carved, multi-armed gods, but we only stayed a few minutes before Buyanto took my arm and guided me into a small hallway off the cavernous main room.

This was where people waited to meet with the lama—whose voice, I now realized, was emanating from behind a closed door. It was an insistent low buzz, rhythmic and monotone, and it went on for minutes in between quick pauses. I figured the sound must be on tape; how much breath could he possibly take into his lungs? But when the door opened and we entered the small room for our turn, I saw that the lama was red-faced and sweating, and the room was sweltering like a sauna, even though the window was cracked open. He had definitely been singing; the evidence of his exertions were thick in the air.

Buyanto introduced me. A handsome young man dressed in a burgundy and yellow robe, the lama asked each of us our first names and birth years, and then he began to chant. I watched in amazement as his neck ballooned wide, like a bullfrog's, and his veins began popping out. I'd never seen anything like this, and in fact it looked painful. The lama rocked back and forth in a kind of trance, singing Tibetan words in that low buzzing hum, and despite the fact that the room was as hot and damp as a gym, he had goose bumps on his arms.

At first, I watched in a kind of detached anthropologic wonder, but as the lama rocked and chanted, I started to feel euphoric. I couldn't take my eyes away from him, as the longer he went on, the more it felt like he couldn't really be doing what he was doing. This was a stunning display of stamina and power, but beyond that, it was simply beautiful. I barely breathed myself as he chanted and chanted, the low buzz becoming louder and more insistent as he rocked.

In the midst of his chanting, the lama handed us each a seed to eat. He then dipped a small broom-like object into water, which he sprinkled on each of our heads. The entire ceremony lasted about 20 minutes, until he finally began slowing down, at last ceasing his rocking, and holding one long note until the end.

Buyanto then handed the lama 200 rubles. Was he paying for me? Or should I pay too? I had no idea, and it felt crass to ask, so I quickly pulled out my wallet, then cringed when I saw that the smallest bill I had was a 500-ruble note. It would feel ostentatious to give that much (about $8), especially given the conversation Buyanto and I had had the night before about money. But what to do? I couldn't very well ask the lama for change, could I? I handed him the 500-ruble bill, and behind me I heard Buyanto murmur, "Ohhh"—though whether in dismay or appreciation, I couldn't tell.

The lama nodded in thanks, then opened the drawer of the desk in front of him and pulled out a small yellow talisman. It was a piece of cloth, folded into a plastic sheath. "This will protect you in your travels," he said. Buyanto again murmured, "Ohhh . . ." We thanked him, bowing to each other, and when we got into the hallway, Buyanto said, "You are very fortunate. The lama doesn't give such things to many people. You must wear it around your neck, and it will keep you safe."

Each time I'd been in Galtai, Buyanto had given me gifts, including silk scarves and prayer beads. He'd done the same on this visit, giving me a blue silk scarf of the type I'd seen tied around the Five Fingers rock formation. But now that I had this talisman, he had one more gift he wanted to give me. He and Tsypelma went into the little store on the first floor of the datsan, and they bought a piece of yellow string so I could wear the talisman.

As Buyanto tied it around my neck, he said, "Don't take it off." I promised I wouldn't. My trip was nearly half over now, and I was happy to take all the help I could get. And if anything were to befall me, I could only hope I'd be able to face it with the equanimity and courage that Buyanto and Tsypelma had shown in facing their own hardships.

—⚋⚋—

SEVEN

Baikal: Deep Water

IN A ROOM ROUGHLY THE SIZE OF A DOUBLE-WIDE phone booth, I sat stark naked, wearing a pointy wool hat decorated with the face of a crazily smiling bird. Next to me, in a similar state of undress, sat one of the world's premier freshwater malacologists,* Tanya Sitnikova. The two of us were guffawing about something—I can't remember what now, because it was 180 degrees in that little room, and I was sweating like hell and dizzy with the exertion of laughing.

The room was, of course, a tiny sauna, and the hat a goofy take on traditional headwear used to ward off heat. When Tanya and I couldn't take it anymore, we wrapped ourselves in sheets

---

*Mollusk scientist. I'd never heard of this word until Tanya taught it to me.

and scurried out to the back of the boat we were on, a vessel
called *Merlin*, which was anchored in a cove on the Angara
River just west of Lake Baikal. I wanted to jump right into the
chilly water, per Russian sauna custom, but 60-year-old Tanya
screeched, "No!" It was dark, and she was afraid we'd have trouble pulling ourselves back onto the boat. Instead, two of Tanya's
fellow researchers came out to the back deck, dipped buckets
into the river, and dumped the water over our heads. I yowled,
then started laughing again as my skin began to tingle.

This was my third time going on a Lake Baikal expedition
with the scientists of Irkutsk's Limnological Institute,[†] but my
first time on a private boat with its own sauna—which was a fair
indicator of how the institute's funding and research process
had changed over the last 20 years.

—⟋⟍—

In 1995, Gary and I knew we wanted to do a story about Lake
Baikal. It's the largest, deepest, and oldest lake in the world, so
voluminous that it holds one-fifth of the earth's freshwater—
about the same amount found in all the Great Lakes put together, though they have eight times the surface area. Baikal is
one of the world's great natural wonders, a mile-deep gash in the
earth filled with sparklingly clean water and thousands of plant
and animal species found nowhere else. For generations of Russians and Buryats, it's more than just a lake; it is an embodiment
of the sacred and the pristine, a mystical, legendary place.

We decided to drop in at the Limnological Institute in
nearby Irkutsk, the base from which scientists study the lake.
To our surprise, the scientists there not only agreed to talk with
us, they invited us to join an expedition that was about to get

---

[†] The study of inland waters. Don't worry, I didn't know this one either.

underway on their research ship, the *G. Titov*. Gary and I couldn't believe our luck. Short of renting a boat and crew ourselves, there weren't many ways in 1995 to see vast Lake Baikal—but now, through a fluke of good timing and the institute's generosity, we'd be heading out into its waters with the people who knew it best.

The *G. Titov*, a 72-foot cutter, was docked in Listvyanka, a tiny lakeside town near the southwestern tip of Baikal. Standing at the dock, I looked across the shimmering water at the snow-capped peaks that towered on the opposite shore. The view was spectacular, like something on a postcard from Switzerland . . . but my reverie was broken by the bustle of scientists tossing sacks of vegetables onto the boat's deck.

Tanya Sitnikova, a bespectacled 40-year-old dressed in a crewneck sweater under overalls, was the expedition's leader, and she was not happy with our start. The expedition was already three days late, as budget constraints—a new phenomenon for Russian scientists, who'd enjoyed full government funding during the Soviet years—had forced several postponements while institute officials searched for affordable fuel for the boat.

"Once we finally got the fuel, we had to wait for clean sheets, which were late," Tanya told me, her voice rising with irritation. "And then I had to go to the market to get food for the trip. I had to look around for a while to find the cheapest cabbage." This was a sorry state of affairs, that the expedition leader—a PhD and member of the Academy of Sciences—had to do the food shopping.

"I never used to have any idea how much it cost to mount an expedition," Tanya went on. "There was no need to; everything was covered by the institute. But now they can't afford to fund expeditions, so we have to find other sources of money and keep

Tanya Sitnikova, world-class malacologist, on Lake Baikal, 1995
(PHOTO BY GARY MATOSO)

very close track of our spending. We still manage to complete the same number of expeditions each year, but the difference is that now we have to spend many hours writing grant proposals and searching for money."

Tanya was fuming, but as we got under way, her irritation abated. It's hard to be in a bad mood when you're floating on Lake Baikal, with its otherworldly clarity, silvery ripples and endless unpopulated shoreline. And this was a particularly lovely day, the sky clear and the air crisp with autumn. The lake sparkled in the sunshine, while trees along the shore formed a brilliant blanket of yellow, red, and green leaves.

"October is the best time of the year for an expedition," another of the scientists said. This was Marina Podtyazhkina, a plankton specialist with nine years of experience at the institute whose salary, she told me, amounted to about $25 a month. "It's not very much, of course," she said. "But I love my work. I love the lake. How could I leave this for something else?"

Tanya echoed that sentiment. "I studied in Leningrad for a while, and I can remember passing by St. Isaac's Cathedral every day on my way to the institute. The first few times I thought, *Wow, what a beautiful cathedral.* But after that, I found it boring. It's just a pile of stones, a dead thing. But Baikal is alive. It is always changing; it has a life of its own. I couldn't wait to get back here.

"On every expedition, we find something new," she went on. "Just look at the size of this lake! Will we ever be able to say with certainty that we've found everything in it that there is to be found?"

The *G. Titov* was well equipped for expeditions, with bunks for 16 people, a laboratory, a small motorboat, a kitchen, and a shower with hot water. But not all the equipment on the boat was state-of-the-art. The deck was scattered with dented buckets, a mesh bag for collecting samples, and good old-fashioned tweezers and jars for examining and storing tiny creatures. To measure the water's clarity, one researcher threw overboard a simple white disk attached to a rope; we all peered over the side as it went down, down, down, and when everyone agreed we couldn't see it anymore, he pulled it back up. He measured the length of rope that had gone underwater to determine the depth of visibility.

There was one diver on the expedition, a hardy fellow named Vladimir Votyagov who pulled on a bulky wetsuit and placidly leapt into the 47-degree waters. After he jumped in, I could see his yellow oxygen tanks going down into the clear depths, still visible many meters below the surface. He scoured the lakebed, bringing up rocks and sponges for the scientists, who would scrape tiny mollusks and other creatures off them into glass jars.

Gary and I spent three days on the *G. Titov*, and the expedition was scheduled to go on for eight more, heading into the far northern reaches of the lake, but we needed to get on with our trip. After much deliberation, Tanya agreed to dock the boat at the village of MRS—the Russian abbreviation for Malomorskaya Fishing Station—on the western shore, so we could check the bus schedule there.

MRS was a tiny, dusty town with one store, a smattering of cottages, and pigs roaming freely through the unpaved streets. It felt like we'd landed on the set of an old Western B-movie, and the few inhabitants we encountered looked at us, with our backpacks and fancy cameras, as if we'd come from another planet. At the town's lone bus stop, we learned that we'd just missed the bus to Irkutsk—and the next one wouldn't come for another two days.

Tanya was reluctant to leave us here, as there was no hotel and no obvious place for us to sleep. Yet if we went farther north with the *G. Titov*, it might take us days to get back. Worst-case scenario in MRS, we could at least catch the bus to Irkutsk in two days' time—and we might find someone here with a car who'd be willing to take us earlier. As it turned out, there was another pier near the village, where a ferryboat arrived every three hours from nearby Olkhon Island, so we could try to hitch a ride with a car coming off the ferry.

Tanya hurried with us to the pier, but the first ferry disgorged only two motorcyclists and a dog. The second, three hours later, had a couple of cars, but none had room for two extra travelers. It appeared we were well and truly stuck.

The sun began to cast long shadows, and Tanya told us she couldn't hold up the expedition any more. She made inquiries in the village, finally managing to secure a place for us to sleep on the floor of an abandoned, unheated house. With temperatures plunging into the thirties overnight, this was, to put it mildly, not ideal. But what choice did we have? We gathered our things from the *G. Titov*, hugged everyone goodbye, and walked back to the pier to await the last ferry of the day.

The wind whipped fiercely as the sun began to set, and a truck driver waiting to catch the ferry back to Olkhon took pity on us, beckoning us into his vehicle. We sat with him, snacking on candy and sipping from a bottle of vodka he passed around, and as the sky became streaked with pink and purple, the 6 p.m. ferry arrived. To our great relief, there was a lone driver in an empty vehicle, and after a quick negotiation, he agreed to take us to Irkutsk for a small fee.

As we drove off, I marveled at how remote and untraveled this part of Russia felt. Baikal was one of the most beautiful lakes I'd ever seen, but there was no tourist infrastructure here at all. I wondered how long that would last.

—⁓—

Tanya Sitnikova was one of the few people I contacted in advance of the 2005 trip. I e-mailed her to say I was coming again, and asked whether it might be possible to join another expedition on the lake. She wrote back right away, putting me in touch with Dima Sherbakov, a colleague of hers who was leading an expedition in early October. This was unbelievable luck—what were the chances that the timing for catching an expedition would work out not just once, but twice?

When David and I got to Irkutsk, we headed over to the Limnological Institute. As we strolled through the corridors I saw dozens of young scientists, some in lab coats, working in offices equipped with microscopes, glass beakers, and flasks—as well as the first Macintosh computers I'd ever seen in Russia. At the same time, the place still had a slightly ramshackle feel, with homemade posters on paint-chipped walls detailing the latest scientific discoveries, and a modest café on the ground floor selling fish soup for the equivalent of 30 cents a bowl.

We were granted an interview with the institute's director, a heavyset man with a messy thatch of gray hair and Coke-bottle-thick glasses named Mikhail Grachev. Grachev looked like a classic Soviet bureaucrat, but from my first question, he showed off a supremely dry humor.

"How long have you been the director?" I asked.

"Oh, they give shorter sentences for killing a person," he replied.

Grachev had headed the institute since 1988, and he told me he'd seen many changes during his tenure. "The first amazing thing is that we survived," he said. "And moreover, we have become much younger. More than half of our people are now younger than thirty-five." He was proud of how they'd survived the lean years of the mid-1990s, and he told me they'd recently acquired a fair amount of new, expensive equipment. When I asked how it was funded, he said, "The state paid for it. Mr. Yeltsin and Mr. Putin."

He told me that more money was flowing into not only the institute, but the area around Baikal as well. In 1995 Listvyanka, the lakeside town where we'd boarded the *G. Titov*, was little more than a few dozen houses and an open-air market. Now, Grachev told me, "Listvyanka has become successful in the market economy. There's business there: 'Want to see the Shaman Stone?‡ No problem! I've got a boat, it'll cost you just one hundred rubles!'

"It's a bit like America at the end of the nineteenth century,"

---

‡ The Shaman Stone is a large rock protruding from the water at the mouth of the Angara River, just west of Listvyanka. Some people believe it has mystical powers, one of which is apparently the ability to draw fee-paying foreigners to look at it.

he said. "There are some cowboys, and some gangsters." This, I had to see.

On the morning of October 1, 2005, David and I boarded a bus with the expedition's research team: biochemist Dima Sherbakov, four graduate students, two divers, and Professor Judith Smith of the University of Leeds, who'd come to collect tiny shrimplike amphipods for her research.

The bus set off from Irkutsk at 9:30 a.m., and as we chugged into Listvyanka a little more than an hour later, I saw that the town had a new landmark: a gigantic electric-pink castle, complete with turrets. This, Dima informed me, was a private home being built by a wealthy Russian. And the castle wasn't the only new structure in town; there were also hotels and restaurants, catering to the new influx of tourists.

When the bus wheezed to a stop at the docks, everybody pitched in to lug gear down to the *G. Titov*. Then Dima said, "OK, now we must go get some important supplies." I remembered Tanya's quest to find cheap cabbage, and I assumed Dima must be prepping for a grocery run. He was, in a way. "We need some fish," he announced, "and some beer."

Dima was a freshwater scientist with a rock-n-roll heart. He'd recently cut off his graying ponytail, he told me, but he still favored purple-tinted sunglasses. The scientists had brought all kinds of equipment for the expedition, but the most important, Dima said, was the pair of portable speakers he'd packed, so he could blast Guns N' Roses below decks while he worked.

We walked to the outdoor market, which had grown from a few fish vendors in 1995 to a bustling tourist bazaar selling postcards, wood carvings, prayer beads, and refrigerator magnets. "We need *omul*," announced Dima, as he perused the piles of smoked fish on the tables.

"Rock-n-Roll Dima" Sherbakov, on the deck of the G. Titov, *2005*
(PHOTO BY DAVID HILLEGAS)

Omul is the prized catch of Baikal, a delicious whitefish en-
demic to the lake. Freshly smoked omul is a tender, flavorful
delicacy, but rumors abounded that you had to be careful when
buying from vendors here, as they'd sell older fish that could
make you sick. Several people had reportedly fallen into comas
recently after eating spoiled omul, and when David and I were
in Ulan-Ude, Oleg had warned us to stay away from it. I asked
Dima if we should be worried. "Eh, I think it's probably OK," he
shrugged. "If we eat it and don't die, we'll know it's safe."

The *G. Titov* set off under a brilliant blue midday sky. Sunlight glinted off the water as we pulled away from Listvyanka,
and once again I could see the soaring snow-capped mountain
peaks on the lake's southern shore. The air was crisp, though the
smell of oil from the boat's engine wafted across the deck.

The goal of the expedition was to collect worms and amphipods from the lakebed. First, a crewmember would attach a specially designed mesh dredging bag to a winch, then lower it to the lake bottom. After ten minutes or so, he'd crank the winch to pull the bag back up, then dump its contents—a mixture of sand, silt, and rocks—into buckets. The grad students and Judith would leap into action, hunching over to sort through the muck with tweezers, plastic spoons, and sieves. The dredging brought up plenty of little creatures that first day, and the mood on the boat was one of excitement.

The next day, after breakfast, the research team gathered again on deck with spoons and tweezers in hand. The crew sent the dredge back down, but when it came time to pull it up, something was wrong. The line was taut, yet the dredge bag wouldn't budge.

For 15 minutes, the crew struggled to bring up the dredge. The captain turned the boat to and fro, and a crewmember pulled on the line, but nothing seemed to work. Finally, the winch began turning again. What came up, however, was an empty line—the dredge bag was gone, stuck 80 meters below the lake's surface, too far down for the divers to recover it.

This wasn't a catastrophe, but it was a serious setback. There was another dredge bag on board, but it was only a third of the size of the one that had been lost. The researchers could still gather samples, but now they'd have to dredge three times as often to get the same amount of material. Dima's face betrayed his disappointment, though he said little about the loss.

Given how much it must be costing to undertake this expedition—fuel, salaries, and supplies—it seemed a shame that the loss of a simple dredge bag might drastically impact the results. I found myself wondering why the institute didn't have more of these bags; perhaps the current financial situation was more precarious than it had seemed.

I asked Dima what had changed between 1995 and now. "In 1995, it was impossible to work," Dima told me. "There was just no money. I took photos of the lake and made them into post-cards to make money on the side. I also sold aquarium fish." This was unfathomable: Imagine the PhDs at Woods Hole Oceano-graphic Institution being forced to sell postcards to support themselves. Now, Dima said, the Limnological Institute was getting more money from the government, though less from the international organizations that helped it through the leanest years.

"We survived in the end due to foreign money," he told me, "but nothing is free in this world, and we still suffer the results of that. But we don't have the wild immigration anymore of everyone moving abroad. Things have gotten back to normal."

The crew continued to dredge with the smaller bag, manag-ing to pull up scores of wiggling worms and amphipods, and the earlier good mood was mostly restored. While the researchers worked, the wind picked up sharply, and the sky changed from blue to cloudy to blue again in minutes. October brings unpre-dictable weather to the lake, and squalls began darting wildly across the water, creating dark patches of ripples on the surface.

In mid-afternoon, the *G. Titov* glided toward the dock of MRS—the tiny village where, ten years earlier, Gary and I had been briefly stranded. I strained to see whether the village had changed, but I needn't have looked farther than the *G. Titov*'s deck; as we drew close, everybody whipped out their cell phones, because MRS was one of the few places along Baikal's shore that had a cell phone tower.

Stepping off the boat for a walk into town, I saw a sign for the Hotel Edelweiss—which would have been a tremendous comfort for Gary and me if only it had been here ten years earlier. The hotel had five rooms, all of which, as the owners proudly advertised, "contain a shower with a lavatory," no small feat in a village where most homes still had outhouses.

David and popped into a store, and I mentioned to the woman behind the counter that MRS had grown over the last decade. "Yes, we're like New York now!" she exclaimed. "We have *five stores!*" Yet most of MRS looked exactly the same. Pigs still wandered the dusty roads, and the wooden cottages, with their brightly painted shutters and flowers in the windows, stood unchanged. All was quiet except for the occasional mooing cow, barking dog, or sputtering motorbike.

I'd have loved to spend the night at the Hotel Edelweiss, but we had one more day on the *G. Titov*, after which Dima planned to drop us off at the village of Khuzhir on Olkhon Island, the largest island in Baikal. With a population of 1,500, Khuzhir now had not only daily bus service to Irkutsk[§], but a couple of hotels as well. One of these, called "Nikita's Homestead on Olkhon," was where David and I would spend the night.

When we arrived at the Homestead, the first thing we saw was a cheery mural of smiling Baikal seals, painted with the words "Welcome Hello" in English. We entered through a wooden gate and found ourselves in a most un-Russian hotel.

It was as if a backpacker's hostel had been picked up from Bangkok or New Delhi and dropped into this small Siberian village. Whimsical folk art, including carved totem poles, painted farm tools, and a "sunken ship" planter with a riot of wildflowers, dotted the grounds. Flyers advertised ping-pong lessons, horseback rides, and a "Buryat folk show." As I stood

---

[§] For most of the year, the buses travel from Olkhon to the mainland via ferry—the same ferry that Gary and I had waited for in MRS back in 1995. In deepest winter, however, when Baikal is frozen, the buses drive directly across the ice.

gaping at the sprawling compound, three young Irish guys strolled by, and I also heard a couple speaking French.

So, Baikal was finally becoming an international tourist destination, complete with backpackers' lodges. Stuck in MRS ten years before, I remembered thinking we were truly in the middle of nowhere. Now, though it wasn't yet what you'd call a tourist mecca, it was certainly starting to become a destination.

—∽—

The pink castle in Listvyanka is no longer pink, but it is most definitely still a castle—a turreted, fortified, multistory monstrosity that towers over the traditional Siberian wood cottages standing on either side. It's a subtle chocolate-milk-brown now, making it less ostentatious, though only marginally so.

I saw the castle as I rode the bus into town, one day before meeting Tanya Sitnikova for my third expedition on Lake Baikal. As in 2005, I'd decided to e-mail Tanya in advance of the trip, to ask if there were any expeditions I might join. Happily, the timing was working out once again, although this expedition wouldn't be on the G. Titov, which had been deactivated for the winter. This time, we'd be going out on a private boat.

Listvyanka had changed since 2005, though not drastically. There were more hotels now—a fact I'd discovered online, when I booked a place to stay for the night. There were more restaurants too, and I was amused when the bus passed by something called the USSR Pub, a squat little brick place with a picture in the window of Barack Obama waving a Russian flag. Next door to the pub was another small building, with a sign out front advertising LIVE BEARS: for a fee, you could walk in and gawk at a couple of bears kept in cages. Not exactly bears in the streets, but closer than anything I'd seen so far.

The live bears weren't the only odd tourist attraction in

Listvyanka. There was also the Retro Park museum, with a yard full of antiques, old cars, and folk-art figures crafted from metal scraps. The nearby Theatre of Original Songs advertised concerts featuring "Songs for smart women and sober men!" And the Nerpinary, a submarine-shaped building, housed an aquarium show featuring *nerpa*, the native seals of Lake Baikal. All this was set against a backdrop of blazing yellow, green, and red foliage on one side and the vast, magnificent lake on the other. Listvyanka was a fun, quirky town, a breath of literal fresh air.

The next morning, Tanya came to pick me up at my hotel. She looked fantastic, certainly not 20 years older than the last time I'd seen her, with dark hair cropped short and wearing white sneakers and a fleece vest. We hugged, and she said, "Well, come on! Let's get to the dock."

I asked Tanya about the boat we'd be on, and told her I'd miss the good old *G. Titov*, my floating home on Lake Baikal. "The *Titov* is bigger than this one, and more expensive," she said. "I've been wanting to rent a private ship for a long time, to avoid dealing with the bureaucracy." Renting private boats for research had always been against the institute's rules, but two years ago, Tanya had requested a policy change.

"It used to be that all the grant money went directly to the institute," she said. "Then I had to write up requisitions, and the institute would tell me what they would and would not pay for. Now, all the money goes directly into my cart, and I can decide for myself." She liked having more control over the process, she said, although "now I'm not just a scientist; I'm an investigator, a bookkeeper, an organizer. It's more work, but I prefer it this way." I asked if she was still cabbage-shopper-in-chief, and she laughed. "No, we pay the team of the ship to do that now."

We boarded the boat, a 50-foot cutter named *Merlin*, and I met the researchers and crew. There were three divers: Big Igor, who owned the *Merlin*; Skinny Igor, an ichthyologist; and a soft-spoken, bespectacled fellow named Valery. Tanya was the expedition leader, and she'd brought along a graduate student named Natasha Maximova to assist her. Rounding out our collective was the captain, Vasya; the cook, Vera; and a fireplug of a man wearing a red-and-white RUSSIA hoodie, an underwater artist named Yura Alekseev.**

We all squeezed around a big wooden table in the middle of the boat, and almost immediately I got lost in the flurry of slang, scientific terms, and inside jokes that began flying around. As Vera served cups of tea and slices of cake, Skinny Igor, a handsome, wiry man with silver hair and a manic, chatty energy, cracked jokes and waved his hands wildly as he told story after story. Everyone seemed excited to head out onto the lake, but as the boat rocked, I began to wonder if I should head out to the deck for some air.

The rocking wasn't violent—in fact, we were still tethered to the dock. But it was uncomfortably warm in the room and the curtains were pulled shut, so I couldn't see the horizon. As I sat listening to everyone talk and laugh, I found myself in a conundrum: Do I embarrass myself by going out to get some air, even though the boat is barely moving? (Weak American, indeed.) Or do I stay, and risk embarrassing myself even more if I actually get sick?

I sipped my tea and trained my attention on a framed photo montage hanging on the wall. To my surprise, it was snapshots of film director James Cameron, who'd apparently come to Baikal in 2010 to explore the lake in a submersible. I asked whether anyone here had met Cameron, and both Tanya and Big Igor said they

---

** Not only does Yura Alekseev paint underwater landscapes, he is actually underwater while he paints them. He's one of a handful of artists in the world who don scuba gear, then carry canvases and paint under the water to create their art.

had, and that he'd impressed them as a "regular guy" and a true explorer. Tanya said she had some video footage taken from the submersible, and offered to show it to me on her laptop. Watching a video of undulating vegetation in Baikal's depths calmed my stomach, and to my relief I was soon feeling hale again.

After tea and cake, we finally got under way. As the *Merlin* motored northeast, I watched little Listvyanka slide past to our left, and a half hour later we dropped anchor just off the shore of a tiny settlement called Bolshiye Koty ("Big Cats"). Tanya had warned me that this expedition wasn't going nearly as far as the others I'd been on; in fact, Bolshiye Koty was our sole destination. I didn't really mind, as simply being on the lake itself was a treat—though I did feel a little cheated that I wouldn't get to see MRS again, to find out whether pigs (if not bears) still wandered the streets there.

Now we had lunch, and I began to think that this was going to be a very leisurely expedition indeed. But soon after we ate, Big Igor, Skinny Igor, and Valery began suiting up for a dive. As he pulled on his wetsuit, I noticed that Skinny Igor was wearing what appeared to be bad catalog pajamas from the seventies—a tight brown knit turtleneck and matching long-underwear-style pants. Catching my quizzical look, he said, "They're wool. They keep me warm underwater. I'm skinny."

Seeing the men suit up reminded me of the diver from the 1995 expedition. "Do you still work with Vladimir Votyagov?" I asked Tanya.

"Ohhh," she said. "He died two years ago, in an accident on the lake." This was a horrifying thought, especially as the two Igors and Valery were just about to leap into the water. "Was it a diving accident?" I asked, trying to keep my voice down. She shook her head.

"He was in a truck, driving across the ice on the lake, and it

(L-R) Me, Tanya Sitnikova, Natasha Maximova, and Yura Alekseev on the deck of the Merlin, *2015* (PHOTO BY LISA DICKEY)

fell through," she said. Driving on Lake Baikal is a common activity in midwinter, as the ice normally ranges from two feet to two meters thick. But, inexplicably, there had been a thin spot, and while others in the truck managed to escape after it plunged, Tanya said, Vladimir couldn't get out in time. He had drowned.

We watched as the three divers leapt into the water, then tracked their movements through their bright yellow tanks and the clouds of bubbles ascending to the surface. I found myself pondering Vladimir Votyagov's death, wondering whether, if the truck had driven a yard or two on either side of that thin ice, it wouldn't have plunged through. One never knew whom fate would touch with tragedy, a fact that seems especially clear when you drop in on people only once every ten years. The thought made me melancholy.

At long last, the divers returned to the boat, their lips blue from the chilly waters. They hoisted up buckets full of rocks, which Tanya and Natasha began picking through with tweezers, in a scene exactly the same as those I'd witnessed 20 years earlier. The scientists' work had changed little, but the state of the lake had changed a great deal, according to Skinny Igor. Baikal, he said, was experiencing a "genuine ecological crisis."

He explained that around 2008, divers and researchers started to notice that the lakebed was changing. "We weren't even sure yet if it was a problem," he said. "But by 2010, it was impossible not to notice that something was wrong."

"What had changed?" I asked him.

"I'll show you," he said. Igor often carried an underwater camera on his dives, and he opened his laptop to show me videos he'd shot. First, he showed me healthy sponges from a few years back. They were green, plump, and plentiful, creating a lush underwater forest of vegetation. Then, he showed me how they looked today.

The difference was startling: these sponges were brown, scarred, and disintegrating. Many lay dead on the lake floor. Others were completely covered in some kind of grassy material, smothered by heavy strands that swayed gently in the water.

The death of so many sponges, Igor told me, was a looming disaster, because sponges provide filtration for the lake. "They are crucial to the health of the lake," he said, "but they are dying. There are places where more than 80 percent of the sponges have died."

The scientists didn't know why they were dying, though some suspected that blue-green algae was the cause. "It must have a connection," Igor said, "but it's still not completely clear why." Another possibility was human interference with the lake. "Consider this," he went on. "It's not happening everywhere along the lake, so it can't be global warming. Global warming isn't selective like that. No, it's happening specifically where there are more tourists."

So far, he said, "We don't know what exactly the cause is. There are many possible factors." Since they didn't know what was killing the sponges, they couldn't act to halt the process. And even if they could, the damage was already catastrophic.

"Healthy sponges grow at a rate of 9 to 11 millimeters per year," Igor told me. "Larger sponges can be 1.5 meters long, and the biggest are even taller than I am. So, even if the sponges started to grow healthy today, it would still take seventy-five to one hundred years to grow back to the size they were.

"Baikal is sick," he concluded, "and it's an irreversible situation."

I thought back to my first two trips here, when the most serious problem seemed to be whether these scientists could find enough funding to explore the lake. Baikal was one of the cleanest bodies of water in the world, due in part to the lack of human habitation along its shores, and there had never seemed to be a reason to worry about its health. Until now, it hadn't occurred to me that this vast, magnificent lake could ever be in danger.

I asked Tanya about the health of the lake, and she confirmed what Igor had told me. "About five years ago, Lake Baikal started changing," she said. "No one is sure why, but there are hypotheses. There's more methane now. Also, there's much more spyrogyra [a type of freshwater algae], and the sponges are sick. This may be a result of climate change, or it may be because the villages along the shore are dumping unclean water into the lake." Nobody knew for sure, and as a result, there was a lot of debate—and arguing—among scientists at the institute.

That evening, Captain Vasya steered the *Merlin* out into deeper waters, so the men on board could fish for omul. The two Igors, Valery, and Yura stood out on the deck, casting their lines and reeling them in, smoke curling up from the occasional cigarette into the chill night air. They cast and cast, swapping stories and cracking jokes, but no one was catching any fish. Long after I retired to my bunk, I could hear them talking and laughing out on the deck.

The following morning, we were docked back at Bolshiye Koty. The lake was churning, with whitecaps stretching as far the eye could see, and waves were sloshing up on to the *Merlin*'s stern as Tanya scurried about, trying to secure the buckets and other equipment. It felt like we were on the ocean, with waves and troughs buffeting the boat.

Tanya had decided the water was too rough for us to go out today, but Skinny Igor disagreed. "It'll be calmer farther out," he said. "We just have to get past this part." The two scientists engaged in a heated discussion, but Tanya was the expedition leader, so her decision was final. Igor shrugged, clearly disappointed. The expedition was short to begin with; now we'd be losing a day. Natasha, Vera, and I set out into the woods near Bolshiye Koty to hunt for mushrooms—not exactly how I'd expected to spend time on a Baikal expedition, but not an unpleasant diversion either. When we returned, we found that the men had decided to dive from the docked boat, as this was better than not diving at all.

By evening, the water had calmed enough for the *Merlin* to ease back out into the lake for more fishing. And this time, the guys started reeling in omul almost immediately. Nearly every time someone cast a line, it came back with a big silvery fish hooked to it. The men filled bucket after bucket with the fish, which would make for some stellar meals in our time remaining—including a breakfast sashimi the next morning of omul slices dressed in oil and onions, which turned out to be much more appetizing than I would have imagined, had I ever imagined raw fish for breakfast.

—m—

In the afternoon, I decided to pay a visit to Captain Vasya, who was at the *Merlin*'s helm steering us back toward the southern part of Baikal. Vasya was a calm, steady presence on the boat, a diminutive man who exuded quiet confidence without ego. I had liked him right away, and over the past few days I'd been looking for a chance to chat with him. Now, as I peered through the window of the bridge, he motioned for me to come in.

He told me he'd been a captain on these waters since 1972, and that he owned a house on the Angara River, which flowed out of Baikal toward Irkutsk. "We'll go right by it later today," he said. "I'll show it to you." Big Igor also had a house nearby, he told me, and the two men not only worked together frequently, they had become friends. It was amusing to think of these two hanging out—trim Vasya with his close-cropped hair and gentle demeanor, and burly, bearded, intimidating Igor, who towered over Vasya and owned the boat that he captained.

As if on cue, Big Igor poked his head in to ask Vasya about our course. Seeing me, he entered the bridge. He asked how I was enjoying the expedition, and whether Captain Vasya was answering all my questions. We engaged in small talk for a few minutes, and then he abruptly switched topics.

"Liza, what do you know about Ukraine?" he asked. I wasn't sure how to answer; was this a real question, or a challenge? I didn't immediately respond, so he tried again: "What do Americans know about Ukraine?" He stared at me, waiting.

"That's a pretty broad question," I said.

"Then let me ask you this," he said. "What if the bears suddenly came to Canada, and started handing out money, paying people there to fight against America? Would you like that? Would that be a *good* thing?" By "bears," he obviously meant Russians, and he was setting up an equation: Americans wouldn't want other countries stirring up trouble on their doorstep, so why should we stir up trouble on Russia's? Meaning, more specifically, why does America think it's OK to send guns and money to Ukraine?

"Let me ask you another question," he said, still staring at me. "How many Russian military bases are near American soil? None. And how many American military bases are near Russia? Many." This was true: the United States has multiple bases in Japan, South Korea, Turkey, the Middle East, and all over western Europe. "How would Americans like it if Russians had military bases in Canada and Mexico?" Igor asked. "Would they like that?" We both knew the answer: of course not. The Soviets once had a military presence in Cuba, after all, and look how well that had gone. The Russians had closed their base there in 2002, and one didn't need a top-secret security clearance to know that the American government preferred to keep it that way.

"America wants to spread its influence all over the world," Big Igor went on. "But we just want to be left alone." He wasn't the first to express that sentiment to me on this trip. Both Pasha in Chita and Vasily in Vladivostok had argued the same thing: that Russians want to be left alone, but we Americans keep poking our nose in their business. One could certainly argue that if Russia wanted to be left alone, it ought to leave Ukraine alone. But this much was abundantly clear: as little as Americans trust

Vladimir Putin's motives, Russians are every bit as distrustful of ours.

"How is it America's business what happens in Ukraine?" Igor asked, his voice rising. "We have centuries of history with Ukraine. Why can't America just mind its own business there—and in Iraq, and everywhere else?" I continued to sit silently, while Vasya began squirming in his captain's chair.

Igor was on a roll now. "And let's not even get started on how America treated the Indians," he said. "We have hundreds of ethnic groups in Russia, and we've left them all alone. Buryats, Tatars—they have their own autonomous regions. Why destroy the culture? What purpose does that serve?" Well, this was a stretch. I flashed back to Tsyren-Dulma Dondagoy telling me about Soviet repression of the Buryats, and the Jews of Birobidzhan describing how they were driven underground. And how about present-day Russia, where darker-skinned Chechens and others from the Caucasus region face regular racial profiling, including beatings, arrests, and expulsions?

But I didn't bring any of this up. For one thing, America certainly has its own problems with racial profiling. For another, it felt like a fool's errand to get in a battle over whose country has historically treated its ethnic minorities worse. Instead, I just said, "Yes, the way we treated the Indians was horrible. You're right about that."

"Cruel," he said. "It was cruel."

With this, gentle Vasya couldn't take it anymore. "Come on now, let's not talk about sad things!" he said. "It's such a lovely day, and we're out on this beautiful lake." Neither Igor nor I responded, so Vasya went on, turning to me to chirp, "Liza, did you know, my grandmother's name is Elizabeth? Like yours!" I smiled weakly, and Igor, sensing that the moment was over, abruptly turned and left the bridge. A few minutes later I excused myself and walked out too, to get some air on the deck.

At that moment, I felt bone tired. I was halfway through the trip now, and my Russian skills had recently seemed to deteriorate, leaving me grasping to understand the slang-filled conversations going on around me. I was sleeping poorly on the boat, as someone in our tiny four-bunk compartment—I'm not saying who—snored.[††] Lake Baikal was ailing, Ukraine was in flames, and suddenly I felt overwhelmed and homesick. I stood out on the deck for a long time, feeling the breeze in my face as the boat motored toward the Angara. I never imagined I could feel so sad in such a spectacularly beautiful place.

Later, Big Igor found me alone at the dining table and took a seat next to me. He wanted me to know, he said, that while he disagreed with the American government, he didn't dislike American people, and he was very glad I had come on the expedition. I told him I wasn't angry about our earlier exchange, just curious. Many of the Russians I'd spoken to had trodden gently around these issues, most likely to avoid getting into a quarrel with me. But Igor had spoken frankly and with passion, and I appreciated that.

"I want you to feel welcome here," he said, and I found myself unexpectedly touched at his concern. Because he'd been so honest about his dislike of America, his effort to make nice with me felt genuine. He stuck out a meaty hand, and we shook.

I asked him what was planned for the rest of the expedition. "The work part is finished," he said. "Now we will move to the cultural part of our program."

"The cultural part?" I asked.

[††] It was Tanya.

"Yes," he said, smiling. "*Shashlik, pivo, i banya.*" Shishkabob, beer, and sauna.

That evening, Captain Vasya docked the boat in a small cove on the Angara River, where we could make some noise without bothering anyone. The guys pulled out a portable grill, and they began building a fire to roast the shashlik. Once again, Natasha, Vera, and I headed to shore to hunt for mushrooms, and Skinny Igor serenaded us loudly from the boat as we traipsed through the woods. Later, after we all gorged on sizzling hunks of shashlik and ice-cold beer, everyone took a turn in the tiny sauna, as Yura the artist plucked at his guitar and sang Russian folk songs. It was a pleasant end to what had been an up-and-down expedition.

The next morning, after the *Merlin* arrived in Irkutsk, we all posed for a selfie on the dock. Big Igor gave me a bear hug, lifting me off my feet, and invited me to come back any time. Valery the diver, who had said so little during the expedition, volunteered that I was an American who "broke the stereotype"—a rather backhanded compliment, I thought. It was almost time to head to my next destination, Novosibirsk. But first, there was one more person I needed to see: Rock-n-Roll Dima.

—⁂—

Dima hadn't been able to come on the expedition, so when he and his wife invited me to stay with them a couple of nights in Irkutsk, I gratefully accepted. Tanya dropped me off at his apartment, and Dima greeted me looking much the same as he had ten years ago, with graying hair, an impish smile, and a professorial wardrobe of corduroy pants and a brown jacket.

"We will have lunch," he declared, reaching into the freezer and pulling out a bag of *pelmeni*. He put a pot of water on to boil, then opened a couple of liter bottles of beer. It was barely noon, but this was Dima.

He was never one for small talk, so soon we launched into his usual roller coaster ride of conversation, which was invariably sprinkled with puns, jokes, and iconoclastic observations. For some reason, he began telling me a long story about a mountain expedition he'd gone on decades ago with a group of American Vietnam War veterans and Russian veterans of the war in Afghanistan. He went into great detail about the mountain, the equipment, and the men, and just as I was wondering why he'd chosen to tell me this, he was on to the next story, a tale about how serious the young people in Russia are these days.

"I recently went to a dissertation party," he said. "All of us were sitting around, talking, and the young ones—even the ones who look weird, with blue hair and tattoos—they took one sip of alcohol, and that was it. Then they went off to play ping-pong. Much later, they came to scoop up the older generation, which had been drinking all night.

"The younger generation doesn't smoke, doesn't drink, exercises, thinks about money, works hard," Dima said, then took a long gulp of his beer. "This is a very big difference, generationally.

"Kids in their twenties now are like an Englishman in his eighties," he went on. "And when has there ever been a generation like this in Russia? I don't know, maybe never. If a professor doesn't show up to teach a class, they all say, 'Why isn't there a substitute? We are here to learn.' Can you imagine?" He chuckled. "For me, it's a culture shock. In my time, we'd have gone off somewhere to have a drink and celebrate."

After lunch, Dima suggested we go for a walk to downtown Irkutsk. Having been cooped up on a boat for three days, I was happy for the exercise, but out of curiosity I asked, "Do you drive?"

"No," he replied. "How can I? I only have two legs, and there are three pedals." Of course. Silly question.

As we walked along a busy highway, we passed a large shopping mall, a boxy, mustard-yellow-painted building with towering red letters that spelled out KOMSOMOLL. I burst out laughing—was this really the play on words it seemed to be? *Komsomol*, the abbreviation for the Soviet-era Young Communist League, turned into a Komso-Mall? "Yes!" Dima exclaimed. "Although you might also read it in French, as *Comme-ça* Mall." I was starting to suspect that, whatever one thought about a particular subject, Dima was likely to offer a contrary view—a suspicion that was confirmed when the conversation next shifted to global warming.

"As humans, we give ourselves too much credit," Dima announced. "We like to think we are the cause of global warming, but we're not that powerful." He went on to tell me about a volcanic eruption in Indonesia a few years earlier that, according to him, released as much carbon dioxide per minute as had been released "over all of human history." This seemed unlikely, but I didn't have enough information to counter him. Instead, I said, "Whatever the case, surely it makes sense to try to minimize our ecological impact anyway?"

"Of course," he replied. "Let's put it this way: the fact that we are all mortal and will die does not mean we should go around shitting in our trousers."

We arrived at the jewel of downtown Irkutsk, a gleaming new row of restaurants, galleries, and stores built to resemble old-style Siberian cottages, and our walk soon turned into a pub crawl. We stepped into the Kruzhal bar, and Dima ordered two double-shots of vodka. Even the hipster bartender, in his pork-

pie hat with a feather sticking out, seemed impressed, respond-
ing with a hearty "Oho!" He brought us the drinks, and after
we toasted, I asked Dima what he thought about Vladimir Putin.

He responded by telling me about a viral YouTube clip he'd
seen, in which the famous Russian rock star Yuri Shevchuk apparently told Putin—to his face—to go fuck himself. Apparently,
the rocker hadn't suffered any official consequences for his
outburst. "So, is this not freedom of speech?" Dima asked.

Perhaps, I countered, but surely Dima didn't truly believe
that Russia had complete freedom of speech? "No, we don't,"
he agreed. "But I think that is best." Really? How so? "We don't
have enough stability in Russia for freedom of speech right
now. It could tear things apart. Freedom of speech is wonderful for the countries that are strong enough to sustain it. But it
could lead to disaster here. It's not worth the deaths that would
result."

The longer I talked with Dima, the less I could get a handle
on him. I decided to ask him about the activist punk collective
Pussy Riot, several members of which had been arrested and
thrown in jail for staging a political protest in Moscow's Cathedral of Christ the Savior. In America, the women of Pussy Riot
were considered heroes, but in Russia, they were more com-
monly seen as troublemakers. Dima was an iconoclast, but was
he enough of an iconoclast to embrace them?

He grimaced. "I didn't want them to be jailed," he finally
said. "But I wanted someone to give them a good spanking."

Our shot glasses empty, we left the bar and meandered on-
ward, under a chilly gray sky. "They said there'd be snow today,"
I remarked.

"They said I'd never marry!" Dima shot back.

He took me to a favorite haunt of his, a beer bar tucked away
on a side street. Inside, he ordered two large beers, and we slid

into a booth in the darkened bar. "I'm an adherent of Cervezya-nity," he told me. Cervezyanity?

"The religion of beer," he explained.

"I'll be the second adherent," I said, and we toasted, our giant steins making a clunking sound.

There was one more thing I wanted to ask Dima about. "Igor tells me that Lake Baikal is facing an ecological catastrophe," I told him. "What do you think?"

"Ah," he said. "Igor is . . . poetic. He may be overstating the problem." He took a sip of beer. "Sometimes his research isn't entirely systematic. I believe the problem may be more compli-cated than what he suggests."

Like Tanya and Igor, Dima too said that scientists weren't completely sure what was causing the changes. I told him about Igor's remark that they seemed to be happening specifically where there were more tourists.

"Well," Dima countered, "tourists tend to concentrate at places that are most attractive for tourists—shallower, warmer water, more picturesque. The question is, does shit appear where there are more flies? Or do flies appear where there is more shit?" Per usual, Dima distilled the question into the most colorful—and scatological—terms possible.

"There are major changes happening in the lake," Dima concluded, "but it is still possible they are part of a larger natu-ral cycle." Yes, he said, sponges were dying, but it wasn't necessar-ily cause for alarm. As we sipped our beers, I didn't know whom to believe. But I was relieved that at least one scientist at the Lim-nological Institute felt relatively sanguine about the lake's future.

—⁓—

EIGHT

Novosibirsk: Circle of Life

THE BEDROOM DOOR SWUNG OPEN. A WOMAN EMERGED, her tight black dress accentuating her slender hips and long, shapely legs. She looked around seductively, her dark eyes set off by thick lashes and lush layers of eye shadow, her lips painted a provocative red. She glided toward the center of the living room where, as she well knew, every eye was on her. Then the music started.

How many times do I have to try to tell you . . . crooned Annie Lennox. The woman sashayed to the couch, mouthing the lyrics, then eased down to the cushions as the music swelled around her. She ran her hand through her cascading black hair, lip-synching perfectly as the small audience watched, enraptured.

When the song drew to a close, another woman—also in a tight black minidress—put down her drink and started clapping wildly, which quickly led to an ovation and shouts of "Brava!" in the living room. The first woman tossed back her head demurely and laughed, her voice surprisingly deep.

This was 27-year-old Grisha, a young gay man in Novosibirsk who agreed to let Gary and me profile him in 1995. From the beginning of that trip, we'd known we wanted to do a story about gay life in Russia, but we weren't sure we could find any Russians willing to step that far out of the proverbial closet. To our surprise, Grisha not only let us trail him around the city snapping photographs and asking questions, he also staged a private drag show for us with one of his close friends, Valera— the other "woman" in a black minidress.

Grisha and his friends had started dressing in drag a year earlier. There were no gay bars or discos here in Russia's third-largest city, so they were looking for ways to entertain them-selves. "We all sort of had the idea together," he told me. "We bought some clothes from secondhand shops and then put on our own little show. It's a lot of fun to dress up and just goof around, but that's all it is, really."

"We only do this for ourselves," he said. "I would never dance in a club, and have never even been to see a drag show." Then a sly smile crossed his face.

"Once, we did decide to go into the street in drag," he said. "We decided to drive to another part of town, then argued about whether to just go out in dresses, or carry them with us in the car," he told me. "Finally, we decided to take the stuff with us, since I didn't want to be seen walking out of my apartment in a dress.

"That turned out to be a lucky decision, as the car ended up breaking down in an intersection on our way. Can you imagine

Valera in drag, with Grisha (left) getting ready while Zhenya looks on,
1995 (PHOTO BY GARY MATOSO)

if we had had to get out and push the car, wearing our dresses
and high-heeled shoes?"

—⚉—

Homosexuality in Russia has, for the most part, always been
concealed. Sex between men* was illegal for most of the twentieth century, outlawed by Article 121 of the criminal code, and
during the Soviet era, many gay men and lesbians were sent to
psychiatric institutions to be "cured." The Russian government
repealed Article 121 in 1993, leading to limited blooms of tolerance, with a few new gay clubs and discos opening in Moscow
and St. Petersburg. A disco opened in Novosibirsk too, but it

---

*Sex between women was not outlawed, presumably because lawmakers either
(a) didn't believe it existed, or (b) considered it more titillating than threatening.

Grisha walks to work in downtown Novosibirsk, 1995 (PHOTO BY GARY MATOSO)

lasted for only a month before the owner closed it for "financial reasons."

So it was that in 1995, gay people here had no public place to congregate—aside from the park in front of the Novosibirsk Opera and Ballet Theater. For years, Grisha told me, that park was the gathering place for gays, who shared the space with punks, drunks, and prostitutes. "But now we just gather at each other's houses, or spend evenings at home," he said. "There was a period when I wanted to meet new men all the time, and would go out to the park in front of the theater and other places, but I don't do that anymore." He smiled coyly and added, "I've become mature."

Grisha lived with his boyfriend of two years, Zhenya, a soft-spoken man with angular good looks and a swoop of blond

Duran Duran hair. I asked if they were able to live openly as a gay couple.

"It's possible to be more open now than it was in the past," Grisha replied, though he acknowledged that he hadn't come out to his colleagues at the pharmaceuticals company where he worked. "It's not that I'm afraid of their reactions," he said. "It's because it's none of their business who I live with and what kind of life I lead."

He had, however, told his mother four years earlier. "She kept saying, 'Are you gay? Are you gay?' and so finally I admitted it," he said. "She's not very happy about it, so we don't talk about it very much. But we are very close otherwise." The same wasn't true of his father, who "doesn't know anything," said Grisha. "And I'm certainly not going to tell him. He would not take it well."

Grisha's living room was a veritable entertainment center of Western gay culture, with stacks of magazines such as *10 Percent*, *Genre*, and *The Advocate* piled next to videotapes of films such as *Priscilla, Queen of the Desert*; *My Own Private Idaho*; and *The Crying Game*. His collection also included homemade videos of a few of their drag shows, one of which he popped into the VCR to show Gary and me.

In the grand tradition of high camp, the video was a masterpiece of whimsy and self-parody: CNN clips of supermodels gliding up and down the Spanish Steps in Rome were expertly intercut with clips of Grisha and his friends wobbling drunkenly up and down the steps of his apartment building at 4 a.m. The supermodels had the edge in designer wear and venue, but it was the images of the graceful, tipsy men in the dimly lit Siberian stairwell that would be difficult to forget.

Grisha also had a collection of porn films—or, as he called them, "erotic films"—which a friend had brought him from

Poland. This, he told me, had led to a rather interesting episode with the local police two years earlier, after thieves broke into his apartment.

"The thieves stole my two VCRs and a bunch of videos and CDs," Grisha said. "When the police arrived, they had only two questions: 'Why are you wearing an earring?' and 'Why do two men live here with only one bed?' They didn't seem to care at all about the robbery.

"But the thieves were eventually caught, and my stuff was recovered," he went on. "So I went down to the police station to pick everything up. When I told them who I was and that I had come to pick up my videos and VCRs, the policeman behind the desk gave me a funny look and said, 'You have some *interesting things* here.' Then he wouldn't give them back unless I brought him two bottles of champagne as a bribe, which I did.

"He gave me my things, but then I noticed later that one of the erotic tapes was missing," Grisha said with a shrug. "They say that one in every ten men is gay, so I figure some policeman has added a new video to his collection."

—∽∾—

On that 1995 visit, Grisha introduced Gary and me to his closest friends, including 32-year-old Valera, who worked as a salesman at the Max Mara clothing store, and 23-year-old Natasha, a college student.

At first, Natasha was reluctant to speak with us. "Where will this story be published?" she asked. I told her we'd be posting it to something called the World Wide Web, then attempted to explain, in Russian, the concept of modems and dial-ups and browsers. She stopped me in the middle; this was obviously too weird and esoteric to worry about. "Write what you want," she told me.

I did, and we also posted photos of everyone, including beautiful images of Grisha and Valera dressed in drag. We didn't reveal anyone's last name, but even so, Gary and I were impressed—and grateful—that these people were willing to open their hidden lives to us, a couple of random American journalists passing through.

Natasha told me that although she'd realized she was gay at age 16, she didn't meet another gay person until she was 19. "For those three years, I felt very alone," she said. "So when I read that Martina Navratilova was a lesbian, and open about it, I couldn't believe it. Here was somebody I had always admired as a tennis player and as a person, and she was a lesbian! Just knowing that made a very big difference for me."

Like Grisha, Natasha had told her mother she was gay. "I had thought she suspected it, but it turned out it had never even occurred to her. She was very upset." No one else except her gay friends knew her secret, she said, and she was eager to keep it that way. Yet at the same time, "I want to be able to hold hands with my lover in public, to kiss her on the street if I feel like it," she said. "Basically, I want to be able to do anything a straight couple can do without getting stared at or beat up. In American cities, people can do that.

"When will Novosibirsk get to that point? Maybe in five years, maybe ten," she said, wistfully. "Maybe never."

Tall, slim, nattily dressed Valera was also in the closet. He'd married a woman when he was 20, and although they'd separated nearly a decade ago, they had never divorced. "She lives with my 11-year-old son in Moscow, but neither has any idea that I'm gay," he told me. "I think my wife might suspect, but we haven't ever talked about it." He and his boyfriend of nearly two years had recently broken up, he told me, and he was still mourning the end of the relationship.

For all the hardships they faced, these friends took obvious joy and comfort in each other. And in truth, I took comfort in them too. Because on that 1995 trip, I was deeply closeted as well: In nearly two months on the road, I hadn't told any of the Russians in other cities that I was gay. Gary knew, of course. But it had quickly become wearying to be asked, time after time, whether I had a husband, when all I really wanted was a girl-friend.

Spending those few days with Grisha, Valera, Zhenya, and Natasha was a balm, a wonderfully soothing respite from forever playing it straight in Russia. We had our own language, our own shortcuts that everyone understood, and no matter how late the evenings went, I never wanted them to end. As much as I'd liked the other Russians I'd met on this trip, I felt bonded to these friends in Novosibirsk. I desperately wanted for them—for all of us—to be able to live openly, wherever we were.

Grisha told me that a few years earlier, he'd considered trying to emigrate to Sweden, but after Article 121 was repealed he decided to stay. "These days, it actually seems possible that Russia will eventually come to a point where we can live as openly as gays do in the West," he said. "It may take a while, but that seems to be the direction we're headed in.

"At least," he concluded, "we can hope for that now." This was a touching—and very un-Russian—burst of optimism. I hoped, for his own sake, that Grisha was right.

—⟨∞⟩—

Four years later, in November of 1999, someone named Aleksey posted a comment to the original Russian Chronicles website. Gary and I had stopped updating the site when the trip ended, but readers continued to send the occasional question or remark to our Mailbox page. We got a lot of random comments, mostly requests for advice from people planning to travel to Russia. This one, however, was different:

> Hi,
>   I just thought that you might want to know this. The Russian gay guy Grisha from Novosibirsk was killed about a couple of weeks ago. We were friends while I was living in Russia.
>   I do not know details.
>   I can let you know if you wish when I find out.
>   Sincerely,
>   Aleksey

Oh, god, I thought. *Please let this not be true.* I quickly wrote back to the e-mail address Aleksey had provided, hoping that this was a mistake, or even a horrible joke. But his next missive was even more chilling: Grisha, he wrote, had been murdered.

I had home phone numbers for Grisha, Valera, and Natasha, and I tried them all but couldn't reach anyone. The Internet was useless; this was 1999, so Novosibirsk's newspapers didn't have any significant Web presence yet, or at least none that I could find. For a while, I was frantic with worry and frustration. But then, in a strange flash, I suddenly realized that I'd rather not know for sure. Call it denial, call it self-delusion, but that's the stance I took for the next six years.

In 2005, when I decided to do the Russia trip again, I dreaded getting to Novosibirsk and finding out the news was true. I kept hoping, no matter how unlikely it seemed, that Aleksey had somehow been mistaken.

David and I had made plans to stay in nearby Akademgorodok, at the home of an American acquaintance and his Russian wife. When we arrived, I called someone in Novosibirsk's gay community whose number I'd managed to track down—I don't even remember now who it was—and learned that Aleksey had been telling the truth. Dear, sweet, brave Grisha was dead.

I needed to see Valera and Natasha. I still couldn't get through on the old phone numbers, though, so the next day I went to the Max Mara store in downtown Novosibirsk, where Valera had been working ten years earlier. When he saw me walk in, his face lit up with surprise, and he hurried over and enveloped me in a hug.

"You came back!" he exclaimed.

"Yes," I said, and we looked each other up and down and laughed. Then his face turned serious, and before he could speak I said, "I heard about Grisha." He nodded, then hugged me again. But of course, here at his workplace, we couldn't really talk.

"Let's have dinner tonight," he said. "We'll talk then." We exchanged cell phone numbers, and he told me he'd be in touch after making arrangements.

That evening, we met at the apartment of a woman named Elena, whom Valera affectionately introduced as *Kuzina*, or cousin. She had been married to one of Grisha's cousins, so she'd known him since he was young, and over the years, she had become close not only to Grisha, but to his friends as well. Six years after his death, she still socialized with Valera, Natasha, and the rest of the group.

We gathered in Kuzina's living room, and over plates of homemade *pelmeni* and salad, she and Valera told me the terrible story.

On the evening of October 20, 1999, Valera had visited Grisha at his apartment. He had a few people over, and they all sat around talking until about 11 p.m. After everyone left, Grisha went out again, and somewhere along the way he met a couple of other young men. He invited them back to his place, and the three of them hung out there, listening to music. Grisha seemed fine; around 2 a.m. he called in to a local radio station, where Natasha was working as a DJ, to make a music request: "Ne Me Quitte Pas," by Nina Simone. That was the last time anyone heard from him.

The next morning, another of Grisha's friends stopped by to pick up a pager he'd left there earlier in the week. He found the apartment door ajar, pushed it open, and saw Grisha's body lying in a pool of blood. He had been stabbed dozens of times.

"Did they find who did it?" I asked.

"Yes," Valera told me. "He was a soldier." He said that the man had been caught, convicted, and was now serving time in a Novosibirsk prison. The motive was unclear, although several of Grisha's things had been stolen. I pictured Grisha's neat, orderly living room, where he and Valera had put on that fun, fabulous drag show for us a decade ago, and I couldn't imagine the horror that had taken place there.

And Grisha's death wasn't the only horrifying thing that happened during that terrible week, as I learned two days later, when we again gathered for dinner at Kuzina's—this time with Zhenya and Natasha.

—⟨ornament⟩—

"The police arrested me for Grisha's murder," said Zhenya, in the same soft voice I remembered from before.

I stared at him, my mouth agape. "Why?" I asked.

Valera jumped in. "They just figured, 'Eh, a gay guy's been killed. Here's his ex-boyfriend, he must have done it.'" Zhenya and Grisha had broken up well before the murder, but the two had remained close. The night Grisha was killed, Zhenya was alone in his own apartment, so no one could corroborate that he wasn't the murderer.

The police didn't really care who'd murdered Grisha, Valera told me—they were just in a hurry to arrest someone. "When I went to Grisha's apartment to clean it up, after he was found," he said, "It was obvious that the police hadn't even looked closely for evidence. As I was trying to clean the blood off the carpet, I picked it up and found the knife under it. How could they have not found the murder weapon, if they'd really been looking?"

"You had to clean up the blood?" I asked him, horrified at the thought.

"Of course," said Valera. "Who else would do it?"

The police arrested Zhenya the day after Grisha's body was found. They brought him in for questioning, and when they learned that he'd left work early the night of the murder and had no one who could confirm where he'd been, they threw him into a jail cell. Zhenya was in shock from his dear friend's violent death, to say nothing of suddenly finding himself in a filthy, cramped, communal cell. Day after day, the police questioned him, insisting that he confess. They wouldn't even let him out of jail to go to Grisha's funeral.

"I knew I would be convicted if they took me to trial," Zhenya told me. "I had no alibi." At the time, Russia's court system returned guilty verdicts in more than 99 percent of criminal trials decided by a judge, and more than 84 percent of those decided by a jury, which meant that he would almost certainly have been convicted, and might still be in prison today, if it weren't for what happened next.

On Zhenya's ninth day in jail, the police brought another man into the cell. "Whenever someone new comes in, the men start asking, 'So, what are you in for? What'd you do?'" he recalled. The man told them what he'd been arrested for, but then he started bragging that he'd also "killed this gay guy, in his apartment down on Krasniy Prospekt," said Zhenya. "It was him." In a scene that would be unbelievable if it hadn't actually happened, Zhenya just sat there quietly, listening as the man described how he'd stabbed Grisha to death.

Shortly after that, the police came and let Zhenya out. "They'd found their killer," he said, "so there was no need to keep me anymore." The murderer's perverse need to brag about what he'd done was the only thing that had saved Zhenya from potentially spending years in prison.

This whole situation seemed outrageous, but Zhenya was philosophical about it. "Things happen," he said. "We can't go back and change them. Life goes on."

The good news was that Valera, Natasha, and Zhenya were all doing really well. Valera was now the manager at the Max Mara store, and he was making enough money to renovate his apartment. He was still single, but he didn't seem as sad about that fact as he'd been ten years ago.

Natasha, who'd been deeply closeted back in 1995, was now openly, proudly gay. She worked as a DJ on a Radio Maximum talk show cheekily titled *Girls on Top*, dispensing advice and talking about gay issues. "The president of the radio company wanted something scandalous, for ratings," she said with a smirk, "and what was more scandalous than homosexuality?"

Over the summer, Natasha had begun dating a woman named Lena, an interpreter who lived in Moscow. Lena was in the process of moving to Novosibirsk to live with Natasha, the first step in the couple's plan to emigrate eventually to Canada. "Why Canada?" I asked her. "It's one of the few countries that offers gay marriage," she said simply. Ten years after she'd declared her desire to "be able to hold hands with my lover in public,

*Zhenya, Kuzina, Valera, and Natasha, after dinner at Kuzina's house,
2005* (PHOTO BY LISA DICKEY)

to kiss her on the street if I feel like it," Natasha had decided that
Russia was moving too slowly in that direction.

—⁓—

In 2007, two years after the second Russia trip ended, I joined
Facebook, and not long after that, I connected there with Valera
and Natasha. So, unlike with most of the people I'd met on the
first two trips, I was able to keep up with what was happening in
their lives.

Natasha and Lena left Russia, moving to Prague in 2009.
Over the years, it was wonderful to see their many photos and
posts, to see how happy and relaxed the couple seemed in their
new home. I knew they came back to Novosibirsk periodically
to visit Natasha's mother, so in the summer of 2014, I sent Natasha a message. "I'm hoping to make the big Russia trip again
next fall," I wrote. "Meet me in Novosibirsk?"

"Yes, we can plan the trip and meet each other in Nsk," she wrote back. "We can go to Altai Mountains. It's awesome there."

Yet in the summer of 2015, when I messaged her again, she told me she and Lena wouldn't be able to make it. I was hugely disappointed, but then she added an intriguing note: the reason, she wrote, was "a surprise, one that you will like."

And so it was. That August, I saw on Facebook that Natasha had given birth to a daughter, Lea. She messaged me privately to say, "My dear, I promised you a surprise, so you got it. You and my Lea were born on the same date! That's why I can't be in Nsk during your trip."

Life, death, and now a beautiful new birth—on my own birthday, no less. I couldn't have been happier than if the baby was my own.

—᧞—

Two months later, I took a taxi from the Novosibirsk train station to the Shalé hotel, one block from Valera's apartment, and when I arrived, he was there waiting for me. We shrieked and hugged; it felt like a miracle that we were together again. He helped me get settled in my hotel room, then said, "Have a rest, then come over for dinner. Kuzina will be there too." I was excited to see her—and to meet Valera's boyfriend of six years, Danya.

A few hours later, I buzzed at the front gate of Valera's building. Kuzina came down to let me in, and when she saw me, she screamed *Leeeeeeza!* loud enough to be heard in the next dimension. She lifted me off my feet with a hug, then pulled me by the hand into the building and up the stairs. The door to Valera's was cracked open, so we went right in, and in the kitchen I saw Valera, dressed in a T-shirt and drawstring pants standing next to a darkly handsome, wiry young man with a black Mohawk and three-day stubble. This was Danya, and although his look was hard-edged, he had an endearingly shy, boyish grin.

We all hugged hello, and then Valera gestured for us to sit at the small table. He picked up a bottle of opaque yellow liquid. "Limoncelllllo," he said, drawing out the word in a fake Italian accent. "I made it myself. Do you want some?" I nodded, and he smiled. With a flourish, he poured me a tiny glass.

"Tell me everything," I said, as we sat down to a feast of roast pork loin, mashed potatoes, and homemade pesto. Valera went first.

He and Danya had been living together for six years, he told me, and though his family members had all met him, they were still trying to convince Valera to find a nice woman and settle down. "It's always, 'Why don't you get a wife?' " he huffed. "I tell them, 'Why do I need a wife? I have Danya.' Then they say, 'Danya will get married, and then you'll be all alone.' "

"Can you just tell them the truth?" I asked. "Wouldn't that be easier?"

"I could," he said, "but it would be such a trauma for my parents. Why do that to them?" I asked Danya about his parents, and he told me they were no longer living. Valera was the only real family he had now.

Perusing Valera's Facebook page, you wouldn't necessarily know he was gay. He didn't often post photos with Danya—most were from work, or from his travels to Thailand with friends. Throughout my trip, I'd been revealing 20-years-later updates about people on Facebook, and I asked Valera whether he'd mind if I revealed his. Sure, he'd already let us post photos and stories online in 1995 and 2005—but because we'd never published his last name, there was almost no chance his colleagues and acquaintances would ever see them. Posting to Facebook would be a step further into officially and permanently outing himself, and I wanted to make sure he was OK with that.

"Write whatever you want," he said. "On Facebook, or in the book you're writing, it doesn't matter. What do I have to be afraid of?" He took a sip of limoncello. "I'm too old to worry about that stuff anymore."

We toasted to that. But I was still worried. What about Russia's new anti-gay law? I asked him. Passed in the summer of 2013, the law banned the "propaganda of nontraditional sexual relations to minors." It had been covered extensively in the Western press, which painted it as a catchall measure that was being used to persecute gay men and lesbians all over Russia. Had that affected him at all?

"Eh," he said, "that law didn't change anything. We live the same way we always have."

When Valera and I first met, back in 1995, I sensed an uncertainty in him. In private, he could be outrageous, dressing in drag and making off-color jokes, but otherwise he took pains to present a straight face to the world—in more ways than one. Now, at 52, he had blossomed into a confident man, more sure of his work, his financial situation, and his life in general. He'd recently gotten a new job as the manager of a high-end men's fashion store, and he had a stylish, expensive wardrobe that accentuated his obvious sense of self-assurance. He wasn't willing to be explicitly out, loud, and proud about his sexual orientation, but he certainly didn't mind letting people know that he didn't care what they thought of him.

He told me about having words with his nosy neighbor, who liked to crack her door open and spy on whom he brought to his apartment. One night, a famous designer came over—a man whose face is familiar across Russia from television and gossip magazines. The next day, the neighbor asked Valera why the man was there. He said, "I told her, 'You should mind your own business because with the work I do, you could get in serious trouble by poking around.'" He cackled, remembering how the neighbor slunk back into her own apartment, convinced that Valera was some kind of government spy.

We talked and laughed late into the night, Danya telling me about his work as a fashion designer and Kuzina telling me about her grown son and daughter who, she said proudly, both spoke perfect English. She'd been divorced from their father—Grisha's cousin—for years, and although she didn't mind the single life, she told us with a wink that she had a date with a new man the following night.

After dinner, Valera brought out a photo album, and we flipped through photos from my first visit. There was 32-year-old Valera, looking alluringly at the camera, taking a drag on a cigarette. There was Gary, posing with Valera and Grisha in their black minidresses, his giant digital camera hanging around his neck. And there I was, with my big round glasses framing my impossibly young face. It seemed like a lifetime ago.

It was well after midnight by the time I walked back to my hotel, a block away. I was tipsy and in a great mood, thrilled to be back here with Valera and Kuzina. *I want to keep coming back forever!* I thought, absurdly. Then I remembered a more prosaic task, and went into the bathroom to brush my teeth.

When I looked in the mirror, I was startled to see a woman of almost 50 gazing back. I suppose, having just looked at all those old photos, I expected to see that fresh-faced 28-year-old from 1995. But in a flash, I realized that she, too, was gone forever—and that realization unhinged me. I don't know if it was the alcohol, midtrip exhaustion, or my first true recognition of the shock of middle age, but I started to cry, suddenly overwhelmed by the visceral understanding that we're all aging, and we all will die—not just Grisha, or the diver Vladimir Votyagov, or Buyanto's brother, or that grand dreamer Valery Bukhner— but all of us, including me. For a few moments, I was crying so hard I couldn't catch my breath. When the wave of grief finally passed, I lay in bed a long time, staring at the ceiling in my little hotel room, before finally drifting off to sleep.

—ᕪᕪ—

My visit to Novosibirsk happened to fall during a slow work-week for Valera, so he decided to show me the local sights. "How about the zoo?" he asked brightly. This seemed random; why the zoo? "I had no idea where to take you, so I looked online for top tourist attractions in Novosibirsk," he said with a laugh, "and that was number one!" So we went to the zoo.

But first, he had a few errands to run downtown. As we strolled around, I took note of all the high-end stores: Armani, L'Etoile, Mon Plaisir, Rive Gauche. There was also a Marriott, a Hilton, and a DoubleTree, as well as an endless array of American fast-food joints, from McDonald's to Burger King to Pizza Hut. A city of 1.5 million and the capital of the Siberian Federal District, Novosibirsk was a bustling, crowded, capitalistic wonderland, and everywhere I looked, I could see construction cranes towering over the skyline. "New housing," said Valera. I had never seen so many new construction projects concentrated in one area, in Russia or anywhere else.

When Valera finished his errands, we walked to the train station, where we caught an ancient, creaking trolleybus to get to the zoo. With its chipping paint, cracked windshield, and torn vinyl seats, this trolleybus seemed to have driven through a time warp to pick us up, and as the weary-looking ticket-taker got into a screaming argument with a passenger in the back,

Valera raised his eyebrows high. "Ah, public transportation," he whispered. Then, the trolleybus suddenly shuddered to a halt, blocks away from the next stop.

We sat waiting, and after a few minutes the driver exited his little enclosed driving cabin. *"Elektroenergii nyet,"* he announced—there was "no electricity."

At this, Valera and I burst out laughing. No electricity? My god, how will the city continue to function? "Oh, no, there's a *defitsit*," I said, using the Russian term for shortage—a word every Russian who lived through the Soviet era knows all too well.

"How far is the zoo?" I asked Valera.

"Maybe a kilometer?" he said.

"Then let's walk." It seemed absurd to wait, especially if the zoo was so close. Valera was reluctant—it was a cold, uphill walk—but at my urging, we disembarked from the trolleybus. We started tromping up the hill, and a few minutes later, our trolleybus trundled by.

"I guess they found some electricity," Valera said, and we laughed again, our breath making little vapor clouds in the cold.

We spent the whole day at the zoo, and while it was far from the worst one I've been to, I don't really recommend Russian zoos if you like animals. The enclosures were small and unheated, which had to have been deeply unpleasant for the animals in the winter weather, and they all seemed to do quite a bit of anxious pacing. The only one that seemed relatively content was the polar bear, who had a comparatively large area with a big pool. A bored-looking girl in an apron was selling pieces of fish for 100 rubles a pop, so I decided to buy one. When else in my life would I ever get to feed a polar bear?

The girl handed me a bloody tail, and I chucked the thing into the enclosure. The bear rumbled over and swallowed it in a gulp, and now I was left with fishy-smelling hands and a piece of bloody paper. I looked around, searching for a bathroom, and she pointed laconically to a spigot about 20 yards away. I rinsed my hands in the painfully cold water, then belatedly realized there was no towel—so now I had freezing, dripping wet hands in the 34-degree weather. Valera, clad in his impeccable black coat and Prada hat, just shook his head in dismay at the clueless *Amerikanka*.

He suggested we duck into a café to warm up. We ordered *shashlik*, French fries, and green tea, and sat down at a table in the wood-paneled room. All around us, in another absurd touch, were the severed heads of deer, bison, and boars, mounted like hunting trophies.

"This zoo is OK," I told Valera. "But I'm a little disappointed that they don't have a giraffe." I said this mostly because I enjoyed the sound of the word in Russian: *zhiraf.*

"Sure, they do. Or, at least, they used to," he said. Then he gestured to my shashlik. "There's your *zhiraf,* poor thing. But at least he tastes good." He cackled again.

Valera was quick to laugh, and he never seemed to take himself too seriously. For that reason, I was surprised by his reaction when we later went to see *The Martian* at a theater in Novosibirsk. I enjoyed the film, munching on popcorn and marveling at the special effects that made it seem like Matt Damon was really on Mars. But when it was over, I found myself wondering whether Russian viewers found its rah-rah American can-do story a little over the top.

When I asked Valera how he'd liked it, he rolled his eyes. "It's propaganda," he said. I figured he meant that it was essentially an advertisement for the American space program. But it turned out his complaint was more specific than that.

"Why would the Americans ask *China* for a rocket?" he demanded, in reference to a plot point in which the United States must seek help from another country to make it back to Mars. "Everybody knows the Russians have the greatest rockets in the world. We were the pioneers in space!" I told him that I honestly didn't think this was meant as a slap at Russia, and that as far as I knew, the Chinese also had a pretty impressive space program. But Valera—who was as apolitical as anyone I knew in Russia—was having none of it.

"Anyone who needed a rocket would *of course* ask Russia," he said, shaking his head. To him, this was a clear insult, a choice made deliberately to belittle the Russians. To me, it seemed akin to the notion that Americans think there are bears wandering the streets here: not necessarily true, but certainly indicative of what Russians *think* we think.

—∽—

The next day, both Valera and Danya had to work, so I decided to explore another of Novosibirsk's attractions: the Museum of the USSR.

Soviet nostalgia has become a big business in Russia. In just about every city, you can find a throwback *stolovaya* (cafeteria) with USSR-themed décor and maps. You can play 1980s video games such as *Submarine Battle* and *Sniper* at museums of Soviet arcade machines. You can hire Lenin impersonators, such as Pasha in Chita, for your parties, and you can chug the Soviet classic Zhiguli beer at USSR-themed bars and pubs all over Russia.

In 1995, such things didn't exist; it was both too early for nostalgia and too close to the bad days of the Gorbachev-era USSR. By 2005, there were a few throwback bars, mostly in Moscow and St. Petersburg. Now, they were absolutely everywhere, serving as both a paean to, and gentle poke at, those times.

Novosibirsk's Museum of the USSR was located on Gorky

Street, in a traditional wooden Siberian cottage. The front door was locked, but a little paper sign to the right instructed visitors to ring once for the museum, or twice to see the stamp collection. I rang once, and waited. And then I waited some more.

Eventually, I heard footsteps shuffling up to the door. It swung open, and a woman stood there, looking at me expectantly.

"I'm here for the museum," I said, confused. "Is it open?"

"Ah, yes," she said. "Come in." She led me into a small office, where I paid the 150-ruble (about $2) entrance fee. She then walked me down a dark hallway to the door of what she called the *communalka* room.† "You can look around this room, then go downstairs to the museum," she told me. "There are clothes you can put on—uniforms, hats—to take photos or whatever you like. Spend as much time as you want."

This didn't feel like a museum exhibition; it felt like I'd walked through a door into 1978. The tiny room was crowded with period furnishings: a Moskva refrigerator, a slide projector, a rotary-dial phone, a short-wave radio, and an old Kvarts 306 television with rabbit-ear antennae. In a marvelously corny touch, someone had taped a black-and-white printout of Leonid Brezhnev to the TV screen, to approximate what we might have been watching in our communalka.

I sat down in a blanket-covered chair, gazing at the World War II posters on the walls and the homemade bead curtain hanging in the doorway, and after a while I decided to peek into the refrigerator, to see if it had vintage Soviet food items in it. To

---

† Communalkas were Soviet-era apartments shared by multiple families, with common kitchens and bathrooms. They were crowded and lacked privacy, but they also gave rise to classic jokes, such as: "A woman was taking a bath in the communalka when a man cracked open the door. 'Get out!' she screamed. 'I'm just making sure you're not using my soap!' he yelled back."

my surprise, it had Tupperware containers—the museum staff's lunches, brought from home.

Eventually, I wandered downstairs to the main room of the museum. It was an absolute wonderland of Soviet-era stuff: antique radios, Lomo cameras, abacuses, calculators, 1980 Moscow Olympics souvenirs, Raketa clocks and watches, record players, dolls, stuffed bears, all sitting out on tables and bookshelves, as if begging to be fiddled with. There were also clothes to try on, mostly for men—Red Army uniforms, old overcoats, fur hats, railway worker uniforms. I decided against dressing up, mostly because it seemed silly to do so alone.

When I got back upstairs, I poked my head into the office to thank the woman who'd let me in. "Did you dress up?" she asked.

"No," I said, smiling apologetically. She looked stricken.

"Then get back down there and do it!" she ordered.

Chastened, I went back down the stairs. There were two outfits for women: a bureaucratic-looking skirt suit, and a brown Pionerka dress with a white pinafore. I chose the latter, and dutifully removed my coat and scarf to try it on. The Pionerkas were the Soviet equivalent of Girl Scouts, so of course the dress was far too small for me. I decided to improvise, just slipping my arms in, then pulling the pinafore over my head and tying the red kerchief around my neck. I saluted with one hand, snapping a few selfies with the other, then pulled everything off, put back on my coat, scarf, and hat, and went upstairs.

I went into the office and showed the woman the selfies I'd taken.

"Oh, no," she said. "That's an improper salute."

"Excuse me?" I said. I wasn't sure I'd heard her correctly.

"Pionerkas don't salute like this," she said, mimicking my U.S. military–style salute, fingers touching her temple. "They do it like *this*." She raised her arm higher, so her wrist was level with her forehead, her hand extending diagonally above her head.

"Ah," I said, nodding. "Interesting. Well . . . thank you."

"Get back down there and do it again," she said. "Go on!"

What could I do? I went back down the stairs, and for the second time, I took off all my outerwear and struggled halfway into the Pionerka outfit. I saluted properly, taking a few more photos.

I headed back upstairs, anxious to finally pass the Pionerka test, though I was worried that I'd improperly tied the scarf or had the wrong arm angle for my salute. When I got to the office and showed the woman my latest round of selfies, however, she crowed with delight. "Will you send this to me?" she asked. "For our website." I did, entitling it *"Amerikanskaya Pionerka."*

The woman clapped her hands with glee. I felt as proud as if I'd been a real Pionerka.

—⚬⚬—

That night, Valera and I took a long walk, ending up at an Italian café owned by a friend of his. As we ordered drinks, I found myself thinking about how much his life had changed in these past 20 years. But it troubled me that he still felt the need to be so secretive about his relationship. I couldn't help but wonder whether he'd be better off revealing it, at least to his family. After all, both Grisha and Natasha had come out to their parents—Grisha more than 20 years earlier—so it wasn't unheard-of among this group of friends.

I asked him about this, and for the first time in any of our visits, he seemed exasperated. "Liza, it's nobody's business but ours," he said. "What would be the point of telling everyone?"

"Well," I said, "you wouldn't have to avoid talking about

Danya. You wouldn't have to lie when people ask whether you had a partner." Having been deeply in the closet myself when I was younger, I was filled with the annoying zeal of the converted.

"But this is Russia," he said, as though explaining to a five-year-old. "We stay out of each other's business. People don't ask questions, because they don't want to know." His words called to mind the purges of the 1930s and '40s, when people's best chance for staying out of prison—even staying alive—was just to keep their heads down, mind their own business, and not ask any questions. This habit had become deeply ingrained in the Russian character.

"Listen," he said. "Let me give you an example. All week, you've been asking me how Kuzina's date went with that guy." This was true: I hadn't seen Kuzina since that first dinner, and I was curious how her date had gone. Each time I saw Valera, I would bring it up.

"I would *never* ask her that question," he said. "It's none of my business! If she wants to tell me, she will tell me."

I felt embarrassed. It had never occurred to me that what I thought of as friendly curiosity might seem like culturally ignorant prying. Perhaps it wasn't just gay people who were in the closet here; in some ways, *everyone* was, to the extent they chose to be. The way Valera described it, Russian culture—gay or straight—was "don't ask, don't tell" writ large.

"There was a girl at work who asked if another guy we work with was gay," Valera went on. "So I snapped at her, 'How would I know what that guy does in his bedroom? How is it any of our business?' That scared her off. She never asked again."

I mulled this for a moment, and once again my Western biases took over. "Well," I said, "that kind of response implies that there's something wrong with being gay." I told him that in

Los Angeles, where I live, the girl's query could be considered just a general-interest question, rather than prying.

"No, Liza," he said, shaking his head. "That's not why she was asking. She was smirking." He rubbed his forehead, clearly tired of the conversation.

For a moment, we both were silent. When Valera spoke again, he said simply, "I just want to live my life, not make waves. Why make a fuss?" It wasn't the first time I'd heard a Russian say this, but it was perhaps the first time I really, truly heard it.

—m—

On the same night Valera and I were talking at the café, an extraordinary scene unfolded four time zones away. A brown bear somehow broke into a closed shopping mall in the Russian Far East city of Khabarovsk, and security videos showed the animal rampaging around the empty stores. Eventually, it burst through two sets of glass doors and went running down the street.

I'm just saying.

—m—

On my last night in Novosibirsk, Valera and I went to Kuzina's for dinner. Danya couldn't come, as he had a cold, and while I'd hoped to see Zhenya on this trip, he was out of town on vacation the entire week I was here. So it would just be the three of us tonight, with a possible appearance later by Kuzina's 21-year-old daughter, Alisa.

Kuzina was 56 now, but she looked far younger. With her wide smile, sturdy build, and inexplicably tanned face, she reminded me of those apple-cheeked farm girls from Soviet propaganda. She was endlessly energetic, even bouncy. Dinners at her house went on for hours, and they typically involved truly

Kuzina, Valera, and me, making one of many, many toasts on my last night in Novosibirsk, 2015 (PHOTO BY LISA DICKEY)

copious amounts of alcohol, with Kuzina taking the lead in consumption.

We started the evening by looking at the photos I'd taken at the Museum of the USSR, but as I proudly showed off my Pionerka selfies, Kuzina barked, "You tied the scarf wrong!" She hustled out of the kitchen, returning with a red scarf. "*This* is how you tie it," she said, looping the thing around my neck. "It's very important. Every true Pionerka knows how to tie the scarf!"

"Hey, now!" I said, "I am a proud Pionerka! Don't insult my *pionerzhnost!*" This last word was made up, roughly translatable as "pioneer-ness." I pouted, and Valera jumped in, saying, "*Kakaya zhopa*, eh?" Translated literally, this phrase means "What an asshole!" But what it means to Russians is, essentially, "What a fucking mess!" This quickly became the running joke of the night.

We drank like there was no tomorrow. Alisa joined us midway through dinner, but when offered a drink, she demurred. "I have more work to do tonight," she said, shrugging. *"Kakaya zhopa!"* shouted Valera. We all guffawed, and Alisa, blushing, said, "OK, OK, I'll have just one."

Eventually, as often happens at Russian dinner parties, a guitar appeared. We all strummed and sang and danced about, ending every song with *"Kakaya zhopa!"* which fit a number of songs surprisingly well. "House of the Rising Sun": "It's been the ruin of many a poor boy, and god, I know I'm one"—*kakaya zhopa!* "Yesterday": "Now I need a place to hide away, oh I believe in yesterday"—*kakaya zhopa!*

At one point, we all meandered to the living room, where Kuzina threw open a window so we could reach out and touch the snowflakes that were starting to fall. Kuzina's apartment overlooked Novosibirsk's main square, and we could see the massive dome of the Opera and Ballet Theater and, in the distance, the statue of Lenin. The cold air was bracing, and when we finally came back into the kitchen, our hilarity had subsided into a more reflective mood.

We started talking about Grisha. I asked Kuzina whether her ex-husband was Grisha's first cousin, or more distantly related. "First cousin," she said.

"But you know," Valera interjected, "after Grisha revealed to his family that he was gay, Kuzina was the only member of the family who continued to see him." She nodded.

"Everybody rejected him, except for her," Valera went on. "Then, when he died, and they all came to the funeral, they all took their seats up front, but she wasn't invited to sit with them. She sat in the back, with us."

Kuzina wiped her eyes. "Grisha always told me, 'Kuzina, you're a beautiful woman, you live in the center of town. You should dress yourself well,'" she said quietly. "He would give me advice on what to wear. So, for his funeral, I dressed up, put on makeup. My husband was jealous. 'What are you dressing up for him for?' he said. 'He's dead.'

"I was so sad when Grisha died," she went on, almost in a whisper. "At the funeral, I said, 'My Grisha is gone. Who will call me Kuzina now?' And Valera said, 'I will.' And he always has, and so has Zhenya." Valera now moved toward her, putting his arm around her shoulders.

"Me too," I said, raising my glass. "To Kuzina."

I left Novosibirsk the next day, hung over and sad, but happy that we would all still be in touch through Facebook. Valera and Kuzina walked me the ten snowy blocks to the train station, and after I got settled in my *kupe*, they stood on the platform to wave good-bye. As the train started to pull away, they offered—in unison—perfectly angled Pionerka salutes. "This is how you do it!" Valera yelled.

"Kakaya zhopa!" I screamed back. As the train picked up speed, I looked back until I could barely see the two friends in the distance, walking arm in arm as they headed off the platform and back toward the city.

—\\\\—

NINE

Chelyabinsk:
Meteors and Missiles

O N THE MORNING OF FEBRUARY 15, 2013, PEOPLE IN the city of Chelyabinsk were startled by a massive streak of flame shooting across the sky. Dash-cam videos captured a ball of fire curving low over the city, the sky flashing a blinding white. Security-camera videos showed windows shattering and people diving for cover, as the fireball exploded in an earsplitting boom during its short flight.

The Chelyabinsk meteor was a spectacular cosmic show. Because it appeared at 9:20 in the morning, thousands of people saw it—and thanks to the magic of YouTube, millions more all over the world have seen it too. I was one: I obsessively clicked on all the videos I could find, unable to get enough of watching that meteor streak wildly over the city I'd first visited in 1995. Now that I was once again coming to Chelyabinsk, I couldn't wait to ask people whether they'd seen the meteor that day.

As it turned out, I'd get to do more than just ask about it; I could see the thing for myself. The meteor had crashed into nearby Lake Chebarkul, and nine months later, scientists managed to pull a huge chunk of it out of the lake bottom. That chunk was now on display at the Chelyabinsk Regional History Museum, a short walk from my hotel, so on my first morning in town, I strolled over for a look.

The pocked, metallic-looking meteor is about the size of a stuffed-full laundry bag, but it weighs more than 1,300 pounds. It is housed in a glass pyramid, which adds to its otherworldly aura, and as I snapped photo after photo, I kept thinking, *This came from* SPACE! I noticed a docent watching me—a tiny, white-haired woman in a smock and sensible shoes. I went over to speak with her.

"Did you see the meteor when it fell?" I asked.

"Well, of course," she said, as if the question were absurd. "I was out in the city, and it flew right overhead. Everything became very hot, which was strange because it was February." She told me she was on a public bus at the time, and that everyone crouched down in fear.

"When I got home," she went on, "my windows were broken. There were two parallel windows with a space between, and all the glass fell right into that space. But at my neighbor's, the blast blew the glass *into her apartment*. Everyone experienced something different." She raised her eyebrows and paused to let this sink in. Then, lowering her voice, she added, "People still say it might actually have been shot at us."

"Like, a missile?" I asked. She nodded. "Do you think that?"

"Oh, I don't know," she said. "But it was *very strange*." Meanwhile, the actual meteor was sitting right here, under glass, not 20 feet away. Given the available evidence, this was some seriously bold conspiracy-theory conjecture.

Rumors that the object was actually some kind of missile started circulating almost as soon as it fell from the sky. The right-wing politician Vladimir Zhirinovsky declared the following day that "those aren't meteorites falling. It's the Americans trying out a new weapon," adding that U.S. Secretary of State John Kerry had tried to call Foreign Minister Sergey Lavrov to "warn him that there would be such a provocation." Zhirinovsky is a professional provocateur himself, so it was perhaps predictable that he'd try to stir things up.* Yet I did find myself wondering whether, if the Chelyabinsk meteor had fallen in 1995 or 2005, the Russians would have been so quick to suspect it was an American weapon.

I mulled this over as I left the museum and strolled toward Kirov Street, referred to by locals as the Arbat, after the famous walking street in Moscow. Like many walking streets, this one felt cloying and touristy, with little folk-art statues, a souvenir kiosk in the shape of a giant *matryoshka* nesting doll, and the requisite coffee shops and McDonald's. There was, however, one inspiring piece of public art: the *Tankist*, a statue of a muscled young fighter standing atop a World War II tank, urging the troops forward with a shout and upraised arm. This was where Anya and I had arranged to meet.

When I'd first met Anya at her family's apartment in 1995, she was a skinny 11-year-old with a plain brunette ponytail.

---

*Among Zhirinovsky's greatest hits: his proposals to reclaim Alaska and ship the Ukrainians there; to turn the Baltic States into a nuclear waste dump for Russia; and to flood the United Kingdom by dropping nukes into the Atlantic Ocean. He has publicly stated a desire to see the Russian empire expand to where Russian soldiers can "wash their boots in the warm water of the Indian Ocean," and, in 2014, he advocated the rape of a pregnant journalist.

She was quiet and shy around the American visitors, and my strongest memory of her was the afternoon she sat at her family's piano, dutifully practicing while Gary and I worked nearby on our laptops. Her serious expression, combined with an utter disinterest in attracting attention, made her seem more miniature adult than child.

I already knew what the now-31-year-old Anya looked like, having recently connected on Facebook. But when she walked up, I was still stunned. She was blonde, her long hair curling voluptuously over her shoulders, and she was dressed in tight jeans and a gorgeous gold-colored coat. Her dark eyes were accentuated with makeup, her fingernails perfectly manicured. She was, for lack of a better term, a knockout.

Yet Anya wasn't just beautiful; she also carried herself with the supreme self-assurance of the Girl Who Has Everything. She's one of those Russian women you see not only in Russia, but in New York, or Monaco, or Ibiza—the ones in designer clothes, carrying expensive bags, gliding past with chins held high and leaving traces of expensive perfume in their wake. I've always been fascinated, and intimidated, by these women, who in ordinary circumstances would walk right by my Gap-button-down-wearing self. But because I'd known Anya since she was a girl, she came right up to me with a big smile and a warm hug.

—⚭—

In 1995, Anya's father Sergei was working as a business consultant, while his wife Lyuba stayed home to raise 16-year-old Masha and 11-year-old Anya. The family lived in a nice, though not opulent, apartment on Revolution Square in the center of town, where Gary and I stayed on that first visit.

When we first came to Chelyabinsk, I knew only two facts about the city: First, its economy was industrial, driven by metallurgy and military production. And second, a nuclear catastrophe had occurred nearby in the 1950s—an incident that the Soviet government tried to hide, but which was later revealed to have spewed a vast radioactive cloud over the region. When it happened, the Kyshtym disaster was the worst nuclear accident in history, contaminating thousands of square miles of territory and leading to evacuations and illnesses in the villages of the Chelyabinsk Region.[†]

Given this information, why would anyone want to come here? In truth, the only reason Gary and I did was because Sergei and Lyuba—who were friends of a friend in St. Petersburg—had offered to let us stay in their apartment. We arrived expecting to find smoggy skies, chemical-belching factories, and glowing green water, but Chelyabinsk turned out to be a charming city, with vast parks, plentiful pine trees, and a sparkling river running through the center. About a million people lived here, and the vibe seemed laid-back.

The same could be said for Sergei and Lyuba. They were a friendly, down-to-earth couple who, unlike many Russians in the mid-nineties, seemed deeply content with their lives. They'd been proud Soviets—Sergei a Komsomol leader and Lyuba active in the Communist Party—but once the USSR fell, they easily made the transition to capitalism. At dinner on our first night, Sergei regaled us with tales of their recent vacation to Italy, and Lyuba showed off her wallet full of credit cards. These were rare at the time, especially outside Moscow and St. Petersburg, but the couple insisted that their post-Soviet lives weren't really so different.

"For me personally, not a whole lot has changed," said Sergei, whose mustache, dimpled chin, and sturdy good looks gave

---

[†] It would later be surpassed by Chernobyl and Fukushima.

him the air of a Russian Tom Selleck. "I lived well then, I live well now. There are a few things that have changed for the worse; it's not safe on the streets anymore . . . But there are many things that are better too, like now people can earn as much as they will work to earn."

He had little patience for those who spent time bemoaning the fall of the USSR, including the ragtag group of Communists that gathered on nearby Revolution Square each weekend to protest. "I can understand why they're complaining," Sergei said. "But that's all they do, just cry. They don't make any constructive proposals. Russians have a saying: 'When your head's been cut off, why cry about losing your hair?' But the Communists just cry about the little things anyway."

When I asked Lyuba how her life had changed, she told me, "The main difference between now and then is that before, things were calmer, more stable . . . If I could have things the best possible way, I would have the security and peace of mind we had then, with the opportunity and freedom we have now." But like her husband, she added, "As far as I'm concerned, my life hasn't changed too much. I was happy then, and I'm happy now. And if I lived in Tsarist times, I'd probably have been happy then too."

Sixteen-year-old Masha told me about her seventh-grade class's mini-rebellion at the end of the Soviet era, when she and her friends decided to stop wearing their uniforms and red Pioneer scarves to school. "Some of our teachers got upset, and told us, 'You are Pioneers, you need to take these things more seriously.' But in the end, they only really scolded us a little bit. A month later, they changed the rules at school so we didn't have to wear the uniforms and scarves anymore."

In her Doc Martens–style boots and miniskirt, with an angular short haircut, Masha was the picture of teenage cool.

"People my age don't really think too much about politics," she told me. "Other than making fun of Yeltsin or the Communists or whoever, we really don't think about these things. When I think of Lenin, I picture this short, bald little guy waving his arms at some tribunal. Even though he was obviously very smart—he got the whole country to follow him, after all—now he's just somebody to make fun of."

With all the economic and societal upheaval in mid-1990s Russia, this family was unusual in its equanimity. Unlike Valya in Vladivostok, who was skittish about spies, or Oleg in Ulan-Ude, who was afraid to let me board a public bus without him, Sergei and Lyuba seemed to take everything in stride. So, ten years later, when I prepared to return to Chelyabinsk, I had the feeling the family would be doing well.

And so they were.

The first indication of just how well came early in the visit. Sergei had invited David and me to stay in the same apartment as in 1995, but the family was no longer living there: they'd upgraded to a bigger, nicer place on Plekhanov Street, less than a mile away. We settled into the old apartment, which we'd be sharing with Sergei's mother, Valentina, and on the second night Anya and Masha came to pick us up for dinner.

I knew the girls would be grown up, but I wasn't prepared for the statuesque twenty-something women who rolled up in a sleek black Land Rover. David and I climbed in, and to my surprise both Anya and Masha began speaking excellent English. Anya's hair was dyed jet black, and she wore a simple black shirt that showed off her slender figure. Masha, now 26, had a rather severe, unsmiling beauty. And both women exuded self-confidence.

When we walked into the family's new apartment, I looked around in wonder: it was bigger than any apartment I'd been to in Russia, immaculately clean, and decorated with a vast assortment of souvenir plates that Lyuba had collected all over the world. As Lyuba made dinner, Anya invited us to surf the Web on their high-speed Internet—the first I'd seen in a Russian home—and play with their dog, a fluffy white Chinese Crested Powderpuff named Busya.

Now that their daughters were grown, Lyuba had gone to work with Sergei at their company, where he was president and she was director of finance. With 170 employees and dozens of big clients, the company provided the couple with a very good living; as Lyuba told me, "We can afford to buy anything we want."

This included a new dacha, or country home, which the couple designed and had built near Lake Chebarkul, about 50 miles west of Chelyabinsk. The dacha was massive: three stories tall, with an indoor swimming pool, a *banya*, and a gazebo in the rear yard. The family had also traveled extensively over the last decade, going abroad twice a year; they'd been to Turkey multiple times, as well as destinations all across Europe. Masha had lived in both France and Germany, and she was now finishing up graduate studies in Moscow. "Should we buy you an apartment there?" Lyuba asked her casually, over dinner.

Yet just as they had in 1995, Sergei and Lyuba still insisted that money hadn't changed their lives. Sergei even said it in almost exactly the same way: "In the Soviet Union, we felt like everything was fine. And now we feel like everything's fine."

"We still have the same circle of children, family, and friends as before," Lyuba added. "We've had the same friends for 25 years! Even without the dacha, the swimming pool and whatever, we still have normal relationships with people."

David and I unfortunately didn't have time to go out to the dacha, but we did manage to set up a photo shoot with Anya and

Masha and Anya on Revolution Square, 2005 (PHOTO BY DAVID HILLEGAS)

Masha on Revolution Square. In 1995, the square had been a mess, undergoing a renovation that had torn up the sidewalks and public areas. The corner where the Communists gathered had been in the shadow of a boxy, abandoned building, which now, in 2005, housed the Museum of Applied Art. Everything was spruced up, and pedestrians bustled across the square, heading into the vast underground shopping mall. As Masha and Anya posed for photos in their designer jeans and fashionable coats, I noticed plenty of passersby stopping to stare.

Smart, beautiful, wealthy, and speaking perfect English,

these two young women had the world at their fingertips. As I prepared to return to Chelyabinsk ten years later, I wondered whether they'd still be there, or whether they'd have left for a more cosmopolitan destination such as Moscow or St. Petersburg—or perhaps Paris, London, or New York.

—᧞—

"Wow," I said to Anya, after we hugged at the *Tankist*. "You look amazing." She smiled, even blushing a little bit, then quickly regained her composure.

"Where would you like to eat?" she asked. After some discussion, we settled on the nearby Turkuaz Grill House, a steakhouse with high ceilings, big booths, and a giant wall sketch showing the beef cuts of a steer. A server hurried over to take Anya's coat, and we settled into a booth for what turned into a nearly three-hour lunch.

I'm not sure whether it was her perfect English, the fact that she's traveled so much in the West, or a simple question of chemistry, but I found it easier to talk with Anya than I did even with some friends back home. Within minutes, we were sharing intimate details of our lives, with Anya telling me about her marriage and divorce, and me telling her about my wedding, and even showing her photos on my phone. I told her that so far, everyone in Russia had said they didn't mind gay people, though others might. She laughed and replied that she didn't think Russians in general had a problem with it, "even older people."

"Oh, really?" I asked. "Like your grandmother?"

"Well . . ." she said, and shrugged.

During the week that David and I had stayed with Anya's grandmother Valentina, she'd been a scowling presence, openly suspicious of us, and as intimidating as any septuagenarian under five feet tall could possibly be. She'd been so unpleasant that just before we left Chelyabinsk, I'd asked David to take a photo of us together, just so I could remember that scowl. The picture, in which she and I are both staring grumpily at the camera, is one of my favorites from the 2005 trip.

I told Anya this, and she laughed. "Do you want to see her? We can go to her house for lunch." I said yes, that I'd try to overcome my fear enough to face her.

Anya gave me updates on the rest of the family. She told me that Masha was married and had a five-year-old son, and that she stayed home to take care of him. Both sisters were still living in Chelyabinsk, though apparently Masha had returned from Moscow only reluctantly, when her husband got a job working for Sergei's company. And Masha's husband wasn't the only one in the family business: Anya, too, was employed there. So, the family was wealthy, but not so wealthy that they didn't have to work. As Anya told me, "Really rich people don't have to keep track of their money. We're not that way."

I asked Anya whether she'd been to the United States, and she said, "Just last month, for the first time!" She'd gone to Miami Beach, Los Angeles, and Las Vegas, but when I asked how she liked it there, she wrinkled her nose. "Not so much," she replied. I asked why.

"My expectations were too high," she said. "I really thought I was going to love it." She'd liked the beach in L.A., but the traffic was terrible, and overall it wasn't as nice as what she'd seen in the movies. In Vegas, she'd stayed at the Wynn and the Venetian, and while she liked the hotels, she'd gotten bored after playing a little roulette. And in Miami Beach, it rained the whole time. All in all, she'd felt disappointed in her U.S. experience.

"Come again, when I'm there," I told her. "You have to see

more than just Vegas and the beach." I wanted her to like America, and was convinced she would if I got a chance to show her around. But she told me that many of her Russian friends who'd emigrated there didn't like it, and some had returned to Russia.

"They say it's hard to make friends with Americans, because they're not really interested in having Russian friends," she said. "So, the Russians all end up sticking together." I'd never thought of this before, but realized it was probably true. Even I, a lifelong Russophile, didn't have any close Russian friends in Los Angeles. And most of those I'd met—particularly the older women I'd spent time with over the summer, when I was trying to improve my language skills—tended to socialize only with other Russians. In fact, many spoke English quite poorly, even if they'd been there for decades, because they never got any practice.

"I like Europe better," Anya told me. "It's more culturally similar to Russia." She felt most at home in France, though she liked Italy too. "My sister loves it there," she said. "It's the only place she ever goes on vacation." At my look of surprise, she laughed. "Seriously, the *only* place. It's a little . . . monotonous."

I got the sense that Anya and Masha weren't close, though they saw each other regularly, often out at Lake Chebarkul, where Sergei had built two more giant dachas—one for each daughter. The family had also constructed a new Russian Orthodox chapel there, so Lyuba would have a place to pray. I desperately wanted to see all this, but it seemed impolite to ask for an invitation, so I just hoped that Anya would suggest going.

We were more than two hours into our lunch when Anya's boyfriend Max showed up. He was a compact, muscular young man with a big smile, but though he clearly adored Anya, her demeanor changed when he sat down. We'd been having a chatty, intimate, girl-talk lunch, but now Anya emanated a slight chill, though Max didn't seem to notice. The two of them were going to see an afternoon movie, but she invited me to come to their apartment for dinner that night, and I eagerly accepted.

She and Max were living in the same apartment where her parents had lived in 2005—the big, beautiful one on Plekhanov Street. Sergei and Lyuba had moved permanently to their dacha on Lake Chebarkul, though Sergei still came into the city to work most days, an hour-long drive each way. "He has a full-time driver," Anya told me, "so it's not too bad."

That evening, when Anya showed me into the Plekhanov apartment, I was amazed to see that it was decorated almost exactly as it had been ten years earlier. Lyuba's souvenir plates were still on the walls. An old tape deck stood in the corner of the dining room. And in the living room, an old doll in a satin dress was propped up underneath an oil painting of a snowy village, just as it had been in 2005. I wouldn't have remembered this, except that I had a photo of 21-year-old Anya and me posing underneath that painting, and the doll was in the picture. I showed Anya the old photo on my phone, and we both started laughing.

"Why haven't you changed anything?" I asked. "Surely you have a different style from your mom?"

"I don't know," Anya said, blushing again. "It just seems wrong to put away all those plates and paintings. They're nice." Even Busya, her mother's dog, was still living in the apartment, though she was old and rather hairless now. It was as if Anya was maintaining the place as an homage to her parents.

As we ate dinner, a television in the dining room was tuned to an episode of *Friends*, dubbed into Russian. I asked if the show was popular here, and Anya said it was. I knew American movies were popular—a stroll past any movie theater confirmed that—but I was surprised to see such a quintessentially American sitcom on Russian TV, especially considering the recent wave of anti-Americanism. But Anya and Max had watched numerous such shows; she told me they loved *The Big Bang Theory*, *Breaking Bad*, and *Mike and Molly* most of all.

Both Max and Anya had seen every episode of *Friends*—all 236 of them. "It's nice, gentle humor," Anya said. "Not mean or coarse." The show aired on Russia's Paramount Comedy channel, which was Anya's favorite for that same reason: she didn't enjoy humor that was snarky or mean. In some ways, she still seemed like that sweet, unassuming 11-year-old girl I'd met in 1995, no matter how glamorous and grown up she looked now.

—⁓—

The next day, Anya, Max, and I went to her grandmother's house for lunch. I was nervous, which Anya found hilarious. "She's my *grandmother*," she teased. "She's not scary!" But I remembered Valentina as one of the few people on that 2005 trip with whom I just couldn't connect. Fortunately, there was one topic I knew we could talk about today: Anya had told me her grandmother had seen the Chelyabinsk meteor.

Anya and Max picked me up in her black BMW SUV, and we headed out of the city center and into the Leninsky District, a run-down area marked by nondescript multistory housing blocks. She steered into a muddy courtyard, past some ramshackle playground equipment, and parked near a two-story, brown-brick apartment building with security grills on the first-floor windows. The neighborhood felt neglected, but it still had a certain charm, with leafy trees and lace curtains visible in apartment windows.

We rang the buzzer, and when Valentina opened the door my first thought was, *She's so tiny!* She was absolutely elfin in her purple housedress, gray floral-patterned cardigan, and plaid slippers, her white hair pulled back with a bobby pin. Anya, wearing a black minidress, black tights, and black thigh-high boots, towered over her. If an alien landed and saw these two creatures, it would not have believed they belonged to the same species.

"Grandmother, do you remember Liza?" Anya asked.

"No," she said, eyeing me with a dour expression.

"Ten years ago, you stayed together at the apartment near Revolution Square," Anya continued, speaking loudly and slowly. "Remember? You stayed there while your apartment was being renovated."

"Ahhh," her grandmother replied. "Maybe I do remember." I doubted that, but at least she was making an effort.

I brought out my laptop to show her photos from that visit— of Anya and Masha on Revolution Square, of Sergei and Lyuba, and finally the one of her and me, both scowling into the camera—which, ironically enough, made her smile, the first time I'd ever seen her do so. Then I showed her a few pictures from my lunch with Anya.

"These were taken yesterday," I told her. She looked at me in shock.

"Yesterday? And you already had them developed? So fast." Anya and I both laughed. Twenty years later, and I still need to explain this digital camera thing?

We took our seats at the small dining room table while Valentina bustled around the kitchen, preparing a lunch of *pelmeni* with sour cream and a tomato salad slathered in oil. She brought out a bottle of semisweet Russian champagne and a dusty Tetra Pak box of red wine. "Have whichever you like," she said, as Max picked up the wine and peered at it. "'The most popular wine in Italy,'" he said, reading off the side of the box. He raised his eyebrows. "Let's have the champagne," he said.

When Valentina finally stopped bustling and sat down, I got right to business. "So, I heard that you saw the meteor . . . ?" I asked.

"No," she replied. "There was a meteor?"

"Grandmother," Anya said, "you did see it."

"No, I didn't." She seemed annoyed that we didn't believe her. "Remember?" Anya insisted. "Two years ago? You saw—"

"Ah, *that one!*" she said, "Of course, I saw that one. I thought you meant there'd been one today." Max, who'd just taken a sip of champagne, nearly did a spit take.

Now that she knew which meteor we were referring to, she gave details. "I saw it fly across the sky, out that window," she said, pointing to a large window covered with a sheer lace curtain. "There was a bright flash, and I was very scared. I even screamed." I asked if it broke the window. "No," she said. "Because it didn't fly right into the courtyard, of course." She thought for a moment. "But it did break my neighbor's windows."

The four of us chatted amiably through the meal, and I began to wonder how I'd found Valentina so awful before. She was a harmless old lady, and probably had scowled so much because she'd been forced to live with a couple of random Americans who kept weird hours and stared endlessly at their laptops. True, she didn't smile much even now, but she was obviously excited that Anya and Max had come to visit. She bounced up and down like a jack-in-the-box throughout lunch, forever making sure we had everything we needed. She was especially attentive to Max, asking him repeatedly if he wanted more pelmeni, more tomatoes, more champagne, a cup of tea, or some cookies.

It was amazing to see how much this family had changed in just two generations. Valentina was a twentieth-century Russian woman, content with her modest apartment, simple meals, and quiet existence. Her life revolved around family, and she didn't appear to desire anything but food on the table and visits from her grandchildren. In contrast, Anya was an utterly twenty-first-

Scowling Valentina and me, 2005
(PHOTO BY DAVID HILLEGAS)

Smiling (?) Valentina and me, 2015
(PHOTO BY LISA DICKEY)

century creation: cosmopolitan, multilingual, eager to explore the world, and blessed with the means to do so. Even Valentina seemed amazed by the difference.

"Have you seen their dachas?" she asked me. "Masha has a three-story house. Anya has a three-story house. Everybody has a three-story house." She shook her head. "I doubt if even Putin has such a place as they do." Anya laughed, and at last Valentina did too, a dry little cackle.

Before leaving, we decided to take a photo mimicking the one from 2005. "Grandmother, you didn't smile in the other picture. So, smile now!" Anya said. But Valentina scowled as usual while Anya snapped a photo with my phone. Then Anya commanded her, louder: "Grandmother, *smile!*" And finally she did—sort of. The resulting picture is another classic, with Valentina baring her teeth as if preparing to bite me.

—𝕞—

The next afternoon, I strolled to the Wild Boudoir Café, where Anya had arranged for us to have lunch with her sister Masha.

From the moment I walked in, I felt self-conscious. With its cool white interior and parquet floors, the restaurant was rather chic, and everyone there was much better dressed than I was. And apparently I was late, because not only were Anya and Masha seated at a table, they had already ordered. Masha said hello, then introduced me to her five-year-old son Nikita, who, I instantly noted, was also dressed better than me in his little oxford-cloth shirt and blue sport coat.

For as easily as the conversation had flowed earlier between Anya and me, the conversation with Masha felt stilted from the start. We exchanged pleasantries, but there was little warmth behind them, and within minutes the talk turned to politics— specifically, the West's sanctions against Russia. "There have been no visible effects of sanctions here," she told me. "We can buy whatever we need; we can make cheese and any other products here. It hasn't affected us at all." She sipped a spoonful of her delectable-looking pumpkin soup, as if bolstering her point.

I asked her if she remembered what she'd told me 20 years ago, when she was 16. She didn't, so I read her the quotes aloud, specifically the part where she said she didn't think much about politics. She smiled a tight little smile.

We ate in silence for a moment, and then she asked, "Are you planning to go to Crimea on this trip?"

"No," I replied. She asked why. I explained that this was a 20-years-later project, so I was visiting the same places as before. Then I added, "I don't think Americans are particularly welcome in Ukraine right now, anyway."

She scoffed. "Of course you can go to Crimea," she said. "There is absolutely no reason not to. You're obviously getting incorrect information from the American press." And with that, the floodgates opened: for the next several minutes, Masha railed against the American media for reporting falsehoods, blindly supporting President Obama, and generally being a tool of the government. "Everything in America is geared this way," she continued. "Movies, TV, everything is all about 'America is great! We're number one!'"

This last point was arguably true, but I couldn't let her statements about the American media pass without comment. I told her it was a bit rich to suggest that the American press is a tool of the government, when Vladimir Putin has systematically shut down independent journalism in Russia. Most major Russian media outlets are state-controlled, which isn't the case in the United States, I argued.

"Well, the Russian press is certainly more free than the American press," she countered. "They can report anything they want." And the American press can't? I asked. "No," she said.

This was absurd. Of all the arguments one could make against the American press or government—and there are many—this was simply not one of them. I was incredulous, not only that she believed what she was saying, but that she'd launched into it within minutes of our sitting down to lunch.

"But, Masha," I said, "what about all the Russian journalists that have been murdered for reporting on Chechnya? What about Anna Politkovskaya?"

"Journalists get killed in America too," she retorted.

"Not like that," I said. "They're not murdered for doing their jobs."

"Journalists *are* murdered in America," she said, her voice rising. "We hear about it over here. Maybe they don't tell you about it there, but I know it has happened many times." I just shook my head. There was no such spate of murders. And if there had been, it certainly wouldn't have been on the orders of President Obama. Yet I truly believed that Putin's government had had a hand in—or at least, had been privy to—the murders of people such as investigative reporter Anna Politkovskaya, Putin critic Alexander Litvinenko, and, of course, opposition leader Boris Nemtsov, who'd been gunned down just outside the Kremlin walls less than a year earlier.

"And you know, it's not just the Russian press that's more free," she continued. "Russians in general have more freedom than Americans."

At this, I turned my attention back to my sandwich, ready to give up on the conversation. Sensing my frustration, Anya jumped in. "Liza, I think I know what she means by that. Let me tell you something that happened when I was in America." She told me that one night, as she and a friend were talking and laughing in her hotel room, a woman called the police on them. "We weren't screaming, nothing out of the ordinary, but suddenly the police were involved," she said. "In Russia, we would have just knocked on the door ourselves and asked for quiet. But in America, people exercise their rights in a way that infringes on other people's rights."

Masha chimed in with another story she'd heard, about a woman and her daughter who'd been lying in the surf at an American beach, when "someone called the police to report that they might be drowning," she said. "This is ridiculous! In Russia, a man would just swim out to take care of the situation."

I ignored the inherent sexism in her solution, but told them they were right about one thing: Americans don't act freely in certain situations, because they're afraid of getting sued if something goes wrong. "We're a very litigious society," I said, "much more so than Russia. It is a problem."

"This is what I'm talking about!" exclaimed Masha. With the possible exception of Big Igor on Lake Baikal, she was the most unabashedly anti-American person I'd met yet—or at least, the most openly vocal one. I'm not a mindlessly flag-waving American, but this conversation was making me angry. "I see some of the points you're making," I told her. "But at the very least, where the media is concerned, I don't believe you have your facts correct."

Once again, Anya stepped in to mediate. "I think you're both right," she said. "Everyone loves their own country. And the press in every country ends up supporting its own government."

"Have you heard of Fox News?" I asked. "Watch a few minutes of that, and you'll see how pro-government the media is. They do nothing but attack Obama, twenty-four hours a day."

"I have seen it," said Masha. "But that is anti-Obama, not anti-America. The media is pro-America." This was a fair, though nuanced, distinction, although the Russian media is no less pro-Russia.

I changed tacks. "You've been to America, right?" I asked. She responded that she'd never been. I wanted to ask how she could claim to know what was really happening there, but I didn't. Instead, I offered an invitation.

"Please come," I told her. "You might feel differently if you visit." She actually seemed touched, her body language softening as she relaxed back into her chair. "I'm not sure we can ever really know what's happening in places unless we go there ourselves," I said. "That's why I'm here. I'm sure most Americans don't really know what's really going on in Russia."

"It's true," she said. "They think we're backward, like we have bears wandering in the streets or something." Despite my irritation, I had to laugh.

Masha and Anya after our contentious lunch at the Wild Boudoir Café, 2015 (PHOTO BY LISA DICKEY)

I wish I could report that this exchange led to a warm and lasting détente, but then the conversation turned to 9/11. When Masha noted that in Italy, where she often vacationed, many people believed the U.S. government had purposefully knocked down the Twin Towers to boost the stock market, it was all I could do not to hurl the remains of my sandwich across the table. Anya was staring studiously at her phone, unwilling to get anywhere near this conversation. Mercifully, the server at last brought the check, and Anya quickly paid the bill.

I figured this would be the last time we saw each other, so I asked Masha if we could take a ten-years-later photo of her and

Anya together. None of us were in the mood—at least, I wasn't—but the sisters dutifully posed in a little square across the street from the restaurant.

To my surprise, Masha then invited me to come see her apartment. Anya drove us there, and although the place was magnificent, with spectacular views over the whole city, what caught my eye was the vast assortment of American toys in Nikita's room, including two Buzz Lightyears, a Woody doll, and a stuffed Garfield the Cat. As Nikita proudly showed them to me, I found myself amazed that Masha allowed them in her home. But I refrained from commenting, having already had that particular can of worms for lunch.

—⋘—

Back in Anya's car, we discussed the lunchtime contretemps. "Masha's at home all day every day with a five-year-old," she said, with a laugh. "She needs to have more conversations with people. Don't think anything of it." Then she asked me if I'd like to spend the night at the dacha. I felt like a child who's been offered a cookie after choking down my spinach.

We picked up Max that evening and drove to Lake Chebarkul. Sergei and Lyuba were out there too, of course, and they invited us to have dinner with them. It was already dark as we drove, so there wasn't much to see; we just rode along in the blackness to an endless soundtrack of pop music. Like the "nice, gentle" humor of *Friends*, Anya also enjoyed old love songs. She wouldn't have said it in front of Max, but later she told me, "When I was younger, I used to think such songs were stupid and sentimental. But now I feel differently. I understand what they're about, because I've lived it." This cool Russian beauty truly was a romantic at heart.

After a little more than an hour, we arrived at the gate

outside Anya's dacha. Before we pulled in, she pointed across the street at a red-brick church with a gold cupola on top. "My mother built that," she said, as I gaped. I knew the family had built a chapel, but I hadn't realized it was a full-fledged onion-domed church "She did it after her brother died," Anya told me. "Also, so people here would have a place to pray."

When we walked into the dacha, I found myself gaping again. The first floor had 15-foot ceilings, a chandelier, and a vast open living room and kitchen, and the walls were covered in contemporary art. Anya gave me a tour while Busya and her other dog, a mutt named Knopa, scampered about. On the second floor, she showed me several bedrooms before we got to mine, which had a curved-wall bedchamber (it was located in the dacha's turret) with a giant round double bed. The floors were heated, even in my private bathroom, and silk curtains surrounded the bed. I put down my backpack, and Anya said, "Do you want to see the cinema room?" *Seriously?*

She took me up to the third floor, where a giant screen covered one wall, with a row of cushy reclining chairs facing it. This was a "dacha" in the same sense that a Cadillac limousine is a "car," and as I *oohed* and *aahed* my way around, Anya smiled, seeming pleased.

Sergei and Lyuba's place was a short walk away, past a banya, through a gate, then past a fire pit and gazebo. Their dacha was equally huge, and the interior was chockablock with art, tchotchkes, and shelves full of books. Lyuba shuffled about the kitchen in a purple housedress and slippers while Sergei gave me the tour.

Like Anya's, this dacha had multiple bedrooms, all of them— as Sergei proudly pointed out—with en suite bathrooms. "The builders told me it would be impossible for each room to have its own bathroom, because of the plumbing," he said. "But I insisted. And now my friends all ask for pictures so they can show their own architects that it can be done." He showed me his "man cave," a book-lined study with curved walls and a view of the lake, and back down on the first floor, the indoor swimming pool. I thought of Anya's grandmother's joke, and while Putin probably does have a bigger dacha, you could totally have him over to this one and not feel self-conscious.

Sergei's hair and mustache had grayed, but other than that he looked great—slimmer than in 2005, and with a perpetual grin on his ruddy face. As we waited for Lyuba to finish making dinner, he fetched a Russian army officer's hat and thrust it into my hands. "Try it on!" he said. I did, and saluted—not like a Pionerka, that much I knew—while Sergei guffawed. He disappeared and returned with a cowboy hat bearing a silver sheriff's star, and we giggled and took photos together in the opulent living room. For a man who'd made so much money and lived in relative splendor, he gave off the air of your favorite goofy uncle.

Lyuba called us to the table, and we sat down to a meal of pork chops, sliced ham, potato casserole, and that Russian classic: *pod shuboy* salad. Pod shuboy, or "under a fur coat," is so named because a layer of herring is covered by an "overcoat" of sliced vegetables, eggs, beets, and mayonnaise. As he took a heaping spoonful, Sergei said, "Lyuba's pod shuboy is better. Someone else brought us this one." Then, as if loath to insult an innocent salad, he said, "But you know, this one is OK too."

We drank wine and champagne out of crystal goblets, while Sergei tossed back vodka shots. The more he drank, the more red-faced and voluble he became, until the evening settled into a rhythm: Sergei would tell a story, waving his arms wildly, and

Lyuba and Sergei, posing at their dacha in 2015 with photos from 1995 and 2005 (PHOTO BY LISA DICKEY)

Lyuba would add dry commentary as the rest of us laughed. It was as if we were playing out a Russian version of the sitcom *Roseanne*.

Toward the end of dinner, Sergei wanted to show me some videos from the old days. We settled into the living room to watch, and the first one flickered onto the TV screen: It was from a friend's fortieth birthday party on October 7, 1995—just three weeks before Gary and I met them. "We're still friends with that couple . . . and that guy," Lyuba said, as the camera panned around the dinner table. "We still see all the same people."

Then there were videos from the years when Anya and Masha were children. The girls wore stretchy knit pants over their diapers, and in nearly every clip, Masha was eating, and little Anya was mimicking washing clothes. "Why am I always washing?" Anya asked, laughing. "And why are our dresses so short?" It was true—in every scene, the girls' little dresses barely came past their hips. "Ah, that was the style then," said Lyuba, laconically.

It occurred to me that Sergei and Lyuba had told the truth, that if you plopped them down anywhere—into a 1970s *communalka*, say, or a Tsarist village—they'd behave no differently than now. They made corny jokes (Sergei: "I lost ten kilograms . . . and Lyuba found it!") while the dogs scrabbled around and barked. They were quick to laugh at themselves, and at each other. At one point, Sergei announced that he had a piece of the Chelyabinsk meteor,‡ and after rummaging around upstairs for ten minutes, he came back down and proudly handed me a small, clear plastic container with a sliver of gray rock. "That's not it!" exclaimed Lyuba. "That's a piece of the Berlin Wall."

"Ah, so it is," said Sergei, peering closer. "Well, they do look kind of similar." Then he broke out into that familiar grin, exclaiming, "Anyway—look, Liza! A piece of the Berlin Wall!" Lyuba rolled her eyes.

—⚬⚬—

The next morning, Anya, Max, and I took a stroll to Lake Chebarkul, to see where the largest chunk of the meteor had fallen. As we walked through a light snowfall, Anya told me that she'd spoken with Masha. "She didn't sleep at all last night," she said. "She's worried that she said too much at lunch, or was too vehement."

"Ah, she was fine," I replied. "She's a patriot of her country. We all are." In truth, I had been startled at the depth of Masha's anger, but the fact that she'd expressed concern soothed whatever raw feelings I had left. In Anya's view, Masha had become

---

‡ Thousands of tiny fragments of the meteor were found in the area around Chelyabinsk, many of which were boxed up and sold as souvenirs.

more fervent about politics since her son had been born, which I could understand. And while I disagreed with much of what Masha believed, I was grateful she'd said it so plainly. I suspected that many of the Russians I'd been spending time with felt the same way, but were afraid of offending the American visitor. Yet I much preferred to hear the truth about what people thought, rather than a sanitized version.

Later that afternoon, I got my wish. Max cooked *shashlik* on an outdoor grill, and the five of us dined in a freestanding glass-walled dining room a short walk from the dacha. Somehow, we got on the subject of racism.

Sergei and Lyuba started talking about the Arabic population in France—specifically, why they didn't make an effort to assimilate, rather than continuing to follow their own customs. "They come to another county and then behave as they would at home," he said. "When I'm in another country, I try to behave according to its standards." I opined that while a certain degree of assimilation was helpful, it wasn't necessary for immigrants to abandon their own culture for that of their host country. Both Sergei and Lyuba disagreed, saying that there were certain standards of behavior people needed to follow.

He then told a story about an encounter on one of his many trips to the United States. "I was riding a bus, and there was a black guy next to me," he said. "When I got up for a minute, he slumped over and took up my seat." This made Sergei angry, and he wanted to throw the man off the bus. But when he confronted the man, "other black people on the bus, in the back, started to make menacing comments." Sergei didn't want to back down, but "then a white guy up front said, 'You'd better come up here.'" He did, though he was furious.

"If I had been in my own country, I would have happily thrown that guy off the bus," he said. "If he was white, nobody would have cared. But in America, people practice reverse racism. Nobody will confront a black person, because they're too scared something will happen." I ventured that the history of race relations in America was long and complicated, and that it continued to infuse modern race relations, but even as the words came out of my mouth, I knew they sounded like so much liberal mush to Sergei. He shook his head. "People should behave properly, no matter their race."

We next got on the subject of Barack Obama. Like everyone I'd met on this trip—and I do mean everyone—Sergei and Lyuba expressed disdain, bordering on disgust, at the mention of his name. "He's not trustworthy," Lyuba said. "You can't believe anything that comes out of his mouth." Both felt that Obama was weak, and a liar. "What about Hillary Clinton?" I asked. Lyuba puckered, then shook her head as if shaking off a bad dream. "She is *terrible*," she said. "I *can't stand* Hillary Clinton." When I asked why, she said, "She's like Obama. She lies."

"Generally speaking, it's not good for Russia when a Democrat is president," Sergei told me. I asked whether they liked George W. Bush better, and both of them puckered again.

"So, which American president did you like, then?" I asked. "Assuming there were any."

"Ronald Reagan," they both said, to my amazement. The "Mr. Gorbachev, tear down this wall" president, the man who took credit for destroying the USSR—this is who they liked? "He stood for something," said Sergei. "He said what he believed. He wasn't sneaky."

Inevitably, the conversation soon segued to Ukraine. "Do you know the history of Ukraine?" Lyuba asked me, in an echo of Big Igor's question two weeks earlier. I responded that I had a general idea.

"There is no such thing as Ukraine!" Sergei and Lyuba

exclaimed, almost in unison. "Ukraine was invented by Lenin," Sergei said. "How can America claim it should maintain its independence from Russia, when it has always been Russian?"

"If there is no such thing as Ukraine," I countered, "then what is the Ukrainian language?" Sergei answered that it was a Slavic language, basically the same as Russian, and only different because there was a mix of people—Poles, Russians, and other Slavs—in those regions. "But it has always, throughout history, been Russia. So what is happening now isn't anything new or different."

Clearly, the Ukrainian protestors on Kiev's Maidan Square disagreed, but once again, as in my discussion with Masha, there didn't appear to be any way to make traction with a counterargument. For as lighthearted as last night's dinner had been, tonight's was a litany of points upon which Sergei and Lyuba and I disagreed. Throughout it all, Anya and Max stared studiously at their phones, though every so often, Anya interjected that we should really get on the road back to Chelyabinsk. But then the discussion would heat up again, and I began to suspect we wouldn't find common ground before it was time to go.

At long last, Sergei raised his glass. "Liza, we are glad you're here. Even if we disagree with your government, we respect you." This was another comment I'd heard consistently on the trip: every time someone criticized the American government, they were quick to clarify that they liked the American people.

I couldn't help but think of my mother's trip to the Soviet Union, all those years ago. Back then, when I was a child, it seemed extraordinary to me that she was able to separate her feelings about Russian people from feelings about their government. Now, I finally realized that that's what Russians had been doing with me all along.

TEN

Kazan: The Soldier's Mother

JUST AS THE RUSSIANS IN 2015 WERE TALKING ABOUT Ukraine, in 1995 they were talking about Chechnya. Everywhere Gary and I went on that first trip, people bemoaned the brutal war there, which started in December 1994 when Russian forces launched air and ground attacks on the capital city, Grozny. The conflict, which became known as the First Chechen War, was fierce and bloody, killing tens of thousands of civilians within the first few weeks and eventually turning Grozny into a bombed-out ghost town.

The conflict had many roots, but primarily it was about sovereignty. Chechens had been under the yoke of Russia for centuries. After the collapse of the Soviet Union, as former republics such as Armenia, Azerbaijan, and the Central Asian "stans" declared their independence, a movement arose in Chechnya to do the same. Former military pilot Dzhokar Dudayev became president of the Chechen Republic of Ichkeria in 1991, and in 1993, his government officially declared Chechnya's autonomy. At first, the Russian government fought back through proxies, sending arms and funds to Chechen fighters opposed to Dudayev. Eventually, when the proxy war failed to achieve its goals, President Yeltsin sent Russian troops to attack Grozny.

Arriving in Kazan in November 1995, Gary and I decided to make the war our topic. Not only was Kazan as geographically close to Chechnya as we'd get, but it was the capital of the Tatarstan republic, which—like Chechnya—had a majority Muslim population. And though the war wasn't specifically about religious differences, the fact that Chechens were Muslim did figure into the conflict.

As soon as we arrived, I began making calls to Russian army offices, hoping to find a returning soldier to interview. Not surprisingly, I was stymied: no one would talk to me, and when I left messages, no one returned my calls. Gary and I even showed up at one office in person, but we were shooed away without help or comment.

Frustrated, we turned to local journalists for help. One young reporter from *Izvestia Tatarstana* (News of Tatarstan) flipped endlessly through her Rolodex, making calls—and being rebuffed—on our behalf. She then recommended another journalist, Vladimir Muzychenko, who worked across the hall at *Vechernyaya Kazan* (Evening Kazan). We dropped by his office to find a stocky man in mended wool pants and a stained sweatshirt, his desk piled high with papers. "Call me Bob," he barked, as he stuck out a beefy hand. "What do you need? I'll take care of it."

He began working the phone, shouting rapid-fire questions

into the receiver, but even he couldn't find anyone willing to meet with us. Then, he pulled a piece of paper from the teetering stack on his desk.

"This is a list of families of soldiers killed in Chechnya," he said, then jabbed his finger at a name. "Here, go talk to this woman. She can introduce you to other soldiers who served with her son." This seemed like a terrible idea, asking a grieving mother to introduce us to her dead son's comrades, and it got worse when he told us the woman didn't have a phone. "Just go to her apartment," he said. "Here, take my card. You'll be fine."

With profound reluctance, Gary and I caught a taxi to a nondescript apartment block on the outskirts of the city. It took a while to find the right place, and then a stout, tired-looking woman answered the door. She eyed us warily, but when I handed her Vladimir's card, she invited us in. As we walked into the living room, I noticed a framed photo of a good-looking young soldier, a black stripe superimposed across one shoulder.

The woman, Natalya, told us that this was her son Zhenya, who'd been killed in Chechnya ten months earlier. Her husband—Zhenya's stepfather, Vladimir—was home as well, and the two of them told us the story.

—⁓—

Born in 1975, Zhenya was a friendly, chubby-cheeked boy with big brown eyes and dark, curly hair. "He looked like a little gypsy boy," Natalya told us. "He always loved to be the center of attention, to be on stage." During his school years, he performed in plays and talent shows, and he taught himself how to play guitar, piano, and drums. Eventually, he began writing his own music. His younger brother, Denis, idolized him.

After high school, Zhenya enrolled in Kazan's Chemical-Technical Institute, where he started a band. He met and fell in

Video image of 19-year-old Zhenya at the Institute party, two months before his death (PHOTO BY GARY MATOSO)

love with a fellow student, Natasha K., and within months they were engaged. Surrounded by friends, his trusty guitar always within reach, the outgoing young musician was the life of the party. Then, in January 1994, 18-year-old Zhenya was drafted. The laws of conscription hadn't changed since the Soviet era, and young men who were drafted typically served two years of service, usually in a location far from their hometowns.

Zhenya was sent to Volgograd, which, considering Russia's vastness, was a relatively close posting—just 30 hours away by train. "We were so happy to have him close by," his mother told me. "We couldn't believe how lucky we were that he hadn't been sent off to Arkhangelsk or some other faraway northern place."

After serving almost a year in Volgograd, Zhenya came home on leave in October 1994. He was a proud, clean-cut soldier now, eager to see his family and fiancée. He didn't tell Natasha K. he was coming, but instead showed up in his army uniform at the

Institute, where she still was a student. Like in a scene from a film, he came and swept her off her feet, to the delight of students and teachers.

Two nights after his return, Zhenya and his buddies gathered at the Institute for a party. His mother showed us a video taken that evening, showing a slightly drunk, very happy Zhenya cutting up with friends and playing the piano. About halfway through the video, he turns from the piano to look directly at the camera, which zooms in on his young, handsome face; as we watched, it was difficult to believe that the man in the flickering image no longer existed anywhere but in memory.

On November 7 a month before the war began—Zhenya's family and friends took him to the Kazan railway station for the train back to Volgograd. "Zhenya promised to try to get back for New Year's," his mother told me. "He thought he'd be able to get leave somehow. And even if he couldn't, his army discharge was scheduled for May, which didn't seem that far off." She sent him off with a hug and a smile, a fact that now haunted her.

"I never dreamed when we went to the station that day that that would be the last time I ever saw my son," she said as tears streamed down her face. "We saw him off that day just as though we'd be seeing him in a few weeks."

Zhenya was sent to Chechnya the first week of December, though in a letter home, he lied so his mother wouldn't worry. "Hello from Volgograd!" he wrote:

> Everything here is fine so far, I'm alive and well, and
> miss you. They've begun to give us a little bit of
> compensation, and now on December 12, the "100
> days" starts—100 days until discharge . . .
> After being home on leave, I am really sick of the
> army. The monotony really gets on my nerves . . . We're

now doing technical and weapon preparation for
training in shooting, and after the New Year we may go
on a training mission, I'm not sure for how long . . .

On December 11, three days after Zhenya posted this letter,
Russian troops launched their assault on Grozny. For two days,
the Russian government pretended nothing was happening, but
on December 13, President Yeltsin officially acknowledged the
fighting. Natalya still didn't know her son was in Chechnya, but
she feared that was where he'd end up. "Calm, peaceful life
ended for us on December 13," she told me. "We watched the
television news every night, trying to get some information
about what was going on there. I just had a bad feeling after the
fighting began."

Two weeks later, the mother of another soldier called Natalya
with the frightening news that her son, who'd been serving with
Zhenya in Volgograd, had been wounded while fighting in
Chechnya. He was recuperating in an army hospital outside
Moscow, and she was traveling there to see him. "She promised
to call and let me know if she found Zhenya in the hospital too,"
Natalya told me.

But Zhenya wasn't in Moscow; he was still in the mountains
outside Grozny. In late December, he wrote a letter to Natasha K.
revealing his location and describing the horrors of combat:

I have been in the mountains 12 kilometers from
Grozny, the capital of Chechnya, for three weeks
already . . . I'm not going to write to my parents, as I
can only imagine what would happen if they knew.
     I've been through four battles, and the scene is
terrible. We've had 16 wounded and 4 killed. One
officer had his leg blown off . . . We wear our bulletproof

jackets and keep our machine guns close even when we
sleep, because at any moment there could be "jazz"—an
attack . . .

This letter is going with the first delivery out of here,
and I don't know if it will get to you or not, since we've
been surrounded for two days. The worst of all is when
they start to shoot, they even shoot innocent people . . .
The Chechens have hired Turkish fighters, who are
professionals at this. We shot at them the night before
last, there's about 40 of them hidden behind a ravine . . .
They usually attack at night, which is convenient for
them as they know the mountains well.

Two days later, on December 31, 1994, chaos erupted in the
mountains. Soldiers were given vodka to celebrate Defense Minister Pavel Grachev's birthday, and a savage battle soon broke out
between the Russian and Chechen forces. The details are murky,
but sometime that night, Zhenya met a brutal death: the head-
less body of the young soldier had to be identified by the tattoos
on his hands and an existing scar on his chest.

From the moment she'd heard from the other soldier's
mother, Natalya had been calling army services several times a
day to ask if Zhenya was on the lists of those wounded, captured,
or killed in Chechnya. Every day for more than two weeks, she
was told he was not. Then, on the afternoon of January 13, she
got a call at work.

"Come to the Military Commissar's office," said a voice. "We
have news for you." It was what they'd been dreading. "Your
son's body will arrive by train at four thirty tomorrow morning," an official informed them. "Go home and prepare to receive his coffin." In shock, the couple did as they were told, going
home and covering the mirrors according to Russian Orthodox

tradition. Realizing she didn't have a formal photo of Zhenya in his army uniform, Natalya arranged for a photography shop to superimpose a photo of her son's face onto the body of another soldier. This was the photo now displayed in their living room.

The following morning, the coffin bearing Zhenya's body arrived at the train station. "I waited at home for my husband and his friends to bring it back here," said Natalya. "The whole time, I kept thinking, 'Maybe there's been a mistake. Maybe they'll get there and find out he's still alive.' But of course, it wasn't a mistake."

Every other day in summer, and once a week when it became cold, Natalya went to the cemetery. On our last afternoon in Kazan, Gary and I went with her. We rode the bus for three stops, then made the long walk across a grassy slope toward the cemetery, where Zhenya's grave was marked off by a wrought-iron fence decorated with lyres. The granite tombstone bore an engraved image of Zhenya's face, his guitar, and two roses. We watched as Natalya straightened the flowers she'd left earlier in the week, muttering to herself, "How could I have known, when we went to the train station a year ago . . . ?"

Although Natalya had at first welcomed us only reluctantly, by the end of our visit, she seemed proud we were doing a story about her son. She wanted people to know what a good person he'd been, and how utterly senseless the war in Chechnya was. "For this stupidity my son died," she said, practically spitting out the words. "It's all the worse that his death was for nothing at all. For nothing."

—m—

Ten years later, David and I arrived in Kazan on a blindingly sunny Saturday afternoon. Before setting out to find Natalya, we decided to take a stroll around the city.

Standing at the confluence of the Volga and Kazanka rivers, some 500 miles from Moscow, Kazan is a fascinating blend of East and West—a riot of churches and mosques, markets and parks, Tatar restaurants and Russian cafés. With just over a million people, it's Russia's eighth-largest city, and it has a cosmopolitan, eclectic vibe that belies a bloody history of fighting among Mongols, Tatars, Bulgars, and Russians.

Kazan's most striking architectural feature is its massive white kremlin, a sixteenth-century walled fortress perched atop a steep, grassy hill. With its stately towers, gates, and cathedrals, the kremlin is spectacular from any angle, and the main gate boasts a stirring statue of Tatar poet Musa Dzhalil struggling to break free from barbed wire. Gary and I had walked around the kremlin in 1995, but when David and I arrived in 2005, I was surprised to discover a new structure there.

Towering above the kremlin walls were the turquoise domes and minarets of the Kul Sharif Mosque, one of the largest in all of Europe. The scale is eye-popping, with minarets rising 180 feet into the sky and a gleaming 128-foot-tall cupola. The vast prayer hall can accommodate 1,500 people for prayers, while another 9,000 can fit into the adjacent square. Tourists flocked to the mosque, where they gazed in wonder at its ornate tile work, massive chandeliers, marble floors, and stained-glass windows.

It was odd to see a mosque inside a classic Russian kremlin, but the location was historic: Kul Sharif was built on the same spot as an earlier mosque that was destroyed in 1552, when Ivan the Terrible's armies stormed across the region slaughtering Muslims in an attempt to spread Russian Orthodoxy. Four and a half centuries after the massacre, the Russian and Tatar governments combined forces—with financial help from oil companies and private donors—to re-create the largest and most beautiful of the mosques that had been destroyed.

The Kazan kremlin, with the new Kul-Sharif Mosque within its walls,
2005 (PHOTO BY DAVID HILLEGAS)

I couldn't help but wonder how it was that Muslim Tatars
now had such good relations with Russians, while Chechens
and Russians were still at each other's throats. Both groups
were predominantly Sunni, and both had historically suffered
slaughter and pillage at Russian hands. But here in Kazan—
which, ironically enough, means "cauldron" in Tatar—Russians
and Tatars mingled easily. Curious, David and I decided to
conduct a thoroughly unscientific survey, asking a few random people in the city's quaint downtown district what they
thought.

We spent a couple of hours stopping people, and one answer

we heard repeatedly was that relations were good because there were many more mixed marriages here. About half the Tatars we stopped told us they were married to Russians, and vice versa. "How can you hate Tatars when your own children are half Tatar?" one Russian woman asked with a shrug.

This didn't really solve the mystery, though. After all, there have always been Russians in Chechnya too, but mixed marriages there are more rare. Yet in Kazan, the question seemed like such a non-issue that people didn't even know how to answer. One 18-year-old Russian named Mark, out walking with his Tatar buddy Artur, said, "It's just always been this way. We don't even think about it." I couldn't help but recall 19-year-old Zhenya and marvel at the fact that if these two teenagers had been born further south, they might have ended up aiming guns at each other rather than strolling around town together.

We happened to stop a historian named Delyara, who gave us a brief discourse on Tatar history. "There have been many governments here over the centuries," she said. "The Bulgars, the Golden Horde, the Kazan Khanate. Under the Kazan Khanate, no churches were ever destroyed. So we have a history of tolerance here." But then she told us there was a simpler reason why Chechnya was more volatile.

"People from the Caucasus are different," she said. "Our blood doesn't run as hot as theirs."

This was a sentiment we heard repeatedly. One middle-aged Russian woman told us that Chechens were "very emotional people, very fiery." And a 20-year-old Tatar woman echoed this, saying, "They're hot-blooded, they want to be free. Tatars are not like them. We're calm people."

In Russia in 2005, generalizations about Chechens abounded, many far more disparaging than "hot-blooded." Dark-haired, olive-skinned men were routinely stopped and harassed by police, and many Russians openly expressed prejudice against Chechens, often in crude and insulting terms, in a cycle of hatred and mistrust that seemed unlikely to break anytime soon.

One of the last people we interviewed, a taxi driver named Mikhail, seemed dismissive of such stereotyping. A self-described "pure-blooded Tatar," he told us, "I went to kindergarten and school with Chechens, Tatars, Russians, everyone. We all got along. Listen, there are no bad nations, only bad people. You can't generalize." Compared to what we'd been hearing, this felt like a refreshingly progressive sentiment. Then he added, "Although, I really don't like Azerbaijanis. They're rude, disgusting, and don't keep their word."

Kazan was full of surprises. In 2005, the city was celebrating the 1,000-year anniversary of its founding; the buildings downtown had been beautifully restored, a new subway system had just opened its doors, and busloads of tourists chugged past billboards proudly proclaiming the millennial jubilee. Yet as we later learned from Vladimir Muzychenko, the 1,000-year number was, to put it kindly, a guesstimate. In fact, in 1977, city officials had spent months preparing for an 800-year anniversary. The celebration never materialized, though souvenir pins were made.

So, how did Kazan manage to age two centuries in just 28 years? Some people believed the 1,000-year anniversary was a political gift from Russia to Tatarstan. The evidence for this was twofold: not only had Tatarstan president Mintimer Shaimiev managed to wangle enough money from the Russian government to completely spruce up the city, he'd also persuaded Putin to allow Kazan to declare itself 150 years older than Moscow—a political concession unthinkable in Soviet times.

But Niyaz Khalitov, an archaeologist at the Kazan kremlin, revealed that there was actually some scientific reasoning behind the new millennial date. In the mid-1990s, he told us, archaeologists here unearthed two coins that dated from the tenth century, indicating that the city was at least 1,000 years old. "Kazan is probably even older," he said, "but a decision was made to mark it as a thousand years." The city had hoped to hold its celebration in 2000, but "it took time to clean up the city and make souvenirs. Then, we thought we might do it in 2003, but St. Petersburg was celebrating its three-hundred-year anniversary that year. So we decided on 2005"—science by committee.

—∞—

The following day, David and I set out to find Zhenya's mother, Natalya. The family didn't have a phone in 1995, so all I had was their address; we'd have to just show up, as the first time. We caught a taxi to their neighborhood in the north of the city, yet somehow I couldn't even find their street, much less their apartment.

The taxi driver drove around and around as we tried in vain to figure out where their building was. Nobody seemed to have heard of their street, which was bizarre. It was like a bad dream, and both David and I were boiling with frustration by the time we learned the problem: the street name had been changed in the late 1990s. We were in the right place, but had no way of recognizing the building, as all the apartment blocks were identical gray boxes.

I rang the bell, and Vladimir, Natalya's husband, opened the door looking exactly the same, except that his hair had turned white. He looked at me blankly, and I said, "Hello. I'm Liza, an American journalist who was here ten years ago. Do you remember me?" He smiled, a casually confident little grin that I suddenly recalled from 1995. "Yeah, I remember you," he said. "Come in."

Photo of Zhenya in his parents' living room, 2005 (PHOTO BY DAVID
HILLEGAS)

Natalya didn't recognize me, but once she realized who I
was, she took me into the living room to show me the photo of
Zhenya. It was still prominently displayed, now with a medal
he'd been awarded posthumously—the Medal of Courage.

We sat at the kitchen table, which Natalya proceeded to load
up with food and drink—a beef-and-potato casserole, salted tomatoes, brown bread, a basket of chocolates and cookies, and
shot glasses that Vladimir filled with vodka. We toasted our
meeting, and Natalya began to tell me what had changed, and
what hadn't, over the previous decade.

Natasha K., Zhenya's fiancée, still came to visit, though she
was married to another man and had a daughter now. "She still
goes down to the cemetery," Natalya said. "I sometimes see
flowers she's left. Her husband has even taken her there." She

thought for a moment, then added, "She had to move on; I'm not sorry she did. We're glad she's happy."

Zhenya's brother Denis was 22 now, and I asked whether he'd been drafted into the army. "They can't draft him because of Zhenya," Natalya told me, "but twice a year, every fall and every spring, they try to anyway. We call and tell them, 'His brother died in Chechnya! He's exempt!' but they always want us to send more paperwork."

Denis was a young businessman, buying and selling goods and splitting his time between Kazan and the Moscow suburbs. He was out of town, so we didn't get a chance to see him, but I got the impression that even when he was here his parents didn't see much of him. "He's different than Zhenya was," Natalya told me. "He's got his own friends and his own life."

Time had eased Natalya's pain. In 1995, she seemed always on the brink of tears, her eyes puffy and red. Now she was able to talk about Zhenya with a kind of warm melancholy, rather than the piercing sorrow of those early days.

"On New Year's Eve," she said, "exactly a year after he died, we had more than a hundred people here for a celebration. Everyone came, all his friends, to remember him." She smiled. "It's gotten easier. Life goes on. But of course, we miss my Zhenka."

And now the tears welled in her eyes. "The pain doesn't go away," she said. "He was my son."

Ten years later, as I was making my way across Russia for the third time, I almost couldn't stand the thought of reaching out again to Natalya. By 2015, her son had been dead for longer than he'd been alive; was I really going to ask her to dip into that well of grief again? The one saving grace was that I now had a cell phone number for her, so at least I wouldn't just be dropping in on the family again. Even so, arriving in Kazan, I decided to put off the call for a day, and instead took a stroll around the city.

A man on the train had told me I wouldn't recognize Kazan now, that it had become like a European city. I assumed he was exaggerating, but walking down central Bauman Street, I had to admit he had a point. Kazan was gorgeous. The Italianate-architecture buildings were brightly painted and spotlessly clean, the vibe was prosperous and calm, and scores of inviting shops, museums, and theaters lined the street. Short of St. Petersburg, Kazan is the most beautiful city I've seen in Russia.

Like Vladivostok, Kazan had a new bridge—the Millennium Bridge, erected in celebration of the anniversary, with a superstructure in the shape of an "M." And across the Kazanka River from downtown, a new Palace of Weddings had been built in the shape of a giant cauldron—arguably not the most appropriate choice of wedding imagery.

Downtown, Western stores and restaurants abounded, from Emporio Armani to Cinnabon to Coyote Ugly. Students from the nearby Kazan Federal University strolled around wearing backpacks, popping into cafeterias serving Tatar staples such as dried horse meat, rice pilaf, and a honey-glazed fried dough confection called *chak-chak*. In 1995, I'd noticed a number of people wearing traditional Tatar clothing of long coats and round hats, but now—at least in the city center— this was a rarity.

Souvenir shops peddled traditional leather slippers next to rows of T-shirts showing Putin riding a bear (slogan: "Not gonna get us"). And quirky museums abounded—the Museum of Illusions, the Museum of Happy Childhood, the House of Entertaining Science and Technology. Perhaps it was the abundance of students, or the influx of cash for the anniversary, but for a 1,000-year-old city (give or take), Kazan seemed unexpectedly young, hip, and fun. I was happy to be back here, even though the story we'd chosen to tell was a sad one.

—ɯ—

After breakfast the next morning, I dialed Natalya's number.

"Hello?"

"Hello, Natalya?"

"Yes?"

"It's Liza Dickey, the American journalist from ten years ago. Do you remember me?"

"Ah, Liza. Of course I remember you."

"I'm in Kazan, and I'd like to see you."

"Ohhh . . . we're far from Kazan. We're on vacation, very far from the city."

"Ah, that's too bad. When will you be back?"

"Not until the end of next week."

It was Friday. Could I stay in Kazan for a whole week or more, for the sake of seeing Natalya? I pondered for a moment, then decided I could.

"So, will you be back on that Friday? Or Saturday?"

A pause.

"Maybe not until Sunday. OK, Liza, good luck. Bye-bye."

Click.

And that was it.

I can't be certain, but I do believe that Natalya was out of town. Yet I also suspect she made a quick calculation that she'd rather not relive the story of her son's death for me one more time.

Eight weeks and nine cities into the trip, Natalya was the first "20 years later" person who declined to speak with me. After hanging up, I felt a swirl of emotions—guilty at having intruded into her life one too many times; stung by her reluctance to talk (though I certainly couldn't blame her); and relieved that I wouldn't be prying open that wound again.

Primarily, though, I felt grateful. There was never a guarantee that any of the people I contacted over all these years would speak with me. Getting turned down, though uncomfortable, made it starkly obvious how fortunate I was that it only happened once.

—⚹—

ELEVEN

Moscow: The Russian Rap Star

T HE MAN ON STAGE AT MASTER DISCOTEC WAS A multicolored sensation, decked out in baggy pants, a double-breasted purple-striped jacket, and a red paisley shirt. Three female dancers gyrated nearby, wearing black go-go shorts and white button-downs knotted at the waist. "Yo! Yo!" the man shouted, as a funky beat filled the packed hall. "Let's dance!"

This was Alexei Pavlov, AKA MD&C Pavlov, the godfather of Russian rap.* A skinny, white, vegetarian Muscovite, he'd taken it upon himself to bring rap to the musically uneducated Russian masses. "People don't understand rhythm," he told me

---

* He started out as MC Pavlov, then changed it to MD&C Pavlov, though now the two names appear to be interchangeable. For the sake of consistency, I'll call him MC Pavlov from here out.

MC Pavlov, Russia's first rap star, 1995 (PHOTO BY GARY MATOSO)

in 1995, in Russian-accented, vaguely hip-hop-flavored English. "They only know how to clap on the first and third beat. But they will learn. We're gonna *teach the people!*"

Pavlov was Russia's most famous rapper, though that wasn't saying much. Rap music was a curiosity then, a thing black Americans did that bore little relation to Russians' lives, and when the first rappers popped up here, they were met with skepticism. "You know, this has no roots at all in our culture," one Moscow artist told the *New York Times Magazine* in 1993. "To see these young people trying to imitate American rappers—it's as incredible to me as it would be to you if you went up to Harlem one day and found everyone there dressed as Ukrainian dancers and strumming on balalaikas."

But Pavlov was determined to bring rap to Russia, and he had the pedigree to do it. In the late 1980s, he was the drummer for the Russian cult band Zvuki Mu (Sounds of Moo), an art-rock ensemble that caught the ear of Brian Eno, the super-producer known for his work with bands such as U2 and Talking Heads. Eno liked Zvuki Mu's funky, jazzy sound, so he arranged for the band to come to the United States. And that's how, in 1989, 23-year-old Alexei Pavlov found himself in New York City, the capital of Western decadence, the city that never sleeps, the Center of Rap on Earth (at least, the East Coast variant).

Pavlov had first heard rap music back in 1984, as an 18-year-old student at the Moscow State Institute of Radio Engineering, Electronics and Automation. A classmate from Cuba had made cassette tapes of pirated U.S. radio while home on vacation, and Pavlov got hooked on the proto-rap stylings of Melle Mel and the Furious Five. "It wasn't even called rap back then," Pavlov told me. "But that's what it was. From then on, I tried to get as much rap music as I could, but it was almost impossible in those days." When he made it to New York with Zvuki Mu, he soaked up as much music as possible, bought himself a pair of black silver-studded shoes, and returned to Russia ready to launch his own rap career. MC Pavlov was born.

His initial efforts to put together a stage show resembled a *Saturday Night Live* skit. "At first, when we were trying to find dancers for the group, we made the mistake of thinking that all black people have good rhythm," he told me. "So we would ask black girls to join our group, but a lot of them couldn't dance at all. I think about 99 percent of the black people here are really white inside."[†] Eventually, he managed to find three girls (as he called them) who could dance—or at least, be taught to dance.

Pavlov rapped in a mix of English, Russian, and a smattering of nonsense words thrown in for rhythmic value. "Who

---

[†] At the time, there were an estimated 40,000 "Afro-Russians" in all of Russia, just 0.02 percent of the population.

cares what the words say? The important thing is, do they sound good together? Words for me are just a phonetic instrument." He initially didn't want to rap in Russian, because "it sounds stupid," he said. "But nobody here understands if I rap only in English. For them, it's like I'm from the moon or something."

Pavlov wasn't from the moon, but he was arguably on a different spiritual plane, because not long before MC Pavlov was born, Alexei Pavlov was reborn—as a Hare Krishna devotee. He told me about his conversion, which happened on a Moscow street corner in 1985.

He'd been the first among his friends to start smoking and drinking, at age 14, and by the time he was 20, he decided to quit. Soon after that, while walking in the city one day, he encountered a man distributing photocopies of the Bhagavad Gita, the 5,000-year-old scripture of Krishna faith. Intrigued, he struck up a conversation, telling the man about his recent conversion to sober living. "So, you've given up smoking and drinking," the man replied. "Now it's time to give up eating meat." When Pavlov asked why, the man said, "Because it's nothing but dead flesh."

"It's dead flesh!" Pavlov exclaimed to me, throwing his hands in the air. "Oh, man, it's so simple! Who wants to put dead, rotting flesh in their mouth? As soon as he said that, I couldn't even imagine eating meat anymore." Pavlov is not a man who does things halfway, so from that moment, he never had another bite of meat, fish, or eggs.

Pavlov invited Gary and me to join him at Moscow's Hare Krishna temple, where devotees could eat vegetarian meals, chant mantras, and pay their obeisances. With a pale robe hanging off his lanky frame, the sides of his head shaved and a skinny braid down his neck, Pavlov looked like a Krishna devotee from central casting. And eight years after joining, he still had the fire of the converted; when we walked into the temple, he immediately prostrated himself in front of a statue of His Divine Grace A. C. Bhaktivedanta Swami Prabhupada, the spiritual master whose image graces Krishna temples worldwide.

Pavlov had even included snippets of Sanskrit on a recent song, "Dance in Extazy"—a catchy, propulsive tune with rapid-fire lyrics set against a *wah-wah* guitar backdrop. At the end of the song came his crowning touch, the ultimate Pavlovian marriage of East and West: a recording of the Swami chanting the Krishna mantra, set to a rap beat. *Hare Krishna Hare Krishna Krishna Krishna Hare Hare . . .*

"Rap is rhythmic chanting, and the mantra is rhythmic chanting," Pavlov told me. "The only difference is that hearing the name of Krishna purifies you. It purifies everything around it, the animals, the trees, the people. So, just by listening to MD&C Pavlov, you're getting some purification!" he concluded, beaming as if he'd just won the lottery—or, more accurately, given me the winning celestial numbers.

I'm not particularly a fan of either rap or Hare Krishna, but I really liked hanging out with Pavlov. The guy exuded happy energy, and on top of that he was making music nobody had ever heard before. His new record, called "Ze Best," was getting airplay, and he spent his nights bouncing all over the city, playing gigs with his "girls." In the artistic hothouse of post-Soviet Moscow, Pavlov was a rare and quirky bloom, and when the 2005 trip rolled around, I wondered just how famous he might have become by now.

—⚭—

Pavlov and I spoke on the phone soon after David and I arrived in Moscow. He seemed surprised (and characteristically excited) to hear from me, and we made a plan to meet the next afternoon at the Dinamo metro station.

When David and I arrived, Pavlov wasn't there. We waited, and then waited some more, and after a while I started getting anxious. Where was he? Had I misunderstood the plan? The platform was empty, save for a heavyset guy standing a few yards away. At last, it dawned on me: Was *that* Pavlov? We peered at each other, and when I uncertainly said, "Heyyyyyyy," his face creased into a smile.

"Ah, it's you," he said. "I wasn't sure." We hugged, and as we pulled apart I noticed that he had a lazy eye, which I didn't remember from before. As we started walking, I noticed his gait had changed too—less spry, more deliberate. He was giving off a very different physical vibe, one that didn't seem totally attributable to being ten years older.

We walked to a nearby studio, and Pavlov took off his coat to reveal bright green overalls, an orange T-shirt, and a neon-orange checkered button-down. He wore tinted glasses, as well as a lanyard around his neck with his cell phone attached, giving him the look of an exceptionally colorful tech nerd. I asked him how things had been going since we saw each other last.

After 1995, he said, his career began soaring. His "Dance in Extazy" video won Video of the Year at a festival of Russian regional TV shows, he got a commercial gig creating musical presentations for the chipmaker Intel, and in 1997, he founded the Festival of Soul and Funk, a three-day extravaganza with shows in multiple Moscow clubs. Through it all, he kept performing and making new music, and in late 1997 he took another trip to New York City.

"I needed to recharge my batteries, to hear some new stuff," he told me. While there, he played with the legendary jazz vibraphonist Roy Ayers and went to numerous clubs. "I would

MC Pavlov, 2005 (PHOTO BY DAVID HILLEGAS)

walk around the city in this orange outfit," he said, laughing, "and people would go, 'Hey, Orange Man from Moscow!'" He even made deals with New York record labels to send him their latest releases, so he could pitch his own TV show about funk music back in Moscow.

The TV show never got off the ground, but Pavlov began hosting a radio show called *Funky Time*. Broadcast in nearly two dozen cities and towns, "it was the only radio show about funk music in Russia," he said proudly. Flush with his growing success, he moved out of his parents' apartment in 1999, rented his own place, and built a makeshift recording studio inside. Then, as a treat, he booked a trip to Thailand with one of his dancers, a beautiful young woman named Polina who'd been performing with him since the early 1990s.

On their first day in Bangkok, the couple visited a Buddhist temple and wandered around the city taking pictures. On the second day, getting ready to cross a busy street, Pavlov looked left, as one does when traffic travels on the right-hand side. In Thailand, however, traffic travels on the left. Pavlov stepped off the curb directly into the path of an oncoming bus. He never even saw it.

The impact nearly killed him. An ambulance rushed the gravely injured Pavlov to a Bangkok hospital, where he underwent three operations. He was in a coma for nearly a month; it was unclear whether he would ever recover.

Almost as soon as the accident happened, friends and fellow musicians in Moscow began planning a benefit concert for Pavlov, who had no way of paying the $1,000-a-day hospital bills he was incurring. "They didn't raise too much money," he told me with a shrug. "But more important was the good energy they sent. All of Moscow was praying for me."

When Pavlov finally awoke from his coma, he was flown back to Moscow to continue recuperating. "I had my fourth operation after I got back," he said. "During that one, they held a special service at the Krishna temple. They lit a sacrifice fire, and chanted special mantras." For a man whose stage act is all clever wordplay and high irony, there's no hint of that irony when he talks about the power of prayer. "It definitely helped," he told me earnestly.

The accident and surgeries left scars running across Pavlov's scalp, but he told me he had no memory loss, save for not remembering the accident itself or the comatose weeks that followed. He referred vaguely to other lingering health problems, though he refused to elaborate or dwell on them.

"Hey, I'm alive!" he said, throwing his arms wide in a pose I remembered well from 1995. "That's what matters."

Pavlov spent a full year recuperating in Moscow hospitals before finally being allowed to go home. Spending a year in the hospital would be a discombobulating, depressing experience for anyone. But as soon as Pavlov got out, he went right back to work. "First thing, we released the CD *I'm Back*"—a compilation of dance and funk tracks he'd recorded before the accident. "There's one track at the end that goes, 'People ask me where I was—I was on vacation! I had a good vacation! I got healthy!'" he told me, laughing. "For those who know what happened to me, they know what I'm talking about. Those who don't, don't."

He also resumed doing commercial presentations for Intel, to pay the bills. "We go in and do this rap about Intel: 'Pentium 4 is the most powerful center of your digital world!'" he exclaimed, waving his hands in excitement. "Then we get someone from the audience to come up and say, 'I love Pentium! I want Pentium!' and right then, during the presentation, we make a mix of that." A sound engineer would then burn a DVD for the audience member to take home as a funky, Intel-branded souvenir.

As startled as I'd been by Pavlov's physical changes, little else seemed different in his life. He was still making music, still a vegetarian, still a Krishna. But the music scene around him had changed dramatically. In 1995 he was an anomaly, but now Moscow was flooded with rappers and DJs—some of whom were too young to remember their predecessor's heyday.

"They're like, "MC Pavlov? Who's that?" he laughed. "They maybe have heard of Public Enemy, but that's about it." He was still able to find work in clubs, though now he was switching his focus from rap to funk music. "Russia wasn't ready for funk a few years ago," he said, "but it's time now!" *We're gonna teach the people!*

When I started preparing for my third trip, I wondered how different Pavlov's life might be now. We hadn't been in touch, so I had no clue—but one thing I did know: Moscow had changed, yet again. Each time I went there, it was like visiting a completely different city.

—⚭—

The first time I set foot in Moscow was in the summer of 1988. I was 21, fresh out of college, and had scored a job working as a nanny for the family of a U.S. diplomat. Mikhail Gorbachev was the Soviet leader, the Cold War was in full swing, and Moscow was a drab, gray city where stores had thrilling names like "Meat," "Bread," and "Milk." At the official exchange rate, set by the Soviet government, one U.S. dollar bought 60 kopeks—less than a ruble. On the black market, a dollar was worth more than 20 times that.

I lived on the U.S. embassy compound, a walled-in, city-block-sized Little America that boasted not only apartments and offices, but a cafeteria, gym, bowling alley, swimming pool, and barbershop. There was also a small grocery store where we could buy treats from home such as Oreo cookies, California wines, and Lay's potato chips. None of these items could be bought elsewhere in Russia, yet it didn't occur to me how exotic they were until the day I unthinkingly walked out of the embassy with a can of Coke. When I popped it open while strolling down nearby Kalininsky Prospekt, people stared as if I were clutching a glowing alien baby in my hand.

One of the only American brands Russians could buy back then was Pepsi, which had been sold in the USSR since the 1970s—though many people probably didn't even know it was an American product, as it was bottled locally and bore the name in Cyrillic: пепси-кола.‡ There was a Baskin-Robbins near Red Square, but locals were forbidden from buying ice cream there; it was a "hard-currency" store, meaning you had to pay with foreign money, which was illegal for most Soviets to own.§ I took a Russian friend there as a treat one evening, and she nearly wept with excitement. On another night, I walked by after closing time and noticed that the long mirror behind the counter was backlit; it was actually a two-way mirror, presumably so Soviet authorities could keep an eye on who was coming and going.

Moscow's wide boulevards were already choked with traffic by the late eighties, though the vehicles were almost exclusively Russian—Zhigulis, Ladas, Volgas, Zils. Red Square was the heart of the city, and the heart of Red Square was the blocky marble mausoleum of Lenin's Tomb, where people still lined up for hours to see the Soviet leader's waxy, embalmed corpse. Across the square was the Gosudarstvenny Universalny Magazin, better known as GUM—a vast shopping mall that in 1988 contained rows of stores such as "Shoes," "Linens," and "Clothing." With its glass roof and dramatic archways, the building was a gorgeous specimen of pre-Revolutionary architecture. But as a shopping experience, it was as dull as a box of dirt. In the few snapshots I took there in 1988, crowds of women in overcoats and knit hats swarmed around the entrance of one shoe

---

‡ In 1959, in what would have made a beautiful TV commercial, Vice President Richard Nixon urged Soviet leader Nikita Khrushchev to try a sip of Pepsi at an exhibition of American products in Moscow. Khrushchev loved it, and in 1972, the USSR struck a deal to manufacture and sell Pepsi in Russia in exchange for PepsiCo's agreement to import and sell Russian vodka in the United States.

§ Payment in hard currency was intended to guarantee a stability the ruble couldn't offer. There were other hard-currency stores in the Soviet Union, called *Beriozkas*, which sold souvenirs and imported goods.

store, which had happened to get a shipment of boots from somewhere in Eastern Europe that day.

Soviet Moscow was a stately, sprawling, serious place. I loved the history and grandness of it, but four years into Gorbachev's perestroika, the economy was in shambles, and people were frustrated. Upon seeing a line forming on a sidewalk, Russians would automatically join it; even if they didn't want whatever was being sold, they could use it as barter. A popular joke relayed how one Muscovite, standing in yet another queue, announced to his comrades, "Enough! I'm going to murder Gorbachev!" Twenty minutes later he returned, complaining, "The line there was even longer."

I left Moscow in April 1989. Nine months later, in January 1990, Russia's first McDonald's opened on Pushkin Square, and 30,000 people showed up for what became the largest restaurant opening in history. Less than two years later, in August 1991, Boris Yeltsin stood on a tank at Russia's White House, thwarting a coup attempt by Soviet hard-liners. And in December 1991, the Soviet Union collapsed.

So, by the time Gary and I arrived in Moscow in November 1995, Russia was nearly four years into its new, capitalist phase. The transition had been rough. The ruble had plummeted in value, wiping out people's life savings. Inflation was in triple digits, and while there was a slim layer of extremely wealthy people at the top of the economic food chain, most everyone else was struggling to make ends meet. People were freaking out about the new uncertainty afflicting their jobs, pensions, housing, education, and health care. For all the agonies they had suffered under the Soviet system, many now found themselves missing the security of it.

One of the most maddening developments for Muscovites in the nineties was the fact that although imported goods now abounded, nobody could afford to buy them. In GUM, those drab Soviet-style stores were being replaced with sparkling brand-name Western boutiques, where one pair of jeans might sell for the equivalent of a month's salary. Expensive restaurants were popping up all over the city, but few Russians could afford to eat in them. The streets, once austere and ad-free, teemed with billboards and neon, and newly wealthy Russians were tooling around in their Mercedes sedans and BMWs, while thousands of others trudged to the subway in old boots they couldn't afford to replace.

Yet for all the angst it engendered, this transitional period also brought an exciting new energy to Moscow. Artists, writers, and musicians could express themselves more freely than under Soviet rule, and there was a real sense—both refreshing and terrifying—that anything could happen. MC Pavlov rode that wave in 1995, exploring the wild new world of artistic possibilities that post-Soviet Russia had to offer.

Returning in 2005, I was struck by how much more stable Russia felt. With very few exceptions, everyone I interviewed on the trip was better off financially than they'd been ten years earlier. Most cities we visited had been spruced up—old buildings renovated, new bridges and highways built. People seemed, if not contented, then at least not as fatalistic as usual. Russia had placed a bet on an oil-based economy, and it was paying off like a slot machine spewing out silver.

Yet as improved as those other Russian cities were in 2005, nothing prepared me for what Moscow had become.

Led by Mayor Yuri Luzhkov, a bald, compact fireplug of a man, Moscow was in the midst of a construction frenzy. Manezh Square, just north of Red Square, housed a new, massive underground shopping mall, topped by a row of above-ground fast-food restaurants and a gleaming glass cupola. Cranes towered over the city, building dozens of new apartment and office buildings. The gigantic Cathedral of Christ the Savior, dynamited into oblivion by Joseph Stalin in 1931, had been rebuilt in the exact same spot, brick by brick, at a reported cost of $360 million. And a little farther down the Moscow River, artist Zurah Tsereteli had constructed a gargantuan, 320-foot-tall statue of Peter the Great.

The statue is a monstrosity. It's a life-sized sailing ship, perched atop a column of stylized waves and ship prows that resembles nothing so much as the stem of a giant mushroom cloud. Bestriding the ship's deck is a colossal Peter the Great, inexplicably dressed in Roman garb and clutching a golden scroll. As a monument to the tsar, the statue is, shall we say, of questionable artistic merit. As a monument to kitsch, it is picture-perfect, especially considering the fact that it often has a "Karaoke Party Boat" moored right in front of it.

Moscow in 2005 was like the guy who'd finally made enough money to buy the Corvette he'd wanted since high school. You're happy for him, but the Corvette smacks of overcompensation, and although it's good-looking, it's got a whiff of un-hip braggadocio to it. As David and I strolled down the New Arbat—formerly Kalininsky Prospekt, where I'd walked 17 years earlier with my alien can of Coke—I stared in amazement at all the nightclubs and garishly lit casinos, evidence of a wave of gambling that was sweeping Russia. Luxury vehicles jammed the streets in the city center, and two blocks from Red Square, Bentley and Ferrari dealerships abutted the ultrarich shopping street Tretyakovsky Pereulok. Thanks to the oil boom, Moscow had real money now—and it wanted the world to know.

In 2015, as I was making my way across Russia for the third time, I saw plenty more new construction: Vladivostok had its

two brand-new suspension bridges, Irkutsk had its newly renovated downtown, and in Novosibirsk, you could hardly see the
sky without peering through a thicket of cranes. Yet the ruble
krizis had thrown a wrench into the Russian success story.
While the people I'd met on the trip had, almost universally,
become better off between 1995 and 2005, in 2015 they fell
somewhere into the murky middle.

Moscow, however, seemed richer than ever.

—∾∾—

My train arrived in Moscow's Kazan Station at 9:30 in the morning, and as I rode in a taxi to my hotel, I was struck by a wave of
nostalgia. We passed by the beautiful baroque Yaroslavl train
station, the stylistic twin of the Vladivostok train station more
than 5,000 miles away at the other end of the track. We crossed
the massive Garden Ring Road, then the smaller Boulevard
Ring, with its grassy, tree-lined medians. Then we rode by Pushkin Square, with Russia's original McDonald's on one side and
the modernist Rossiya Theater on the other, and I remembered
walking along the plaza here in 1988, savoring one of my first
Moscow snowfalls. With a start, I realized that memory was
more than a quarter-century old.

I checked into the Marco Polo Presnja, a historic hotel within
walking distance of my old stomping grounds, the U.S. embassy.
It was also, according to Google Maps, an easy 20-minute walk
from here to Red Square, so after a quick shower, I headed out
into the brilliant autumn sunshine to explore.

Strolling through the Patriarch's Ponds neighborhood,
I couldn't believe how clean, renovated, and, well, *cheerful*
it seemed. Wine stores, restaurants, cake shops, and cafés
abounded, but instead of the air of ostentation that permeated
Moscow ten years earlier, the city felt more relaxed.

As I walked past the TASS** building, with its familiar globe and arched entryway, I gaped at a sight I'd never seen in Russia: bike lanes. A little farther down the block was another shock—a row of gleaming bicycles in a bike-share rack. Freshly painted pedestrian crosswalks allowed people to cross the street at their leisure, a big change from the sprint-for-your-life system of years past. I might as well have been in Amsterdam, or Vienna; this certainly didn't feel like the Moscow I'd known for decades. It reminded me of how New York's Times Square felt after then-mayor Rudy Giuliani swept in and "cleaned up": gleaming, wealthy, but sanitized.

After ten more minutes of strolling, I arrived at Manezh Square. The giant underground shopping mall was still there, of course, with its row of fast-food joints. I walked by a Sbarro, then found myself eyeing, of all places, McDonald's. I hadn't eaten breakfast and was starving. I couldn't remember the last time I'd eaten at a McDonald's, so in the name of research, and hunger, I headed in.

The place was a madhouse. People swarmed everywhere, crowding the cashiers' counter, hovering for tables, and waiting their turn at automated kiosks where you could order on a large touch screen and pay with a credit card. I decided to order at the counter, taking my place among a horde of people that resembled a crowd of bees pushing its way into a hive.

Waves of chatting, laughing teenagers came in, families scurried about, and tables were packed with every kind of diner imaginable—young and old, foreigners and Russians. Overall, the age skewed young, and as I hunted for a table after getting my meal, I had the unwelcome thought that most of

---

** The Telegraph Agency of the Soviet Union, or TASS, was the main newsgathering organ in Soviet times.

my fellow diners probably weren't born yet on my first visit to Moscow.

Suitably (or unsuitably) nourished, I headed back out. I walked up the cobbled passageway by the red-brick State Historical Museum and emerged onto Red Square. Even though I'd been there dozens of times, I was still struck by how beautiful, sprawling, and impressive it was. To my right was a line of people, and like a good Soviet, I immediately got in it, though I had no idea what we were queuing for. This turned out to be the line to see waxy Lenin in his tomb—one of the few elements of Moscow that, even 25 years after the fall of the Soviet Union, remains unchanged.

In the evening, I ate dinner at the Margarita Café—a restaurant I'd first visited back in 1988. It was a modest little eatery back then, serving flaky pastries and muddy coffee in thin plastic cups, popular primarily because it was near the author Mikhail Bulgakov's old apartment. In the Soviet days, Bulgakov's apartment building was a hangout for disaffected youth, who gathered to smoke, drink, and talk in a stairwell covered with graffiti homages to the author's banned masterpiece, *The Master and Margarita*. This whole area—Bulgakov's building, the streets around Patriarch's Ponds, the Margarita Café—felt like a secret haunt for the literary set, a raw and magical place where devotees could imagine themselves as characters in the novel.

By 2015, the area had officially become a monument to Bulgakov. Now there are not one, but two Bulgakov museums—one in the apartment where he lived, the other in the building next door. The two apparently compete, engaged in a spitting match over which is the "official" museum. And while graffiti still covers the stairwell walls, the scrawlings are relatively new, as the drawings and quotes from earlier generations have been

unceremoniously painted over. A few blocks away, by Patriarch's Ponds, a posted sign declares DON'T TALK TO STRANGERS—
a nod to chapter 1 of *The Master and Margarita*.

I found these changes amusing, though there was something
artificial about them too; what once was a spontaneous, unoffi
cial shrine to a beloved author now had a whiff of Disneyland to
it. As I sat in the Margarita Café, where the wobbly metal tables
and plastic plates had been replaced by polished wood, gothic
paintings, and a menu of seasonal "Russo-European" cuisine, I
pondered how we all love to pine for the old days, building them
up in memory as some kind of golden time. Then I took a few
photos with my phone, uploaded them instantly to Facebook,
tagged some friends from the embassy days, and enjoyed a real-
time cross-global conversation with people in London, New
York, Massachusetts, and Los Angeles.

—⟡—

The day I arrived in Moscow, I called MC Pavlov. We'd spoken
briefly by phone a week earlier, and now it was time to make a
plan to meet. "Oh, there's a special service happening at the Hare
Krishna temple tomorrow. We can go to that," he said, with
enthusiasm. Then he asked, "Are you married?"

This threw me. To the best of my recollection, I hadn't told
him I was gay, and while I was pretty sure he wouldn't care, it
felt weird to tell him over the phone. Besides that, it was one
thing to be gay, and quite another to actually be married; even
people who were unfazed by the first sometimes balked at the
second. So I dodged the question, saying, "It's complicated."

"Ah, OK! Sorry!" he blurted, seeming embarrassed. "I didn't
mean anything by that. It's just that the service is for women
who want to pray for their husbands. But if you don't have a husband, you can pray for a family member or a friend or whoever

you want." I told him that sounded perfect, and we made a plan to meet at 10 a.m. at the statue of Pushkin, not far from my hotel.

Arriving the next morning, I saw to my relief that Pavlov looked the same as, if not better than, he had in 2005. He appeared to have lost weight, and he smiled brightly as he handed me a long-stemmed rose. We headed off the metro speaking English together, though he struggled to come up with words. I offered to speak Russian, but he said he wanted the practice. So we chatted amiably, if slowly, on the metro, and by the time we arrived at the Krishna temple I was feeling at ease with him.

Arriving at the temple, he said, "Hey, I didn't mean to make you uncomfortable, asking if you had a husband."

"Don't worry!" I replied, smiling. "Let me explain: I am married, but I don't have a husband. I'm married to a woman."

Pavlov looked stunned, cocking his head to one side. "Wow, OK," he finally said. "So . . . who's the man?"

Now I was stunned. Had he misunderstood? "Neither of us," I replied. "There is no man. We're both women."

"Yeah, but I mean, who's the man in the relationship?"

Now I was annoyed. "Neither," I said, an edge creeping into my voice. "That's not how it works."

"Ah, OK, OK," he said, grasping my irritation. "So, let's go in!" he chirped. He held the door for me, and we entered the lobby of the temple.

Of all the people I'd worried about telling on this trip, Pavlov hadn't been one of them. As a jazz-funk musician, and a person who'd demonstrated plenty of openness to new ideas, he seemed like the kind of guy who'd be chill about it. I was dismayed, but also realized I'd made an unfair calculation. Why should I assume that a person who's grown up in an anti-gay society, who may or may not know any openly gay people himself, will automatically be accepting of it?

MC Pavlov in Moscow's Krishna Temple, 2015 (PHOTO BY LISA DICKEY)

We took off our coats and shoes and headed into the main part of the temple. He walked me around, showing me the statue of the Swami and offering me some kind of milky liquid meant to purify my system, which I declined. Then he walked me into a small side room, where the special ceremony was about to begin.

The room was filled with young women in colorful, flowing skirts, many of them wearing scarves as head coverings. They sat in a circle around a low, round table laden with trays of apples, oranges, bananas, and grapes. Pavlov, dressed in a bright yellow Hugo Boss shirt and yellow knit hat, and wearing round glasses with no lenses in them (a fashion choice, he said), sat in a corner behind the women. Apart from Pavlov, there was one other man in the room, a young, silver-haired guru in a beige robe, wearing a string of beads around his neck and a long thin braid down his back.

I sat down cross-legged among the women, and the guru opened the service by gesturing to Pavlov. "How many years ago was it?" he asked. "Seven?"

"It was sixteen years ago," Pavlov replied, then pressed his hands together in a prayerful pose.

"Sixteen years!" the guru announced, shaking his head in wonder. "Sixteen years ago, this man was hit by a bus in Thailand. He was almost killed, but we prayed for him here, and now look! He is healthy." Pavlov smiled and nodded his head, as the women pressed their hands together. He'd told me in 2005 that he credited Krishna for his recovery, and it was clear that this was taken as truth at the temple too.

The guru starting chanting, singing prayers from a book. He lit a fire in a square bowl on the table, and every few minutes he tossed on a spoonful of oil, causing it to flare dramatically. Each woman had been given a metal bowl filled with seeds, and at periodic signals from the guru, we tossed handfuls onto the altar. I'd never been to a Krishna ceremony before, and I found the rhythmic chanting mesmerizing—all the more so because it was in Sanskrit, so I couldn't understand a word of it. Staring into the fire, I found myself sliding into a more tranquil state than I'd been in for weeks.

I could have sat like that for hours, watching the fire leap and the seeds clatter onto the altar, but about ten minutes in, Pavlov took my arm and whispered, "They're opening up the altar. Come see."

When we'd entered the temple, a long curtain had obscured the main part of the sanctuary. But now, the curtain had been thrown open to reveal an ornately carved wooden altar, with colorful statues, portraits of the Swami, and a decorative wrought-metal screen with lotuses. Pavlov picked up a double-sided conga drum and started to play, while others joined in with chants and singing.

Pavlov had begun his musical career as a drummer, and his skills were apparent. For the next 20 minutes, he cast a rhythmic spell over the room as devotees prostrated themselves on the smooth wooden floor in front of the altar. He played with a fluidity and ease that belied the complicated rhythms he was producing, and as I watched him sway and chant, his eyes closed in apparent ecstasy, I could understand why he was so drawn to this place. His face was utterly relaxed, more so than I'd ever seen it.

After the services were over, we popped into the vegetarian café. Someone in the temple had handed Pavlov a coupon for two free lunches, so we went through the cafeteria line and got our meals: beet salad, tomato soup, stewed chickpeas, and fruit compote. As we sat at a table, Pavlov piped up, *"Priyatnovo appetita!"*—bon appétit, in Russian. "Do you know this phrase?" he asked. It was as if he'd already forgotten that I speak Russian.

We talked for an hour over lunch, but whenever I asked about his life now, he kept returning to the past; he never seemed to tire of talking about Zvuki Mu, Brian Eno, and the events of the eighties and nineties. I kept trying to guide him into the present, as I was truly curious about whether he was performing and recording anymore, and if not, how he made a living. But nothing worked; he wouldn't, or couldn't, focus on the here and now.

Then a woman walked up and started whispering to him. I couldn't hear what she said, but I heard his reply: "I wish I could help you, sister. But I can't. I'm in the same situation, haven't worked in six months."

Aha, I thought. Perhaps this was why he didn't want to talk about the present. I felt bad for having pressed him, and decided to back off the questioning. And just like that, he brought it up himself.

He told me that six months ago, his *Funky Time* radio show had lost its sponsor, the audio company Sennheiser. "We've been searching for a new sponsor, but they're hard to find," he said. "But I have some meetings set up." He also told me that the Intel gig had ended a few years ago, but that he was continuing to play music and work as a DJ. And then he turned back to the digressions of earlier, going on a long tangent about how he became a vegetarian, the perils of eating meat, and how I should purify my system if I wanted to have a long life.

At last, we finished lunch and walked to the metro. Looking for conversation, I brought up the unusual wallpaper he'd had in his living room back in 1995—a view of New York City's Twin Towers at night. I asked if he still had it.

"Yes," he said. "It's still there." Then he asked me where I'd been on September 11. I told him I was living in Washington, D.C., and that my then-girlfriend worked a few blocks from the Capitol building. At first, she hadn't realized the gravity of the attacks, and I'd had to convince her to leave work and come home—which she'd had to do on foot, as all public transportation was shut down in the chaos. "It was a terrible day," I told him, then added how depressed I'd felt for weeks afterward.

"I saw a documentary," he began, and in a flash of dread, I knew what was coming. "It proved that it wasn't bin Laden who brought down the towers. It was a plan by the American government . . ." I felt the air go out of me. Of all the difficult conversations I'd had with Russians on this trip, this was the one I simply couldn't take. I could readily admit that I didn't know exactly what was going on in Ukraine, and that I wasn't an expert on

Vladimir Putin or Kremlin politics or international relations. But this 9/11 truther stuff simply unhinged me.

"Don't," I said, raising my hand. "It's not true. Let's not discuss it." I made no attempt to hide my irritation—not that I could have anyway. Mercifully, the next stop was mine, and I gave Pavlov a quick hug goodbye.

—∾—

The next morning, I woke up to an in-box of e-mails from Pavlov. They were full of links and attachments to articles written about him in the 1990s—including, oddly, my own article about him that had been published in 1996 in the *Moscow Times*. I spent a long time in my hotel room, reading, watching clips, and trying to figure out what to do next. Pavlov still felt like an enigma, and I wasn't sure that meeting again would provide clarity. But I wanted to try.

I'd hoped to see him perform—either as a DJ, or a drummer, or a rapper—but he didn't have anything lined up for the week I was in Moscow. So we made a plan instead to go to a concert: his old Zvuki Mu bandmate Pyotr Mamonov was putting on a comeback show, with a new group called Otzvuki Mu.[††] I asked Pavlov if we could also get together before the concert, since it was a few days away, but he told me he was busy with meetings.

So now I had a couple of days on my own to further explore Moscow. I took the metro out to VDNKh, the site of the Soviet Union's once-proud Exhibitions of the Achievements of the National Economy. I remembered coming here in 1988, expecting to see a proud monument to Soviet production, and being

---

[††] Literally, "From Zvuki Mu." Not to be confused with "The Brand New Zvuki Mu," which is another offshoot of the original Zvuki Mu band.

surprised at how run-down and sad the place felt then. My most vivid memory was of a claw machine, a glass box with a mechanical claw you could manipulate to pick up a prize; the most coveted treasure, as far as I could tell from watching Soviets playing the game, was a dusty, capless tube of toothpaste.

As I wandered around the pavilions of VDNKh now, the place was gleaming. I watched tourists take selfies in front of the Lenin statue and skateboarders whiz by in the late autumn sun, and I snacked on a *ponchik*—a deep-fried, thoroughly addictive Russian donut—and coffee. Later, I popped into the nearby Memorial Museum of Cosmonautics to see Belka and Strelka, the first two dogs to go into orbit and return alive; the dogs, who became folk heroes in Russia, have been stuffed and put on display next to the capsule that took them into space. Hours later, I finally made my way to the metro, and as I boarded a train to head back into the city center, I happened to pick a car that was set up as an art exhibition, with sketches and drawings from the Russian Geographical Society hanging on the wall across from a bench of passengers, many of whom were staring at their phones, taking advantage of the free metro-wide Wi-Fi. Moscow just kept surprising me.

On my last night in the city, Pavlov came to meet me at the hotel. Once again, he brought me a flower—a giant bird-of-paradise, a wildly exotic bloom for November in Russia. I stashed it up in my room, and we headed to the concert, which was in a hall at the House of Artists, not far from the towering Roman-toga statue of Peter the Great. We filed into the auditorium with hundreds of other fans, and for about an hour, we watched and listened as bald, gravelly voiced Pyotr Mamonov thrilled the crowd with his poetic songs, computer-generated backup music, and minimalist guitar in a show that was equal parts performance art and music. Pavlov knew a few other people there, and it was good to see him in his element, talking about music and reminiscing about his Zvuki Mu days.

I left for St. Petersburg the next morning, so that concert was the last time I saw him. And in the end, I wasn't completely sure what to make of MC Pavlov, circa 2015. I could never figure out how much performing he did, or whether the loss of his *Funky Time* radio show had been as big a financial blow as I feared. I felt a little obsessed with these questions, though it appeared I might never get an answer to them.

Not long after I returned to Los Angeles, Pavlov sent me an invitation to connect on LinkedIn, of all things. I had to laugh; it was as if he'd looked into my soul and seen my existential angst over his professional life. On his page, he was listed as the founder of Pav-Love Muzik and an instructor at the Rainbow Music Agency, though it wasn't clear whether he made a living from either of them. Then, a few months after that, he sent me a link to a four-minute video of himself playing and rapping with a keyboardist named Pavel Hotin. And that cleared everything up. Because as I watched Pavlov jamming at a tiny synthesizer, dressed in a bright yellow shirt and pink newsboy cap, bobbing his head joyfully to the beat, I realized I was being ridiculous to worry. Whatever happened, MC Pavlov was still making great music. He was still *teaching the people*.

—ᴍ—

St. Petersburg: Five Generations

O N NOVEMBER 4, 2015, I ARRIVED IN ST. PETERSBURG—
the place where, 20 years earlier, this whole adventure had
begun with a random e-mail from Gary Matoso. Back then, I
was a desperate young would-be writer, unsure if I'd ever find
my way into print. Now, fittingly, I was returning to my favorite
city in the world, ready to write a book about the experiences
that began and were ending here.

St. Petersburg always felt like home. I'd lived here for two
and a half years in the mid-nineties, and despite epic winter cold
and darkness, the city's magic had captured me. With its meandering canals, Italianate architecture, and Tsarist-era splendor,
there was beauty wherever one's gaze happened to fall. The
city's tragic history during World War II, when German troops

surrounded the city for 872 days, choking off food supplies and starving more than a million people, infused it with a steely survivor's mentality. St. Petersburg felt heroic, strong, enduring. And one of the things I loved most about it was the sense that history lurked around every corner.

At the end of our 1995 trip, Gary and I decided to try to capture some of that history. A Russian friend of mine named Boris had offered to introduce us to his great-grandmother Maria Mikhailovna, a tiny but sturdy woman of 98 who had vivid memories of growing up in tsarist times. This was an amazing, vanishingly rare opportunity to hear firsthand about pre-Revolutionary Russia, and we jumped at the chance.

We spoke with Maria Mikhailovna, then interviewed her 72-year-old daughter Lia, who'd served in Leningrad during World War II; then Lia's daughter-in-law Nina, who'd grown up during the space race era; Nina's son Boris, who'd come of age during the collapse of the Soviet Union; and finally, Maria Mikhailovna's great-great-grandson from another branch of the family tree, Vanya. At the age of six, little Vanya was poised at the edge of a new century, just as Maria Mikhailovna had been as a child nearly 100 years earlier.

To understand Russia today, one must look at what its people lived through in the twentieth century. This was our attempt to tell the story of that century, through the eyes of one family.

—◊—

Maria Mikhailovna Gurevich was born on December 25, 1896, to Russian Jewish parents in the Black Sea town of Feodosiya. "My father was in the working class," she told me, "and my mother stayed home to take care of the children. We had a big family, but we never went hungry, even though we didn't have very much money. Mama knew how to take care of us." Her

*Five generations of a Leningrad/St. Petersburg family: 98-year-old
Maria Mikhailovna, WWII veteran Lia, physician Nina, psychology
student Boris, and 6-year-old Vanya, 1995* (PHOTO BY GARY MATOSO)

mother eventually bore seven children; Maria Mikhailovna was
the eldest.

She was eight years old, studying at a grammar school named
for Tsar Alexander II, when the first rumblings of revolution
began. Labor strikes flared in the faraway capital of St. Petersburg, and on January 22, 1905, Imperial Guards opened fire on
an unarmed crowd of protestors, killing and wounding hundreds. News of the "Bloody Sunday" massacre spread quickly,

provoking violent protests across Russia. "I remember sitting on the roof of my house in Feodosiya and watching fires burn across the city," she recalled of that time, which Leon Trotsky later dubbed the "dress rehearsal for the revolution."

In 1913, the family moved to the Crimean city of Kerch. Maria Mikhailovna was now a pretty, dark-haired young woman of 16, and suitors soon came calling. In 1914, a soldier in the Tsar's army named Naum Ilyich Schneider proposed with the words, "Let's get married or not get married, but I'm tired of just coming over for tea." The couple wed, but their marital bliss was short-lived; Russia had entered World War I, and Naum Ilyich was almost immediately sent to the front to fight.

As Maria Mikhailovna recalled:

> We knew he had to go fight, but we thought we'd have a little bit of time together first. He left two days after we married, and I didn't see him again for almost three years.
>
> He was wounded very badly in the war, hit in the leg with an exploding bullet. One doctor wanted to amputate, but another said it wasn't necessary. He suffered terribly. But in the end, they didn't amputate. I remember when I saw him for the first time after he came back. He had recovered in a hospital in Odessa, but was still in very bad shape.
>
> I was only sixteen when we married, just a girl. But when he came back, I was a young woman. When they told me he was coming, I put on a special dress for the occasion, and a new hat, and then rushed over to see him.
>
> I could not believe what I saw. He was so thin and ragged-looking, and he'd lost some of his teeth. He

was ten years older than I, and he looked to me at that moment like an old man. I thought, *Is this really my husband?*

For any soldier, returning home from a bloody battle must come as a relief—but the country to which Naum Ilyich returned was in chaos. In February 1917, armed revolutionaries overthrew the Russian government, and a month later, Tsar Nicholas II abdicated his throne; the Russian empire was collapsing. In October of that same year, the Bolsheviks, led by Vladimir Lenin, seized control and declared Russia the first "Soviet Federative Socialist Republic." But not all Russians supported the Reds, as they were called, and anti-Bolshevik factions known as the Whites rose up to battle them. Now, in addition to the fighting in Europe, Russia was plunged into a violent civil war—another conflict that nearly took Naum Ilyich's life:

> We were living in Kerch. The Whites had taken the city, and the Reds had retreated to hide in catacombs in the mountains nearby. The Whites stormed through the city, looking for young men to take away with them.
>
> They came into our building, grabbed my husband in the stairwell and started to drag him away. I came running out with our newborn daughter in one arm, and grabbed him with the other. I refused to let him go. I knew that most of the men who were taken away would never return.
>
> They were furious that I wouldn't let him go, and burst into our apartment to look for weapons. They started throwing things out of the bookshelves and closets. Suddenly, my husband's Order of St. George

medal that he had won in the war fell out. When they
saw that, they let him go. That medal saved his life.

The Russian Civil War raged for five years. When it ended in
1922, the Bolsheviks were in power, and Vladimir Lenin established himself as leader of the new Soviet Union. Although the
USSR was envisioned as a Communist state, Lenin launched
reforms known as the New Economic Policy, or NEP, under
which certain people—called NEPmen—were allowed to en-
gage in small-scale private enterprise to help reinvigorate the
shattered economy.

Naum Ilyich became a NEPman. He ran a private mill in the
early 1920s, which enabled the young family—now with three
children—to enjoy a comfortable life. But comfort was fleeting: after Lenin's death in 1924, new Soviet leader Joseph Stalin
abolished NEP and launched a violent backlash against NEP-
men, who were branded as dirty capitalists. The children of
NEPmen were denied entrance to kindergartens, so Lia, the
couple's youngest child, was forced to take her mother's maiden
name of Gurevich. To her father's shame and distress, Lia never
took back his name.

Stalin launched the first of his Five-Year Plans in 1928, rush-
ing to industrialize the country at a terrible cost, eventually
plunging large swaths of the Soviet Union into famine. Naum
Ilyich, whose private mill had been seized, found work in a
quarry, where he was forced to labor 16-hour days for meager
pay. Maria Mikhailovna did her best to feed the children, but the
family had very little; when Lia fell ill with typhus, her father fed
her noodles brought home from his quarry rations.

These were terrible times, and they got worse in 1930 when
Naum Ilyich hurt his shoulder in an accident. No longer able to
work at the quarry, and with no other employment prospects, he

took the dramatic step of leaving his wife and children in Kerch and heading north to Leningrad, in hopes of finding work there.

By now, the young family had already endured war, famine, and devastating economic privation. Then, the Terror began.

Throughout the 1930s, Stalin stoked fear and paranoia across Russia, ordering the arrest, imprisonment, and execution of millions of people, often for no reason at all. In 1932, Maria Mikhailovna's father became one of those arrested when, after noticing a shortage of whistles at the factory where he worked, he'd melted down five-kopek pieces to get enough copper to make new ones. He was charged with the crime of defacing the Soviet seal—the hammer and sickle on the melted coins— and thrown into prison. Yet he was one of the lucky ones, serving just three months for his "crime."

—⌇⌇—

That same year, Naum Ilyich finally scraped together enough money to bring Maria Mikhailovna to Leningrad. She brought their eldest daughter and left the other two children, including Lia, in Kerch with their grandparents. Two years would pass before she could afford to return for the younger two children.

When she did come back, "she brought a suitcase filled with treats for us," recalled Lia, who was a robust, plainspoken woman of 72 when she told me this story. "White bread and buns. I hadn't seen white bread in ages. It was the best thing I had ever tasted."

The late 1930s were a terrifying time for many Russians, but a happy time for Lia. Her family was together at last, living just outside Leningrad in the village of Levashovo. She was a bright young student with hopes of studying at Leningrad State University, a goal she achieved in 1940, enrolling in the university's history department.

Yet once again, comfort was fleeting. During her first year at the university, her father was arrested at their home in Levashovo. When I asked why, she responded dryly, "You don't ask that question in Russia. Nobody was arrested for anything sensible; people were just arrested. They didn't have to have a reason." Naum Ilyich was thrown into a Leningrad prison.

Lia forged ahead with her studies, even as she began hearing alarming reports of Nazi advances throughout Europe. Stalin and Hitler had signed a nonaggression pact in 1939, and the Soviet Union continued to go about its business in the vain belief that Hitler would honor the pact. But on June 22, 1941, the Germans invaded Russia.

"I will never forget that day," Lia told me.

> It was early Sunday morning when they attacked, and one of their planes was shot down between Levashovo and Leningrad. Of course, everybody went to see it, just like we were going to a show. We had an exam scheduled for the next day, and when everyone found out I had seen a shot-down German plane, they wanted to hear all about it.
>
>   It was exciting for us; we didn't really know what war was. But I remember the sad eyes of my professor. He gave everyone a top mark on the exam that day, because he knew grades didn't mean anything anymore. He knew what was coming. He ended up starving during the blockade.
>
>   I didn't know what war was back then. But I know now.

The whole of Leningrad was soon to learn, in one of the most tragic episodes of modern warfare. By the fall of 1941, the city was almost entirely cut off by encircling German troops. When planes bombed the food warehouses, there was virtually nothing for Leningraders to eat. Hundreds of thousands of people would starve or freeze to death before the nearly 900-day blockade was broken.

Like most of her fellow university students, Lia volunteered for the army; she was sent to the outskirts of Leningrad to erect anti-tank barriers. "We wore white uniforms and hats, and Nazi planes would fly over and shoot at us," she recalled. "Many young women died that way. And they would drop leaflets on us, telling us to give up fighting them. I still have some of those leaflets."

In the grueling winter of 1941–42, when the death toll in Leningrad was the highest, Lia worked at the hospital in Levashovo registering the sick, wounded, and starving. "I worked there until I couldn't stand it anymore," she told me. "After a while it was just too much to bear."

> The day I quit, a man who was starving to death had come in. He was begging for something to drink. "Give me some water! Please!" he kept saying, but the doctors said he was too starved and ill to drink. He needed treatment.
>
> But the man dragged himself over to a sink in the corner and suddenly started drinking straight from the cistern, in great gulps. What happened next, I could hardly bear to watch. He started convulsing, screaming, and vomiting, the water coming right back out of him. He died right there, by the sink. After that day, I never worked again at the hospital.
>
> It was a horrible, horrible time. Everywhere, people were dying of hunger and cold. You would

walk down the street and hear a child crying, because
his mother had just dropped dead beside him. Whole
families died.

In Levashovo, there was a warehouse that we used
to make into a dance hall for the young people during
the summer. That winter, we used it as a morgue.
People just dragged their dead loved ones and left
them there. And the worst thing of all, sometimes
people would find bodies there with parts cut out of
them. Cheeks, or thighs . . . People cut out human
meat to sell at the markets, or to feed themselves.

Though these events had taken place a half century earlier, it
was clear from Lia's expression that the memories remained
painfully vivid. I'd read about the horrors of the blockade, but
hearing about them from a woman who'd witnessed them firsthand was chilling.

Lia was next called into service as a radio operator, working
with the brave souls who flew over Leningrad in dirigibles to
report the movements of Nazi troops. One of those flyers, a
young man named Anatoly Shalyopa, became her husband in
December 1944, after the blockade had been lifted from Leningrad, but before the end of the war.

At the memory of May 9, 1945—the day of Germany's
surrender—Lia's eyes lit up.

I was up at the university. There was a whole crowd
of people there. We all knew the announcement was
going to come, and we all were just waiting, ready to
burst with joy. We waited and waited, and finally the
announcement came. Everyone was crying and

cheering, kissing and hugging, even people who didn't
know each other.

You have to understand what we had been
through. You have to understand the suffering that the
people of this city endured, to understand the feeling
that we had on that day. There have been only two
days like that in my entire life. The first was Victory
Day, and the second was the day my son was born.

The war was finally over. Lia's father had been freed from
prison, and the family was, miraculously, alive and intact. But
Lia's marriage didn't last long, as the union forged between her
and Anatoly Shalyopa in the bonds of war soon proved unten-
able in everyday life. She left her husband shortly after the birth
of Gennady, her only child, in 1946.

Lia finished her studies at Leningrad State University in
1948, and in 1950 she was invited to serve as a history lecturer
at a Soviet military institute in China. She accepted and was preparing to go when her father died. Naum Ilyich, who'd survived
a revolution, two world wars, combat wounds, and years in
prison, finally succumbed to heart failure at the age of 64.

After her father's funeral, Lia left for China, taking little
Gennady with her. "I enjoyed living in China," she told me.
"Relations between the USSR and China were relatively good at
the time, and it was interesting to experience another culture."
Lia and her son lived in a compound with other Soviets, but
they took every opportunity to explore Chinese culture during
their four years there.

In 1953, while they were in China, Stalin died. "Everyone
acted as though it was this great tragedy," Lia told me. "But I was
not sad. I knew too well what Stalin was."

—ᴍ—

Thousands of miles away, back in Leningrad, an eight-year-old girl stood among her schoolmates as their teacher announced that Stalin had died. She watched with dry eyes as the teacher hung a portrait of the leader, while her fellow students sniffled and wept.

The girl's name was Nina Gorelik, and in the late 1960s, she would marry Lia's son Gennady. But on this day, she was still just a little girl—one who wasn't sure what to make of all the fuss upon the death of the Soviet leader.

"My grandmother always hated Stalin," she told me.

> She called him the anti-Christ. But my mother and father loved him. When they would broadcast one of Stalin's speeches on the radio, my father would say to my sister and me, "Come listen, children! You may never get a chance to meet Comrade Stalin, but you need to listen when he speaks." My sister and I were never quite sure what to think.
>
> Grandmother wasn't afraid to criticize Stalin, but she always said to us, "Walls have ears. If you repeat what I tell you, they'll take you away and you'll never see your family or your home again." The whole time I was growing up, I had this vision of walls being gigantic ears.

In 1954, Nina's family moved to Tallinn, Estonia, when the army stationed her father there. Though Soviet slogans trumpeted the "brotherhood of nations" and "friendship between peoples" of the USSR, Nina found the Estonians, whose country

Stalin had annexed less than 15 years earlier, antagonistic toward Russians.

"Russians and Estonians went to separate schools," she recalled, "and we always made sure not to walk by the Estonian school, because the kids would taunt us and try to start fights. Before we moved to Tallinn, I didn't even know what another nationality was. But I found out quickly enough that I was different from the Estonian kids.

"I always felt like a second-class citizen in Estonia, and made up my mind during that time that I would never live anywhere but Russia again. We lived there more than ten years, but it never felt like home."

In 1956, Soviet leader Nikita Khrushchev made his "secret speech" to the Twentieth Party Congress, boldly denouncing Stalin and his reign of terror. The period that followed came to be known as the "thaw," as thousands of political prisoners were released, and the atmosphere in Russia became slightly more open.

"There was a different feeling in the air," said Nina. "Students started coming to the USSR from Africa and the Arab states, and people felt more free to talk openly." But even with this thaw, old habits of fear and secrecy remained. Although Nina's parents both professed belief in God, they were afraid to go to the Russian Orthodox church in Tallinn. Even so, Nina went occasionally with her grandmother. "She used to say, 'Let them shoot me, but I will have icons in my house,'" said Nina, who now had a row of icons in her own home.

One day in 1961, when Nina was in her ninth-grade math class, the teacher was called out of the room. When she returned, her eyes were bright with excitement. "Children!" she announced with pride, "Man is in space!" Soviet cosmonaut Yuri Gagarin had orbited the earth in the first-ever manned space flight.

"I was so proud," Nina recalled. "I was the kind of child who cried whenever Soviet athletes won international awards and our flag was raised. I loved my country so much! So when the first man in space was a Soviet man, it made the achievement that much better."

Yet the idealistic young Komsomolka got a dose of cynicism when she went to her first open Communist Party meeting. "I was so nervous. I thought it would be this monumental gathering, where people discussed ideas and really did the work of the Party. But when I got there, nobody was paying attention; people were milling about, reading, playing chess. It was farcical.

"I knew from that time that there was nothing to strive for in the Communist system," she concluded. "If that was what Party meetings were about, there was no reason to want to belong."

As Nina grew older, her cynicism deepened. When applying for admittance to the Leningrad Medical Institute, she wrote as her essay a scathing indictment of Soviet slogans. Thanks to her childhood experiences in Estonia, she viewed them as mindless and hypocritical.

> Those slogans made me sick! "Long live friendship between nations!" "Long live the Soviet brotherhood!"
> So I wrote a critique. When my aunt found out about it, she said, "The black raven is going to come for you," meaning the black Volga sedans that came for people who were to be arrested.
> But nothing bad resulted from that essay. In fact, I got the highest marks.

While studying at the medical institute, Nina met Gennady Shalyopa. The couple married in 1969, and within a few years they had two sons, Boris and Andrey. Life in the 1970s, during Brezhnev's "period of stagnation," was for the most part uneventful. "There were no long lines in the 1970s, no terrible shortages," remembered Nina. "Not in Moscow and Leningrad, anyway. Other parts of Russia had more difficulties as far as getting food products, but things here were fine. We lived modestly, but well."

This was, perhaps, the calmest period of the Soviet century. Yet Russians in the 1970s were still careful not to say the wrong things to the wrong people.

> We didn't tell anecdotes on the trams, where someone might hear. Things weren't nearly so paranoid as in the Stalin years, but all the same, people weren't free to say whatever they wanted.
>
> Once I went to my uncle's house to visit. He had a friend over, and we all sat around drinking wine. I told a political joke—nothing terrible, just poking a little fun. My uncle laughed, but his friend looked at me and said very seriously, "That's not funny. They put people in jail for jokes like that. And rightly so."

The seventies were a time when Soviets passed around mimeographed copies of banned writings and shared cassette tapes with fuzzy recordings of Western bands. "Of course I read banned literature whenever I could," said Nina. "But I wouldn't say it was something I was obsessed with. There was a lot of good literature that could be had legally."

In 1979, when Nina was offered a position as the head of a city medical department, she was invited to join the Communist Party. She declined. "Part of the reason I turned them down," she told me, "is because I didn't want that job. In those days, it was impossible to take a job like that without joining the Party . . . Who knows what I would have done if I had really wanted it? Even I don't know.

"The idea of Communism itself is not bad," she said. "But the fulfillment of it in this country was very, very bad. Once I realized that, I didn't want to have anything to do with it. I remained very apolitical."

—⟨∽⟩—

In the early 1980s, the quick, successive deaths of aged apparatchiks Leonid Brezhnev, Yuri Andropov, and Konstantin Chernenko paved the way for new leadership in the Soviet Union. U.S. president Ronald Reagan began to escalate Cold War rhetoric, and Russia's future looked uncertain. But no one realized just how uncertain until Mikhail Gorbachev came to power in 1985 and started shaking up the government.

"Gorbachev spoke without notes; he just talked. That was the amazing thing," said Nina's son Boris, who was 15 when Gorbachev came to power. "He was young and dynamic, not like Brezhnev, who could barely speak. We had a sense that he would fight against the things that we didn't like about the Soviet Union, and everybody began to be interested in politics."

The twin policies of perestroika (restructuring) and glasnost (openness) became part of the world lexicon, and things began changing quickly in the creaking behemoth of the USSR. For young people like Boris, the transformation was exhilarating. "When Gorbachev initiated perestroika, I thought, *It's about time!*" he told me.

But that enthusiasm turned to disillusionment in the late eighties, years that saw terrible food shortages all over Russia. When Gorbachev declared limits on alcohol production, sugar disappeared from store shelves, snatched up as a vital ingredient in homemade liquor. There were also chronic shortages of butter, flour, tea, and other essentials.

"In the end," said Boris, a handsome, bearded man with a passing resemblance to Billy Crystal, "Gorbachev himself became a barrier to the reforms he started. He was afraid to do more. He lost control of the situation." By the early 1990s, Gorbachev had lost control altogether, and in 1991 he resigned his presidency and dissolved the Soviet Union.

For Boris, the fall of the Soviet Union was no tragedy. "The USSR was an artificially created entity; Kazakhs, Azeris, and other nationalities that were brought into the Soviet Union are completely unrelated to Russians," he said. "They should have their own countries." During the putsch attempt of 1993, when members of the Russian parliament attempted to overthrow President Yeltsin, Boris went to St. Petersburg's Mariinsky Square, where hundreds of people gathered to listen for news from Moscow. After initial anxiety, he decided everything would be fine after noticing "how calm everyone was on the square. Nobody was yelling, or panicking. The whole place was quiet."

Now, Boris said, "Things are better than they were five years ago. The ghost of hunger has disappeared from Russia. If you work, you can earn money, and now you can buy everything here. Yes, there are some pensioners who are suffering, but Russia is enduring growing pains now. It's all part of the historical process. Some will suffer, some will die, but the process itself is unstoppable."

—⁂—

Six-year-old Vanya was born in 1989, as the Soviet Union was wheezing toward its final collapse. When I met him in 1995, his father Dima worked as a distributor of wholesale eyeglasses and his mother, Zhenya, sold Mary Kay cosmetics. His parents planned for Vanya, then in kindergarten, to go to a special school the following year, where students took intensive courses in English—the "language of the twenty-first century," as they called it.

Gary snapped photos as Vanya's great-great-grandmother, Maria Mikhailovna, stretched out her gnarled old hands to pull him close. "Come here," she said, taking his small, smooth hand in hers. "He's a good boy, a smart boy," she said of the child 92 years her junior. "Who knows what the future will be like for this country? But he will do well."

Ten years later, as I prepared to meet with 16-year-old Vanya, I wondered if his great-great-grandmother's prediction would turn out to be true.

—⌇⌇—

When David and I arrived in St. Petersburg in 2005, I called Boris. He had moved into his grandmother Lia's apartment, overlooking the House of Soviets office complex in the south of the city, and he invited us to come for a visit with him and his mother, Nina. The apartment looked much the same as it did a decade earlier, with the small kitchen virtually unchanged and the walls in one room covered with framed photos of Maria Mikhailovna, Lia, and other family members. Boris made tea, and he and his mother gave me updates on the family.

Maria Mikhailovna died four months after our interview, at age 99. The night before she died, she had enjoyed a few sips of cognac with a family friend who'd stopped by; when someone told her she shouldn't be drinking at her age, she'd snapped, "As long as I'm alive, I'll do what I want!" She had hoped to live to see the first day of spring in 1996, but she missed it by one day.

Lia, too, was gone, having succumbed at age 76 to complications from hypertension. She died in this very apartment, in Nina's arms, after months of being ill. "She didn't want to see anyone, or to eat," Nina told me. "She just lay in her bed. I'd say, 'Do you want to listen to music?' and she'd tell me with her eyes." At the memory, Nina's own eyes welled up. "She was very demanding in life, but in death she was just the opposite. She just lay in her bed as I took care of her."

Nina was still working as a physician, at the same polyclinic as in 1995. But she told me that life had "gotten worse. I have so much paperwork now, there's no time to work with the patients. It has become a nightmare." She'd traveled abroad often over the past ten years, visiting France, Spain, Austria, and India, among other places. But the onetime disenchanted Komsomolka still expressed a firm patriotic preference for Russia. "No place is as beautiful as St. Petersburg," she told me. "No museum is as beautiful as the Hermitage."

Boris was working as a psychologist, and in the decade since we'd seen each other, he'd married and gotten divorced. Characteristically, he didn't want to talk much about himself, but instead turned the conversation to Vanya, who was now 16. When I'd met six-year-old Vanya in 1995, he was entering a special school for intensive English language study. Now in his final year of high school, he could speak English with ease.

I decided to make Vanya the centerpiece of the ten-years-later story. And not just Vanya, but his fellow classmates too—young people who had no memory of Soviet times, who were now the future of Russia. I arranged to meet him at a restaurant near his school and asked him to invite some friends to join us.

Vanya was tall, ruddy-cheeked, athletic, and polite enough to field my multitude of questions. In return, all he wanted was a decent translation of a White Stripes song title: "What does

Boris, Vanya, Nina, and Vanya's mother Zhenya, 2005 (PHOTO BY
DAVID HILLEGAS)

'Seven Nation Army' mean?" he asked me. "I can't figure it out."
Sadly, I wasn't sure either, but he graciously agreed to continue
with the interview.

He brought three classmates: mop-haired, mustachioed
Misha; sober Pasha; and shy, curly-haired Tonya—all 16-year-old
students at the Gymnasium for Global Education No. 631. We
met for lunch at a Chinese restaurant, which seemed an appropriately global choice, and for the next hour we talked—in
English—about their hopes, dreams, and fears.

I came into the interview with certain expectations. Having
just completed my 2005 trip across Russia, and having seen
how much better people's lives and economic situations were, I
expected Vanya and his friends to be optimistic about the
future. But from the start, their responses surprised me.

When I asked how Russia had changed over the last ten
years, Tonya spoke first. "The first thing that's changed is the

mind of the people," she said. "Now they don't live for the country; they live for themselves. There's no united country, like there was in Soviet times."

"There's a difference between the relations of people and the government in Russia," Pasha added. "In the USSR, the government was very attentive to people, to their interests. Practically 99 percent of people had higher education.* Education in the USSR was free to all: if you passed exams, you could go to any university you liked. But nowadays it's difficult to enter, because the universities don't have good support from the government."

He went on. "The second thing is, in Russia today, of course we have more freedom. In the USSR, there were a lot of rules people had to follow, but now the rules are minimized. I think that's good." But he did bemoan one development: "There was no such thing as poverty then, but nowadays a lot of people are below the poverty line. It is a problem."

"In our lives now, maybe we have more freedom," Misha chimed in. "But I think we don't need this freedom, because we don't know what to do after university. In the Soviet Union, if you wanted to choose a career, you went to the university and then to work. Nowadays, you can go anywhere—but you don't know what to do. Making a choice is difficult."

Vanya added, "In the Soviet Union, we were like one big society that just tried to solve our own problems with the help of our neighbors. We have democracy now, but it hasn't been developed in the right way."

What did they think the future held? Would the situation in Russia get better, or worse?

"Worse," Misha said, without hesitation. "Practically all the

---

*In 1989, near the end of the Soviet era, the census showed that 64 percent of Soviets had completed secondary education, while 23 percent had completed higher education.

economics in our country is influenced by the course of oil prices. And now we're exporting to practically every country. So, when fuel oil in our country is finished, it will be a very big problem. I think the problems will start in six years, and then in sixty years, we'll have no more oil left."

Misha's pessimism about Russia's one-note economy would prove prescient ten years later—though not because oil was running out, but because a global glut would drive down prices. I expressed surprise that the students were so concerned about oil running out, as I wasn't aware this was a serious concern during our lifetimes. All the students believed it would, however, and Pasha added that he'd read all about it on the Internet.

"Are you all really as pessimistic as you sound?" I asked.

"Not pessimistic," Misha replied. "Just realistic."

Pasha did venture that Russia would become the leader of the world in information technology (IT), which he called "the future of society." "The Russian government has taken steps to achieve this," he told me. "In St. Petersburg, we're building a center of information technology. We'll have the best programmers and specialists. Science is the future of the Russian federation."

"There will be pluses and minuses in the future," Vanya concluded. "Perhaps more pluses. And while people are pessimistic, or realistic, I think they will still try their best to keep Russia strong."

So, where did they think they'd all be in ten years? All four students said they hoped to be living and working in Russia. "I like my country very much," Pasha said, "and I will stay and work only here. Because I want my country to be the best country."

Vanya was more circumspect. "It's a difficult question for me. If I become an engineer, which I hope, I think there's a 90 percent chance I'll be here. I think that Russia is developing not only its

high-tech industry, but construction too, so I hope I'll be able
to find a good job here."

Ten years later, it was time to find out if Vanya's hope had
come true.

—∽—

The night I arrived in St. Petersburg, I checked my iPhone's
weather app to find that the only sunny afternoon in the entire
coming week would be the following day. St. Petersburg is noto-
rious for its wildly changing weather, but the row of uninter-
rupted raincloud icons convinced me that before I sought out
Boris, Nina, and Vanya, I should take that one precious sunny
day to explore.

I took the metro to bustling Nevsky Prospekt, the city's main
thoroughfare, and happily began strolling. St. Petersburg had
been spruced up since I lived here in the mid-nineties, but unlike Moscow, it didn't feel radically changed. I walked past the
Griboyedov Canal, with its onion-domed Church on Spilled
Blood (named after the spot upon which Tsar Alexander II was
killed by an assassin's bomb), then past Dom Knigi, with its rows
of books displayed in the windows. Across the street, the Kazan
Cathedral gleamed in the sun, and a few blocks later, I passed
by the Moika Canal and the Literaturnoye Café, where Alexander Pushkin was said to have had his last meal before being shot
to death in a duel. The café had been there forever, but it did have
one new element: a mannequin wearing eighteenth-century
garb and a curly Pushkin wig had been propped at a window
table.

A block farther, I turned right to walk toward the massive
arch leading to Palace Square. Emerging onto the cobblestoned
expanse, I saw the brilliant aqua-colored Hermitage and the
soaring Alexander Column, topped by an angel bearing a cross.

I'd always loved this glorious, historic vista, but now I noticed something unusual. The low metal fence surrounding the column was covered with piles of flowers, stuffed animals, religious icons, candles, and, most wrenchingly, photographs of smiling people and agonized notes of farewell.

This was a spontaneous memorial to the victims of Russia's Metrojet flight 9268, which had crashed into the Sinai Desert a few days earlier. At the time, rumors abounded that the crash was the result of a terrorist attack, though the Russian government had yet to officially conclude as much. The plane had been en route from Egypt to St. Petersburg, and most of the 224 victims were from the city and its environs.

I walked across the square and past the Little Hermitage, with its massive marble Atlas statues holding up the portico. Following the curving Moika Canal, I again walked past the Church on Spilled Blood, then strolled through the Mikhailovsky Garden and crossed the Fontanka River into the neighborhood where I'd lived during those early, frustrating years of trying to become a writer. I turned left to walk up Mokhovaya Street, then stopped in front of my old building, No. 12. On the first floor of the building next door was a tiny 24-hour store, where I used to buy dill-flavored potato chips, Baltika beer, and Orbit gum. The store had also carried an item that became a staple of my 1990s Russian diet: bags of frozen broccoli.

Broccoli was a true rarity back then; I could remember having Boris and his friend Max over for dinner one night, and Max peering at the tiny green trees in wonder. He'd never had broccoli before, he told me—in fact, he'd never even seen it. He speared a piece with his fork, then held it up while giving the thumbs-up sign with his other hand. I snapped a picture—one of few that I have from that time, in the days before anyone but Gary Matoso had a digital camera.

I decided to pop into the store to see if, 20 years on, they still carried frozen broccoli. To my surprise, they did. I laughed aloud, then, feeling self-conscious, told the woman behind the counter what was so funny.

"I'm American, but I lived in building No. 12 20 years ago," I said. "I used to buy broccoli right here in this store."

She looked shocked. "This store was open twenty years ago?"

At that, another woman emerged from a back room. "Yes," she said. "We opened in the summer of 1995." Then she smiled and added, "Welcome back."

———

The next day, I saw Boris. Now 45, he'd lost most of his hair, and what was left was rapidly graying. Apart from that, he looked unchanged; he was still lithe and fit, and he still reminded me of Billy Crystal.

We hadn't seen each other in ten years, so I expected we'd spend time catching up. Instead, Boris launched into a detailed recitation of his feelings about—of all things—global warming. He declared that climate change is cyclical, and that what the world is experiencing now is nothing more than the natural result of such cycles. "Do you know why Greenland is called Greenland?" he asked. I shook my head. "Because back when it was discovered, thanks to a cyclical warming period, it *was* green."

He, like Rock-n-Roll Dima in Irkutsk, also posited that volcanoes had released far more CO_2 into the atmosphere than humans ever could. "And anyway," he went on, "CO_2 isn't harmful. How can it be, when we drink sodas with CO_2 bubbles in them and don't die?" I had no answer for this. Or perhaps I did, but I didn't see the point of arguing. It hardly mattered, anyway, because now Boris switched topics, to GMOs and hormones in food. He asked if I'd ever heard of "dark rice," which I hadn't, and he proceeded to explain that it's rice treated with beta carotene, which the human body needs, though it's less good for you, because it's modified, and then I don't know what else because honestly I started to zone out.

I couldn't figure out why Boris was leaping so suddenly, and vehemently, into these subjects. I liked Boris; back in the nineties, we'd been good friends, and I remembered having all kinds of fascinating conversations with him. He was well-read, curious, and articulate, and I'd always found it interesting to hear his take on various subjects. But now, whether it was my exhaustion and waning patience at the end of a long trip, or some tone-deafness on his part, we weren't connecting at all.

Next he brought up World War II, venturing that he wasn't a fan of Russia's big Victory Day celebrations. This was truly unexpected; if you can't celebrate a victory over Adolf Hitler, especially when that victory came at the cost of 20 million lives, what can you celebrate? Boris explained: "My grandfather fought on the Eastern front, so the war didn't end for him on May 9." He also didn't like the fact that in his view, Russia "acts like we did it all ourselves—like it was our war, our victory. There were fifty-three countries who fought," he said. I wasn't surprised that he knew the exact number.

Since we were on the topic of World War II, he mentioned that his brother Andrey was making a movie about it—and not just any movie, but the biggest crowd-funded film in Russian history. The name of the film was *Panfilov's 28 Men*, and although I hadn't heard of it, I later Googled it and discovered it was one of the most hotly anticipated Russian films in years. Given his grandmother Lia's history during World War II, it made sense that Andrey had gravitated toward it as a subject.

I asked Boris how his mother, Nina, was doing, and he told me she'd just turned 71 the day before. She was free that evening, so we made a plan to have dinner over at her place. I'd go on the early side, to have a little time to chat with her, and Boris would join us later. He also told me that Vanya, who was now 26, was living in the Netherlands, where he was a graduate student at the Delft University of Technology. I was disappointed I wouldn't get to see him, but Boris promised to help me connect with him so we could Skype later in the week.

That evening, I stopped by a flower shop to buy Nina a birthday bouquet. When she met me at her apartment door, I was thrilled to see that she looked healthy and fit, and not even close to 71. I'd always liked Nina, a physician who had a rare combination of a no nonsense air and empathy: she's the kind of woman who won't listen to any crap, but she'll give you a hug if she senses you need it.

From the start, our conversation was everything my conversation with Boris wasn't. She asked how my trip had gone, what had changed in Russia over the past decade, whether I'd had any difficulties traveling alone. I asked about work and her travels, and we chatted easily over homemade meat cutlets and potatoes and a bottle of dry red wine. In fact, the only odd moment was related to the flowers I'd brought. She cut the stems, put the flowers in a vase, filled it with water, and then placed it on the kitchen floor.

She caught me glancing at the bouquet—she didn't miss much of anything, really—and smiled. "I always put flowers on the floor," she said, "because having flowers at my feet feels like having a garden."

We got on the subject of Andrey's film, and after describing how much money he'd raised through his crowd-funding campaign, she remarked, "It's from God. That's the only way this could happen." Then her face softened. "Liza, I want to tell you a story," she said. "One night, a man had a dream. He was walking on a beach . . ." She began describing how the man, looking

back through his life, saw two sets of footprints in the sand—
one his and one God's—and I thought, *Wow, she's actually telling me the Footprints story?*[†] This was a surprise, not only
because it was a vaguely Hallmark-cardy tale, but also because
I'd never thought of Nina as the proselytizing type.

I asked her whether she'd always had such strong religious
beliefs, and she repeated something she'd told me 20 years earlier. "My grandmother taught us to believe," she said, "but she
told us never to tell anyone else." Nina had been baptized as a
child, but she'd never been particularly devout until 2007, when
she took a trip to Israel. "I wanted to see where Christ had
walked," she told me, her eyes shining. "After that trip, I felt differently." Since then, she'd been back to Israel three more times.

We were midway through dinner when Boris arrived. He
hugged his mother warmly, but the intimate conversation I'd
been having with Nina predictably swerved toward bigger, more
serious issues. Boris started talking about what was wrong with
Russia today, bemoaning the fact that the country wasn't man-
ufacturing anything. "We're not building rockets, not making
new science," he said. "All we have is oil!" He told me about a
new movie being produced by Americans, in which audio from
Yuri Gagarin's first space flight was spliced together with views
of what the cosmonaut would have seen as he was orbiting.
"Why are the Americans the ones doing this?" Boris asked.
"Why aren't the Russians doing it? Why aren't we celebrating
our accomplishments?"

Finally, Nina interjected. "OK, enough with the criticism,"
she said, gently touching her son's arm.

[†] For the handful of people who haven't encountered the story: the man notices that
during most of his life, there are two sets of footprints in the sand, but in the most
difficult times, there's only one. When he asks why God abandoned him during his
difficulties, God replies, "My son, it was then that I carried you."

"It's not criticism," he responded. "It's observation." Boris was simply brimming over with desire to discuss every big global topic; it was as if his brain was filled to bursting, and he had to give vent to his thoughts or it might actually explode. The subject next turned to Ukraine, and it turned out that he, unlike the vast majority of Russians I'd spoken with, was no fan of Putin's actions there. In this, he disagreed with Nina, who believed Russians were being persecuted in Crimea, and Putin was merely taking steps to protect them. But Boris saw Putin as an autocrat, and he groaned when I relayed my conversation in Chelyabinsk, when Sergei and Lyuba had told me there was no such thing as Ukraine.

Of all the Russians I'd spoken with on the trip, Boris was the most outspoken in his dislike for Putin. "Why do you think people love him so much?" I asked.

"Because it's fun to cheer for the winning team," he replied. It was his most succinct, and thought-provoking, utterance yet.

—m—

Two days later, as I was walking down Liteiny Prospekt, I saw a poster showing a man in red pants and a plaid shirt, riding a bear like a horse. Across the top were the words HOW I BECAME RUSSIAN. It was—I kid you not—a new half-hour sitcom about "the adventures of an American in Russia." Because our adventures in Russia naturally involve bears.

I didn't get a chance to see the show, but the plot, as described on the Internet Movie Database, is this:

> Contemporary Moscow. An American journalist, Alex
> Wilson (Mateusz Damiecki), is sent by his employer,
> *The American Post,* one of the largest newspapers in
> the world, on a long-term assignment in their Moscow

Boris and Nina, in Nina's kitchen, 2015 (PHOTO BY LISA DICKEY)

office. In addition to his job there as an editor, Alex starts a blog, where he tries to answer important questions about Russians, Russian culture, and the mythical and elusive Russian soul, such as: Why is useless junk stored on the balcony? Why is there a package in every Russian home that contains other packages? And why do you have to bully people to avoid fights?

Launched in November 2015, the show soon became a hit, and it was quickly picked up for a second season.

⟨⟩

On the afternoon of November 14—the day after terrorists attacked Paris, killing more than a hundred people across the city—I had a Skype call with now-26-year-old Vanya. He'd been living abroad for the past few years, first in Bologna, Italy, and now in the Netherlands, where he was studying structural engineering. Given how eager he'd been a decade earlier to live and work in Russia, I was curious how he felt about having been in Europe for the past few years.

"For the first six months, I was aiming to go back to Russia after graduating," he told me, speaking flawless English. "But I've realized it would be better to use my diploma here for at least two or three years, to gain experience."

Vanya had decided to specialize in structural engineering for the oil industry, since that was Russia's main economic driver. "I'm taking offshore engineering courses," he said, "but it's really frustrating now, because oil prices have dropped, and there are basically no investments in this field, particularly in Russia. It's just easier to find work outside of Russia."

So, in light of what he'd told me as a 16-year-old, why had he chosen to study in Europe in the first place? "Because I felt that the Russian civil engineering market was closed," he said. "We don't design anything, and we don't build anything abroad in comparison to other countries. I wanted to take this opportunity to use my skills not just in the country where I was born, but somewhere else." Yet he reiterated that, ultimately, he wanted to live in Russia. "My generation doesn't want to run away from our country. We want to stay there and do good things."

As news of the Paris attacks was flooding the airwaves, I asked him about the threat of terrorism in today's Russia. "They haven't made any official statements about the plane that crashed in Egypt," he said, "but there's a high probability that it was a terrorist attack." He sighed heavily. "It's terrible. I don't know where these ISIS guys have the money coming from.

"I have a Spanish friend here who studies history and archaeology," he continued. "He's a Stalinist. We fight a lot about that.

But he just left me a voice mail this morning, saying, 'Russians should consolidate in Syria and kill those guys, like you did in World War II and killed the Germans.' They hear the news from Syria, that we're bombing ISIS locations, and they're relying on us to fight the ISIS guys. But as soon as I hear 'land operation,' I think, *There will be Russian people involved in this*, and I don't want that."

I read him parts of the 2005 interview with him and his high school friends, and he chuckled. "It's funny to hear this interview now," he said. "The school we were attending was the Gymnasium for Global Education, the only one in St. Petersburg. They were trying to develop this global way of thinking, teaching us tolerance from the first grade.

"But since I moved to Europe, I've come to understand that people are tired of being tolerant here," he said. "I hear a lot of jokes, going to bars with students in Bologna, in the heart of Italy. It's a city of workers, and all the jokes are either racist or homophobic."

Vanya's plan was to graduate in the fall of 2016, after which he'd look for a job in either Europe or Asia. "There's no point coming back with a European diploma—Russian employers won't even know what the University of Bologna is," he said. He figured he was most likely to find a good job in Asia, though that was much farther away from his family than he preferred.

"It would be best to be an expert for a Western company and work in St. Petersburg," he told me. "But the sanctions have put a fence between Western industry and Russian industry. I'd like to be an employee of Shell and work in St. Petersburg, but there are so many things in the way—oil prices, the *krizis*, the political situation. The sanctions will be in place for years, and they do have an effect."

I told him about a theory I'd heard several times, that the

Western sanctions had served to bring Russians together, uniting them against a common foe.

"Yes, that's true," he said, then laughed. "People were putting stickers on their cars: A picture of a bear giving himself a manicure with a big pair of nail clippers. And across the clippers was the word 'Sanctions'—so, he was showing that the sanctions will only serve to sharpen his claws."

At the end of our interview, Vanya brought the subject back around to his Spanish Communist friend. "I was in Madrid for a week this summer," he said, "and we had a lot of conversations. He said that the Revolution was the best thing that ever happened to Russia, and that Stalin would never allow all the things that are happening now.

"But I told him, that period for us was brother killing brother. My family—my mother's line—was in the Crimea at the time, in Feodosiya. Lots of them were killed, and they lost their property and everything." This, of course, was Maria Mikhailovna's family.

I asked if he remembered my first visit with him and Maria Mikhailovna, when he was just six years old. "No," he said. "In fact, I don't really remember her at all." He told me that the photos Gary had taken were the only ones of them together, and that the family was grateful to have them.

I didn't think to tell him, but wish I had, that his great-great-grandmother had been correct in her prediction all those years ago. "Who knows what the future will be like for this country?" she'd said then. "But he will do well." Vanya is a smart, ambitious, hard-working young man whose fondest wish is to live and work in Russia, the land of his ancestors. I only hope that he will be able to find a job and return there, to help build and shape his homeland in the years to come.

Epilogue

B Y THE END OF THE 2015 TRIP, I WAS EXHAUSTED. For two and a half months, I'd been compulsively focused and organized, taking reams of notes, shooting hundreds of photographs, and keeping obsessive track of my stuff. When the finish line was in sight, I finally allowed myself to relax—perhaps a little too much.

With three days to go, I left my backpack hanging on a chair after lunch with a friend in St. Petersburg. By the time I realized my mistake, I was sure it would be gone—along with my wallet, phone, and iPad. To my immense relief, the bag was right where I'd left it. I couldn't believe my luck, and made a mental note to be more careful.

The next day, I dropped my iPhone in a toilet. And the day

after that, while I was blithely waiting at a crosswalk on crowded Nevsky Prospekt, a thief unzipped my backpack and stole my wallet. I rushed to cancel my credit cards, but this was getting ridiculous. The way I was going, if the trip didn't end soon, I'd lose not only all my valuables, but possibly my sanity as well.

Yet for all the irritation these final incidents caused, they also served as a reminder of how incredibly fortunate I'd been—and how very well I'd been treated here. In the months leading up to the trip, I'd been racked with worry about traveling alone, anti-American sentiment, safety on the trains, homophobia, potential visa trouble, you name it. But in all those weeks of travel, I'd encountered very little difficulty, and a great deal of generosity. People who had nothing to gain by talking to an American writer nonetheless willingly opened their lives to me, even when it was clear they weren't fans of the nation I call home.

So, while it appears to be true that overall, relations between Russia and America are at their worst since the Stalin era, it's also true—at least in my experience—that most Russians bear no ill will toward us. "People are people" was a phrase I heard again and again, whether in the hills of Buryatia, on the waters of Lake Baikal, or sitting in any of the innumerable kitchens where Russians fed me and we toasted our friendship.

We have many more similarities than differences, a truth that, as I write this, happens to be bolstered by an article prominently featured on CBSnews.com: "Wandering Bear Shuts Down Los Angeles Neighborhood."

> A young bear is back in the Angeles National Forest after leading Los Angeles police officers, firefighters and animal control officers on a wild chase through a Sylmar neighborhood Monday night.
> The animal was first spotted around 8 p.m. on the

campus of Mission College on Eldridge Avenue, reports CBS Los Angeles. For two hours, the bear was running through streets, alleys and front yards.

I'm just saying.

Acknowledgments

—∿—

Thank you, Gary Matoso, for including me on your bold and brilliant 1995 journey. It's no exaggeration to say that our trip, and your example of perseverance and daring, changed my life. Thanks also to Tripp Mikich and Chuck Gathard, who made the groundbreaking Russian Chronicles website possible, and to our original sponsors, FocalPoint f/8, World Media Network, Sprint, Kodak, and Leica.

Thank you, David Hillegas, for taking a chance and joining me (on incredibly short notice) for the 2005 trip. And to both Gary and David, thank you for your magnificent photos, and for the permission to reproduce them in this book. Thanks also to Washingtonpost.com, in particular then-editor Jim Brady, for agreeing to run our 2005 blog, and to I-Linx for sponsoring that trip. And a tremendous thank-you to the friends and family who, after my bag was stolen in St. Petersburg, gave generously and without hesitation to make up the cash I'd lost. You know who you are.

To Elisabeth Dyssegaard of St. Martin's Press, thank you for believing in this project, and for having the courage to offer me a book deal even before knowing what would happen on the third trip. To Gail Ross and Howard Yoon, thank you for being wonderful literary agents, but more important, for being great friends. Thanks also to Laura Apperson, Donna Cherry, Lauren Friedlander, and Kathryn Hough of St. Martin's Press.

So many people have offered support over the years—everything from reading drafts to providing a bed in a far-flung place to simply offering encouragement when I needed it most. For these reasons and more, I'm grateful to Debby and Oleg Abramov, Ben Barnes, Laura Birek, Charles Digges, Dana Eagle, Christopher Hamilton, Roz Jacobs, Brad Kessler, Jesse Kornbluth, Karman Kregloe, Dona McAdams, Bridget McManus, Rada Mirzoeva, Pierre Noel, Lynda Park, Marina Ratina, Jill Sobule, Amy Turner, Lusya Verholuk, and Laurie Weisman. Thanks also to my wonderful circle of DC friends, to Nancy Desser of JFS, and to the babushkas of West Hollywood, in particular Roza and Sofia.

Kara Swisher, thank you for persuading me I could write for a living (and for talking me out of applying to law school). To my parents, thank you for the example of traveling fearlessly, and for all you've done over the years to help me make this project happen. To my Uncle Pitt, thank you for a lifetime of encouraging me to keep writing and stop worrying. And to my wife, Randi Barnes, thank you for believing in me, and for offering your unwavering support when I decided to disappear to Russia for

three months. I'm grateful every day to be able to share my life with you.

Finally, this project would never have been possible without the incredible generosity and candor of the many Russians described in these pages. To all of you who welcomed me into your lives, fed and housed me, shared your stories, and never blinked an eye when I just kept showing up, thank you. I can never adequately express what your trust has meant to me over these many years. I'm very grateful to you all . . . and I'll see you in 2025.